LA... ...ERS

Law for Social Workers
Fourth Edition

CAROLINE BALL
School of Law, University of East Anglia, Norwich
and
ANN McDONALD
School of Social Work and Psychosocial Studies,
University of East Anglia, Norwich

With a chapter on Scottish Law by
JANICE McGHEE
School of Social Work, University of Edinburgh

ASHGATE

Published by
Ashgate Publishing Limited
Gower House
Croft Road
Aldershot
Hants GU11 3HR
England

Ashgate Publishing Company
Suite 420, 101 Cherry Street
Burlington, VT 05401-4405 USA

Ashgate website: http//www.ashgate.com

British Library Cataloguing in Publication Data
Ball, Caroline, 1938-
    Law for social workers. - 4th ed.
    1. Social workers - Legal status, laws, etc. - Great Britain
    2. Public welfare - Law and legislation - Great Britain
    I. Title II. McDonald, Ann III. McGhee, Janice
    344.4'1'0313

Library of Congress Cataloging-in-Publication Data
Ball, Caroline, 1938-
    Law for social workers / Caroline Ball and Ann McDonald.-- 4th ed.
        p.   cm.
    Includes bibliographical references and indexes.
    ISBN 0-7546-1777-7 (alk. paper) -- ISBN 0-7546-1778-5 (pbk. : alk. paper)
        1. Social workers--Legal status, laws, etc.--Great Britain.
    I. McDonald, Ann, lecturer in social work II. Title.

    KD3302.B35 2002
    344.41'0313--dc21

                                                        2002024927
ISBN 0 7546 1777 7 (Hbk)
ISBN 0 7546 1778 5 (Pbk)

Typeset by IML Typographers, Birkenhead, Merseyside.
Printed and bound by MPG Books Ltd, Bodmin, Cornwall.

Contents

List of Figures and Tables

Figures

Tables

Preface

The law is organic, developing and changing to adapt to societal, demographic and professional practice shifts. This edition, in which Janice McGhee addresses the many changes that devolution has brought to the very different legal context of social work practice in Scotland, also benefits from the move from sole authorship to the complementing interests of co-authors.

The way in which this text has evolved and expanded since the first edition was published in 1986 reflects massive changes in social work related practice. In particular, since the last edition in 1996, the establishment of separate training for probation officers and the introduction of multi-disciplinary youth offending teams has required substantial expansion of the criminal process and youth justice chapters. Additionally, in recognition of the more diverse needs for up-to-date, relevant, legal information of those working in or training for social work related practice across the statutory, voluntary and private sectors, discrimination, community care and those areas of law such as social security, education and housing which impact on clients' lives are addressed in more detail.

The accelerated pace of the change in social work practice since the last edition in 1996 is reflected in the reform of the statutory framework of most areas of that practice. Since the general election of 1997, the Government has introduced legislation to effect specific and far-reaching reforms relating to most client groups, although reform of the Mental Health Act 1983 is still awaited. In addition, permeating all areas of practice, the Human Rights Act 1998 not only requires the decisions of all public bodies to be compliant with the European Convention on Human Rights but allows breaches to be challenged within the domestic courts.

Implementation of the new enactments is at different stages. The reforms introduced by the Crime and Disorder Act 1998 and the Youth Justice and Criminal Evidence Act 1999 have already resulted in the formation of local multi-disciplinary youth offending teams and wholesale changes throughout the youth justice system. The Child and Family Court Advisory and Support Service (CAFCASS) has, somewhat chaotically (White, 2001; Gerlis, 2002), replaced panels of guardians *ad litem* and reporting officers and probation service court welfare officers. Implementation of parts of the Care Standards Act 2000, which reforms the regulatory system for health and social care services, has introduced some radical reforms including the introduction of Social Care Councils, replacing the Central Council for Education and Training in Social Work (CCETSW) in each of the four countries of the

United Kingdom. The General Social Care Council has become the regulator for social work practice, and the new Care Standards Commission has assumed inspectorial responsibilities for a wide range of adult and child care services. The rest of the 2000 Act will come into force in January 2003. After a lengthy gestation, the Adoption and Children Act 2002 will shortly be on the statute book, as yet without any of the fine detail that will appear in rules, regulations and guidance.

Nor does it stop there. The summer of 2002 has seen two further important developments. In June the government published in draft form a Mental Health Bill to enact proposals set out in the white paper *Reforming the Mental Health Act* (Department of Health and the Home Office, 2000), and in July the long-awaited white paper *Justice for All* (Home Department, 2002) with wide-ranging proposals for reform of the criminal justice system. We have been able to include some references to both of these developments.

Whatever the pace of implementation of what is already enacted, new legislation, and the anticipated new curriculum for social work training, we hope that this new expanded edition, with its cross referencing to relevant research, will assist students and practitioners towards an understanding of social work and probation service related law in its practice context.

Caroline Ball
and
Ann McDonald
August 2002

List of Abbreviations

AA	Adoption Act
A(IA)A	Adoption (Intercountry Aspects) Act
ACA	Adoption and Children Act
ACPC	Area Child Protection Committee
AFH	Approved Family Help
AID	artificial insemination by donor
AO	adjudications officer
ASBO	anti-social behaviour order
ASP	Act of the Scottish Parliament
ASSET	assessment tool
ASW	approved social worker
CA	Children Act
C&YPA	Children and Young Persons Act
CAFCASS	Child and Family Court Advisory and Support Service
CAO	child assessment order
CCETSW	Central Council for Education and Training in Social Work
CCG	community care grant
CDA	Crime and Disorder Act
CDS	Criminal Defence Service
CJA	Criminal Justice Act
CJCSA	Criminal Justice and Court Services Act
CLS	Community Legal Service
CPA	Care Programme Approach
CPO	child protection order
CPRO	community punishment and rehabilitation order
CPS	Crown Prosecution Service
CRAG	*Charging for Residential Accommodation Guide*
CRE	Commission for Racial Equality
C(S)A	Crime (Sentences) Act
CSA	Child Support Agency
CTB	council tax benefit
DCO	designated complaints officer
DfEE	Department for Education and Employment
DfES	Department for Education and Skills
DHSS	Department of Health and Social Security
DLA	disability living allowance
DoH	Department of Health

DSS	Department of Social Security
DTTO	drug treatment and testing order
DWP	Department for Work and Pensions
ECHR	European Convention on Human Rights
ECtHR	European Court of Human Rights
EPO	emergency protection order
ESO	education supervision order
EWHL	England and Wales House of Lords (case)
EWO	education welfare officer
HB	housing benefit
HMP	Her Majesty's Pleasure
HRA	Human Rights Act
ICB	incapacity benefit
IO	investigating officer
IP	independent person
IS	income support
LAC	local authority circular
LEA	local education authority
LSC	Legal Services Commission
MHO	mental health officer
MSP	Member of the Scottish Parliament
NASS	National Asylum Support Service
NSPCC	National Society for the Prevention of Cruelty to Children
PACE	Police and Criminal Evidence Act
PCC(S)A	Powers of the Criminal Courts (Sentencing) Act
PRO	parental responsibilities order
PSR	pre-sentence report
RMO	responsible medical officer
RRA	Race Relations Act
SCRA	Scottish Children's Reporter Administration
SF	social fund
SFO	social fund officer
SLAB	Scottish Legal Aid Board
SMP	statutory maternity pay
SSD	Social Services Department
SWSA	Social Work (Scotland) Act
YJB	Youth Justice Board
YJCEA	Youth Justice and Criminal Evidence Act
YOI	young offender institution
YOT	youth offending team

PART I
THE LEGAL CONTEXT OF SOCIAL WORK PRACTICE

Chapter 1
Nature, Sources and Administration of Law

The law, by which is meant the body of rules whereby a civilized society maintains order and regulates its internal affairs as between one individual and another, and between individuals and the state, consists in the United Kingdom of common law, statute law (Acts of Parliament) and case law, or judicial precedent. Domestic law is also significantly influenced by international treaty obligations. For instance, the Human Rights Act 1998 effectively incorporates the bulk of the substantive rights of the European Convention on Human Rights (ECHR) into UK law (see Chapter 2), and the Adoption (Intercountry Aspects) Act 1999 incorporates the Hague Convention on Intercountry Adoption into domestic law.

For historical reasons the law of England and Wales, and its administration, differs quite substantially from that in Scotland (see Part VI), and in important respects, from that of Northern Ireland; any reference to particular provisions in Parts I to III therefore relate only to England and Wales unless the contrary is stated.

Sources of Law

Legislation

Parliament can, subject in any conflict to the supremacy of European Community law, by statute make or change the law in any way that a majority decision of both the House of Commons and the House of Lords, following established procedure, deems appropriate.

Most legislation (statute law) is introduced by the government of the day to implement its political agenda, respond to crises, or to carry through politically non-contentious departmental policy reforms, often to remedy perceived deficiencies in existing statute law; the Children Act 1989 is a prime example of the latter. The frenetic legislative activity 1997–2000 provides abundant evidence of the first. The Labour government came to power in 1997 committed in their manifesto, amongst other things, to devolution, reform of the House of Lords, and a complete overhaul of the youth justice system. All have been legislated for and most implemented. Legislation may also be introduced, not to make new law, but to rationalize and clarify existing provisions scattered throughout several statutes. For instance the Powers of the Criminal Courts (Sentencing) Act 2000 brought together all the sentencing powers of the criminal courts. This reform was long overdue. The consolidated sentencing powers were previously enacted in 15, mostly much amended, statutes ranging from the Children and Young Persons Act 1933 to the Youth Justice and Criminal Evidence Act 1999, including Criminal Justice Acts from 1982, 1988, 1991, 1993 and 1994 (Criminal Justice and Public Order Act).

Acts of Parliament, or statutes, are primary legislation and have to go through the whole parliamentary legislative procedure. Rules and regulations are made by statutory instrument under powers delegated to the Secretary of State for the relevant government department in the primary legislation. Delegated legislation is subject to only cursory parliamentary scrutiny, although it has equal force in law to primary legislation. (For a helpful account of the legislative process, see, for instance, Partington, 2000: ch. 3.)

Codes of Practice and Guidance

Whether set out in departmental circulars or glossy volumes, guidance and most Codes of Practice do not have statutory status. They are intended to be a statement of what is officially regarded as good practice and followed for that reason. Where guidance is issued under section 7(1) of the Local Authority Social Services Act 1970, local authorities are required to follow it. Although they do not breach the law by failing to do so, their actions may be challenged by complaint to the Ombudsman or weigh against them in legal proceedings. The helpful summary of the relative status of regulations and guidance in *The Care of Children: Principles and Practice in Regulations and Guidance* (DoH, 1989) has not been bettered.

> One might sum up the differences between the requirements of these various official documents like this: – Regulations say 'You must/shall'; codes say 'You ought/should'. When guidance explains regulations, it reaffirms the 'you must' messages. However when it goes beyond regulations setting out good practice, it conveys the message that 'It is highly desirable to …' or 'Unless there is good reason not to, you should …' rather than 'You must'. (Ibid.: 2)

Case Law

The judges of the superior courts, the House of Lords, the Court of Appeal and the High Court, through their interpretation of statutory provisions and legal principles, both define and refine existing law, and may on occasions, where there is no similar case or established legal principle to which they can refer, make new law. Where judges do 'make' law in this way, Parliament may, by statute, subsequently restate the law to its own liking. The process of legislation from political or practical ideas through the democratic process to

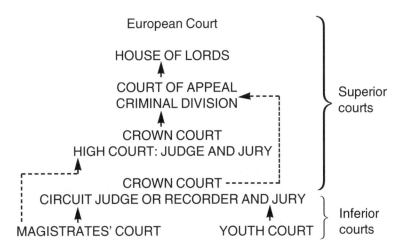

Figure 1.1   The criminal courts

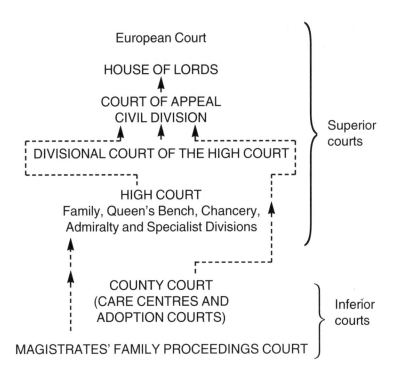

Figure 1.2   The civil courts
Key
Appeals   ----▶-----

enacted statute is a familiar one; the interpreting and occasional making of law by the judges may be less so (for further elaboration, see for instance, Partington, 2000: 50–59).

In order to understand the working of judicial precedent it is necessary to look at the structure of the courts and the way in which decisions in the superior courts have to be followed by those below them in the hierarchy (Figures 1.1 and 1.2). The courts within which the law is administered reflect the essential difference between the civil and criminal law. Civil law, for the most part, involves disputes between individual parties or corporate bodies, with one seeking either an order, or compensation for loss or damage suffered, against another. The criminal law is concerned with the trial and punishment of those who have acted in a way that is unlawful; this includes, of course, besides acts generally recognized as crimes such as murder, rape and theft, a vast range of matters, such as minor motoring offences, which are only technically 'criminal' in nature but nonetheless come within the jurisdiction of the criminal courts.

As can be seen from the figures, the separate systems of courts for the administration of the criminal and civil law now come together only when an appeal reaches the Judicial Committee of the House of Lords (commonly referred to simply as 'the House of Lords'), or more rarely the European Court of Human Rights.

Judicial precedent – the system by which the decisions of superior courts are binding on those below them in the hierarchy – not only clarifies and refines the law, but makes it more certain. Where a point of law has been decided in a previous case, a court subsequently hearing a case involving the same point will be bound to follow that decision or differentiate the circumstances of the current case.

A point of law decided in a case in the House of Lords is binding on all other courts below – but not necessarily on itself on a future occasion (*Practice Statement (Judicial Precedent)* 1966). Decisions in either division of the Court of Appeal bind all the courts below and will generally be followed in their own subsequent decisions. In the High Court, Divisional Court decisions (two judges) are binding on a judge sitting alone, but one High Court judge's decision will not necessarily be binding – although it is likely to be influential – on another.

The inferior courts, which are the county court, lower tier of the Crown Court and all the magistrates' courts are bound by the decisions of all superior courts, but not by their own or those of other inferior courts.

Information on all important judicial decisions is recorded in reports in which the facts of the case, the points of law involved and the decision are recorded and regularly published in hard copy and electronically according to the specialist subject matter involved. There is an elaborate system of referencing to enable lawyers and courts to keep track of developments in case law and to trace decisions relevant to particular situations or legal principles (see page 4). In 2000, a new system of referencing reported decisions in the superior courts was introduced. Cases continue to be reported in specialist reports but will be cited according to the new referencing system. Judgments from the Court of Appeal and the House of Lords are available almost immediately on the Internet, and those from all superior courts can be accessed through a growing number of electronic legal databases.

Jurisdiction of the Courts

Civil Courts

The venue for civil trials will depend either on the nature of the dispute or the sum of money involved, or sometimes both. As an example, it may be helpful to look first at family proceedings and then at other civil disputes.

If the traditional concern of family law was with marriage and its consequences particularly in regard to property, today the term covers a wider area. It encompasses, for instance, such legal regulation as there is regarding the consequences of cohabitation, and the public as well as the private law relating to children. In most family proceedings, although not in divorce in which magistrates have no jurisdiction, all three levels of court (magistrates, county court and High Court) have concurrent jurisdiction. The decision as to which level of court to make application in private law proceedings is a matter for the applicant, although if they are in receipt of funding by the Legal Services Commission (see page 19) they will only be funded for the least expensive proceedings able to provide the order or remedy required. Public law cases start with an application to the magistrates' family proceedings court, and may be dealt with there or transferred to a county court care centre or, exceptionally, to the Family Division of the High Court. Private law proceedings related to family breakdown are dealt with in greater detail in Chapter 7 and those relating to child care and protection in Chapters 9 and 10.

Cases such as those involving claims for personal injury or breach of contract will generally be heard in the county court or in the Queen's Bench Division of the High Court if very large sums of money are involved. Almost all these cases are eventually settled between the parties before the case actually reaches the court, or when part-heard.

Appeals from the magistrates' family proceedings court go to the Family Division of the High Court and from the county and High Courts to the Court of Appeal Civil Division. From there they may, with leave, go to the House of Lords and, if they involve a claim against UK law, which has not been resolved in the domestic courts under the Human Rights Act 1998 (see Chapter 2), to the European Court of Human Rights in Strasbourg.

Criminal Courts

All criminal cases concerning adults (aged 18 years and over) start in the magistrates' court and most are dealt with there. Most criminal proceedings against young offenders (aged 10–17), except the most serious, are dealt with in the magistrates' youth courts (see Part IV). The criminal justice system was reviewed by Lord Justice Auld in 2000. His report with wide-ranging recommendations was published in 2001. In July 2002, the Government published a white paper *Justice for All* setting out proposals for wide-ranging reforms (Home Department, 2002).

Except in inner London and other areas of dense population, where paid, legally qualified, District Judges (Magistrates' Courts) sit alone, judicial decisions in magistrates' courts are made by benches of three unpaid lay justices. There are some 32,000 justices of the peace, appointed, until they reach the retiring age of 70, by the Lord Chancellor, acting on recommendations from local Advisory Committees. In the past the whole process of the selection of justices of the peace was somewhat secretive; over recent years it has been opened up, and now advertisements encourage both the recommendation of people to serve and personal applications. The names of members of the Advisory Committee are published, and selection processes are in most areas designed to encourage the appointment of people who reflect the composition of their communities, although there are serious doubts as to the extent to which this is achieved (Darbyshire, 1997; Sanders and Young, 2000: 531–7). Justices of the peace or magistrates – the term is interchangeable – have to undergo basic training before they adjudicate and are required to undertake appraisal and refresher training on a regular basis. All lay magistrates sit in the adult court and are eligible for election to serve additionally on the family proceedings and youth court panels. They are advised on law and procedure by a legally qualified clerk, although the magistrates bear responsibility for all the decisions they make, whether they have acted on their clerk's advice or have ignored it.

More than 90 per cent of all criminal cases begin and end in the magistrates' court. In more serious cases, requiring more severe sentences than the magistrates have power to impose, or where the defendant chooses trial at the Crown Court, accused persons are required to enter a plea of guilty or not guilty in the magistrates' court. If they plead guilty they will be committed to the Crown Court for sentence. Those who plead not guilty are committed for trial in the Crown Court. Cases committed to the Crown Court will generally be heard in the second tier by a circuit judge or a recorder, possibly sitting with two lay justices and, if the defendant is pleading not guilty, a jury of 12 laymen and laywomen whose role is to determine guilt or innocence. Murder and some other very serious or complex cases will be heard in the top tier of the Crown Court by a High Court judge, with a jury to decide guilt or innocence if the offence is denied.

Appeals against findings of guilt or sentences imposed by the magistrates are heard in the Crown Court, and on points of law by the Divisional Court of the High Court. When a case is committed by magistrates for trial in the Crown Court, appeals against sentence or on a point of law – but not generally against the jury's finding of guilt unless this can be seen to be perverse in view of the way the judge summed up the evidence – are heard, with leave, in the Criminal Division of the Court of Appeal. On a point of law only, and with leave of the court, there may be a further appeal to the Judicial Committee of the House of Lords. From there, if a point of Community law is involved, there is a possibility of appeal to the European Court or, if there is a challenge under the European Convention on Human Rights which has not been resolved in the domestic court, to the European Court of Human Rights in Strasbourg.

Access to Legal Advice and Representation

Unusually, when compared to other jurisdictions, the legal profession is divided into two branches: solicitors who currently have a monopoly on direct access to clients, and barristers who have greater rights of advocacy in the higher courts and are instructed by solicitors on behalf of their clients. Although each branch of the legal profession still has a separate identity, there is less division in regard to the work that they undertake than there was in the past. Although currently the majority of solicitors work outside the courts and most barristers practise as advocates in the courts, it appears likely that the two professions will gradually merge into one.

In order to help the public, most of whom will have occasion to seek professional legal advice only rarely, in the choice of a solicitor suitable to their needs the Law Society publishes lists of firms and legal advice centres, indicating their areas of expertise and whether they are franchised to undertake work funded by the Legal Services Commission, which has replaced the Legal Aid Board. Solicitors who are members of the Law Society child-care panel should be chosen for care and related proceedings in which specialist representation is essential for all parties. Parties who can afford to pay for legal advice and representation are free to choose who will act for them. Public funding of legal services has been reduced substantially over the last decade and was radically altered in 2000.

Funding Access to Legal Services

In April 2000 the Legal Aid Board which administered legal aid for advice and basic assistance, criminal legal aid and civil legal aid was replaced by the Legal Services Commission (LSC) set up under the Access to Justice Act 1999. The Commission has responsibility for two schemes, the Community Legal Service (CLS) and the Criminal Defence Service (CDS). The LSC publishes guides to the two schemes (Legal Services Commission, 2000a; 2000b), and other helpful but more critical accounts can be found (Partington, 2000: ch. 10). There are separate schemes for Scotland and Northern Ireland.

In England and Wales, the LSC administers funding for civil and criminal cases through regional Legal Services Committees which are responsible, under the general guidance of the Lord Chancellor, for planning and delivering cash limited services and reaching and reviewing funding decisions. Some contracted solicitors and other legal advisers are approved to make initial funding decisions without reference to the regional committee.

Community Legal Service

Only organizations with a contract with the LSC are able to provide advice or representation funded by the Commission, and only specialist solicitors' firms are funded to do work in family and other specific areas such as immigration and medical negligence. Unlike its predecessor, Legal Aid, the CLS goes beyond the legal profession; citizens' advice bureaux, law and other advice centres may also hold a contract for the provision of legal advice or mediation services. A range of services exist, on the basis that if the remedy sought can be provided in any other way, formal legal proceedings will not be funded. In family cases, public funding for services from a solicitor will only be available if mediation is found to be unsuitable or impracticable. Details of the services available under the new scheme and of the criteria to be applied in relation to decisions to fund or continue to fund services are set out in the Funding Code. The services available include Legal Help, Help at Court, Family Mediation, Approved Family Help, and Legal Representation.

Legal Help Subject to financial eligibility, initial legal advice and some assistance, for instance writing letters, getting a barrister's opinion or preparing a written case for a court or tribunal, are provided by solicitors or legal advisers who hold contracts with the LSC. 'Legal Help' replaces the former 'green form' scheme.

Help at Court This allows a solicitor or adviser to speak on the client's behalf at certain court hearings without providing formal representation throughout the proceedings.

Legal support under the above schemes can be provided until the charges reach a set maximum (currently £500). Once the limit is reached, further work at that level can only be carried out with the authority of the LSC regional office.

Family Mediation The LSC contracts with trained mediators to provide a service to help families to resolve disputes. Funding is also available to assess whether a case is suitable for mediation.

Approved Family Help Approved Family Help (AFH) may include assistance in resolving a family dispute through negotiation, the issuing of proceedings, and representation where necessary to obtain disclosure from another party. Subject to financial eligibility AFH is available to provide legal advice and assistance in the course of family mediation, or general legal advice on family matters.

Legal Representation   This is the level of service previously provided under civil legal aid. It may be available either for investigating the strength of a claim or for full representation in legal proceedings.

Whatever the merits of the case or the means of the client, some cases will not qualify for public funding. The 'conditional fee agreement', under which personal injury and some other categories of case are not eligible for legal aid but are undertaken by solicitors on a 'no win, no fee' basis is one of the most controversial reforms introduced by the Access to Justice Act 1999 (Partington, 2000: 233–7).

Eligibility

In almost all cases, funding for legal services is dependent on financial eligibility determined through an assessment of income and capital resources. For legal representation, eligibility also depends on an assessment of the merits criteria relevant to the type of case determined by the LSC.

Financial eligibility is set at a level which requires almost everyone except those in receipt of certain benefits, or with very low incomes, to contribute substantially to the services provided. The detailed rules regarding financial eligibility are generally revised each April and can be found on the LSC website (www.legalservices.gov.uk).

There is one important exception to the financial and merit eligibility rules. Parents, or others with parental responsibility, and children who are parties to care proceedings (Children Act 1989, s.31), or emergency protection order (s.44) or child assessment order (s.43) applications are entitled to legal representation without any means or merits test. Children who are the subject of secure accommodation order applications are similarly entitled.

Criminal Defence Services

In a radical shift, the CDS administered by the LSC replaced the previous system of criminal legal aid in April 2000 and is likely to be fully operational from 2003. The main impacts of the reforms are that the previous case-by-case assistance administered through the courts is replaced by the CDS securing advice and representation from solicitors or advice agencies on a contractual basis, or in the longer term employing its own lawyers to represent defendants. As a result defendants will have less choice, and will be expected to keep the same representative from the police station through to trial. Only solicitors firms with a 'general criminal contract' are able to carry out criminal defence work funded by the Commission. The other major change is that, instead of, as formerly, defendants having to be assessed for and pay financial contributions required prior to trial, now courts have the power to order the payment of full or part costs, on the basis of a means assessment undertaken by the Commission, at the end of the trial.

The CDS provides three levels of service: Advice and Assistance, Advocacy Assistance and Representation.

Advice and Assistance   Any person, including a child, who is financially eligible is entitled to free legal advice and limited assistance, such as letter writing, negotiation or obtaining a barrister's opinion in relation to criminal proceedings from a contracted firm of solicitors. The current rules regarding financial eligibility can be found on the LSC website (www.legalservices.gov.uk). Advice and Assistance does not include any representation in court.

Advocacy Assistance   Advocacy Assistance covers the cost of the initial preparation of a defendant's case and initial representation in the magistrates' and Crown Court. It also covers representation of people at risk of imprisonment for failing to obey a court order or pay a fine. Prisoners facing disciplinary charges before the prison governor, and life prisoners or young offenders detained during Her Majesty's Pleasure whose cases are referred to the Parole Board, may also be entitled to representation under this scheme.

Representation   Representation may be applied for on behalf of anyone charged with a criminal offence. The court decides whether 'in the interests of justice' representation should be granted because the case is sufficiently serious to make imprisonment or the loss of employment likely on conviction. Representation may also be granted if the case involves a substantial question of law or if the defendant might not be able to follow the case because of language or mental health problems. Orders for contributions may be made at the end of the trial, depending on the means of the defendant.

Court Duty Solicitor Scheme   Anyone being questioned by the police is entitled to free legal advice which is not means tested. There should also be duty solicitors available to give immediate legal advice to unrepresented defendants in magistrates' courts.

Support in Court

Any litigant in criminal or civil proceedings who is not legally represented may have the assistance of someone, whether legally qualified or not, to sit beside him/her in court, taking notes, offering advice and suggesting questions to be asked. This may be an important role for a social worker to play for an inarticulate client who has been refused funded representation. The adviser is generally referred to as a '*McKenzie* friend', after the case of

McKenzie v. *McKenzie* [1970] in which the principle of litigants' rights to such support was established. A '*McKenzie* friend' may not address the court but may offer all other advice and assistance provided that the assistance is bona fide and not proffered in a way that is 'inimical to the proper administration of justice' per Donaldson MR in *R* v. *Leicester City Justices ex parte Barrow and Another* [1991]. It should be noted that the right to have a *McKenzie* friend is that of the party to the proceedings and not the right of the adviser (*R* v. *Bow County Court ex parte Pelling* [1999]).

Standard of Proof and Rules of Evidence

Since possibly liberty, and certainly reputation, may be at stake, a higher standard of proof is required for a conviction in criminal proceedings than for judgment in civil proceedings. The evidential test in criminal proceedings is that the prosecution must prove their case 'beyond reasonable doubt'. In civil cases, where the issue is one between theoretically equal parties, the court is required to base its decision only on a balance of probabilities in favour of one side or the other.

To non-lawyers, and it has to be admitted to some lawyers, the rules of evidence appear obscure, technical and unduly complex. They are also inextricably interwoven with the procedural rules for different proceedings. Regardless of complexity, social workers, especially those involved or likely to be involved in child protection work, need to be aware of the basic rules of evidence. The effective presentation of relevant facts by social workers called on to testify, for instance in care proceedings, may be critical to the outcome of the case.

Evidence in court consists of the testimony of witnesses, given under oath or affirmation and subject to cross-examination, and, with procedural safeguards intended to ensure validity, photographs and other documentary materials including video and audio recordings. The rules which exclude certain testimony and documents generally hinge on the principle that evidence presented in court must be reliable and the best available. For example, a photocopy or fax of a document is not as good evidence as the original document, and will not generally be admissible as evidence in the absence of the original.

The extent to which the rules of evidence disadvantage and indeed damage children appearing as witnesses, particularly in the criminal trial of their alleged abuser, has long been a matter for concern (Spencer and Flin, 1993). Implementation of Part II of the Youth Justice and Criminal Evidence Act 1999 should improve the position of children as well as that of other vulnerable witnesses (Birch, 2000).

Hearsay Evidence

Evidence of a statement made by a person not giving evidence, is not the best evidence if an attempt is being made to establish the truth of what was said. For this reason it is excluded in criminal proceedings and was excluded in civil proceedings until, in 1991, an exception was introduced in regard to cases concerning the care and upbringing of children. Subsequently, the Civil Evidence Act 1995 abolished the rule against hearsay in all civil cases. The rule has only changed in regard to admissibility; the weight to be attached to such evidence will still be in issue.

Leading Questions

Contrary to popular belief, leading questions are not questions the answers to which might prove embarrassing or incriminating, but those which put words into the witness's mouth or suggest the answer required. In order that witnesses give their own evidence and are not led into making the statements that their advocate might want them to make, leading questions may not be asked of witnesses giving their own testimony where the facts are in dispute. They may be used in cross-examination because the nature of this is to test the accuracy of evidence already given under oath.

The Use of Documents to 'Refresh Memory'

Witnesses may find it difficult to recall exact dates or times or the sequence in which events took place. The rules regarding the extent to which documents may be relied on are treated seriously to ensure that the evidence given accurately reflects the events described by the witness. The rules allow a witness to refresh her memory by reference to a document made or verified by her contemporaneously with the events to which it relates. A social worker may, provided that the judge is content that the conditions are satisfied, refer for instance to the notes of a visit or interview, provided that the notes are written up as soon as possible after the event, or, if recorded and typed up by someone else, were verified by the witness.

Tribunals

Tribunals, 'the adjudicative fora in which the vast majority of disputes between the citizen and the state get resolved' (Partington, 2000: 126) are effectively court substitutes which exercise a quasi-judicial function in specialist areas outside the court system. Tribunals, for instance mental health review tribunals, social security appeals tribunals and employment appeal tribunals, and immigration appeal tribunals, principally exist to determine appeals from administrative decisions and are mostly staffed by experts in the particular field, or by lay people representing the community, generally with a legally qualified chairperson. Proceedings are less formal than in courts, however, although they are not courts of law, they must comply with the rules of natural justice. Many tribunals have built up case law of their own which they follow, and, as public authorities under the Human Rights Act 1998, they have to comply with the requirements of the European Convention on Human Rights (see Chapter 2). Funding is available, for representation before employment appeal, mental health review, immigration appeal and the Protection of Children Act 1999 tribunals. Except for patients appearing before mental health review tribunals, representation is subject to the strict rules regarding financial eligibility for CLS funding. Supporting clients who cannot be legally represented in tribunal hearings is an area in which social workers and volunteers can, provided they have the necessary expertise, play an important advocacy role.

Chapter 2

Social Work and the Human Rights Act 1998

In 1950, immediately after the Second World War, the European Convention on Human Rights and Fundamental Freedoms introduced the first international complaints procedure under which individuals had access to an international court, the European Court of Human Rights (ECtHR), with jurisdiction to hear cases against the state involving abuse of human rights. The Convention was drafted within the context of the widespread abuses of human rights perpetrated within totalitarian regimes throughout the first half of the twentieth century and most recently in Nazi Germany. The fundamental rights protected by the Convention – the right to life, the right not to suffer torture, the right to a fair trial, the right to family life and so on – are, reflecting those abuses, essentially civil and political rather than economic and social rights.

The Convention is not, however, any sort of a relic frozen in the 1950s. A broadly purposive approach to its interpretation makes it a 'living instrument' which is interpreted to reflect present-day conditions. As society changes, so, often very slowly, the ECtHR changes its interpretation of Convention rights. A good example of this is the case of *Marckx* v. *Belgium* (1979), in which the Court found that Belgian laws in relation to children born outside marriage were in breach of the right to family life, largely on the basis that they were out of step with the new approach to the status of illegitimate children which had been adopted by most of the contracting states.

In the interpretation of the Convention, crucial roles are played by two interpretative instruments: the doctrine of the margin of appreciation and the principle of proportionality. In broad terms, margin of appreciation means that a state, when making a decision that involves a Convention right, has a measure of discretion where the right may conflict with legitimate public purposes in its own country. Arguably, therefore the margin of appreciation is a principle of international law not incorporated into domestic law. The principle of proportionality which underpins the whole Convention is concerned with achieving a fair balance. The principle requires that where the Convention expressly permits restrictions on Convention rights (as in Article 8, below) on the basis of necessity, the interference with the right must be proportionate to the legitimate aim the state seeks to achieve.

The United Kingdom government ratified the Convention in 1951 and recognized the right of individual petition to the ECtHR at Strasbourg in

1966. This allowed UK citizens to challenge the legitimacy of UK law, and many successfully, though at great expense and with lengthy delays, proved breaches of Convention rights. As a result, over the years the UK government has had to amend domestic law in order to comply with the Convention: for instance in regard to secure accommodation (*Abbott* v. *United Kingdom* [1990]), parental access to children in care (*W* v. *United Kingdom* (1988)), corporal punishment (*A* v. *United Kingdom* [1998]), and the right to a fair trial for young offenders accused of grave crimes (*T* v. *United Kingdom* and *V* v. *United Kingdom* [2000]).

Throughout the 1970s and 1980s there were many proposals for, and lively debate around the idea of, a Bill of Rights which would wholly or partially incorporate the Convention (Wadham and Mountfield, 1999). In 1996 the Labour Party published a consultation paper, *Bringing Rights Home*, which set out the Party's plans for incorporation. This was included in the manifesto for the 1997 election.

The Human Rights Act 1998

The Act, which came into force in October 2000, does not incorporate the whole of the ECHR into domestic law. Instead, in a complex political compromise, it gives 'further effect' to the rights and freedoms guaranteed under the Convention, without surrendering absolute parliamentary sovereignty. The fundamental principle of the Act is that it is unlawful for a public authority to act in a way which is incompatible with a Convention right (s.6(1)). In general the effect of section 6 is that the Act will bind public authorities but will not regulate relations between private individuals, except in so far as the courts as public authorities are bound by the Human Rights Act 1998 and will interpret private law consistently. Thus any person who is the victim of any act by a public authority which is incompatible with the Convention can challenge the authority in any court. Courts have to decide case compatibly with Convention rights, and have to interpret legislation to conform to Convention rights wherever possible, and take account of case law from the ECtHR.

Where a higher (superior) court (see Figure 1.1, page 5) is satisfied that a legislative provision is incompatible with the Convention, it may make a 'declaration of incompatibility'. The declaration does not, in order to preserve parliamentary sovereignty, set aside primary legislation (see page 3), or even force the government to act, although it should prompt the government to seek to amend the law to make it Convention compliant.

There are three types of public bodies envisaged under section 6:

- public authorities which exercise statutory or prerogative powers (for instance local authorities);

- bodies carrying out public functions (likely to be interpreted using the same principles as those identifying whether a public body is amenable to judicial review); and,
- courts and tribunals.

Key Convention Articles Relevant to Social Work Practice

In terms of social work practice, Articles 3, 5, 6, 8, 14 and Article 2 of the First Protocol are probably the most relevant. They are set out Schedule 1 to the 1998 Act.

Article 3

> No one shall be subjected to torture or to inhuman or degrading treatment or punishment.

This is an unqualified right which cannot, like some of the other rights (see for instance Article 8, the right to family life, below) be derogated from in any circumstance. In *A* v. *United Kingdom* [1998] a boy aged nine was beaten with a garden cane with considerable force by his step-father. The step-father was charged with causing the boy actual bodily harm, but was acquitted, having argued the defence of 'reasonable chastisement'. The nine judges of the ECtHR found unanimously that the treatment amounted to 'inhuman or degrading treatment', and that the state should be held responsible for the beating, since it provided no effective deterrent. The failure of local authorities to intervene to protect children, thus allowing them to suffer ill-treatment has also been upheld as being in breach of Article 3 (*TP and KM* v *United Kingdom* (1996)). In terms of social work practice, there is little doubt that the treatment of children in the public care in Staffordshire under the 'pindown' regime (Levy and Kahan, 1991) would have been regarded as inhuman and degrading treatment had it been referred to Strasbourg, and would now be open to challenge as being in breach of Article 3 in the domestic courts.

Article 5

> Everyone has the right to liberty and security of person.

There then follows a list of exceptions which apply provided that there is compliance with 'a procedure prescribed by law'. The two exceptions most likely to apply in regard to clients of social services departments are:

(d)   the detention of a minor by lawful order for the purposes of educational supervision or his lawful detention for the purpose of bringing him before the competent legal authority;

and,

   (e)   the lawful detention of persons for the prevention of the spreading of
         infectious diseases, of persons of unsound mind, alcoholics or drug addicts
         or vagrants.

Prior to implementation of the Act there had been considerable speculation
that the secure accommodations provisions under the Children Act 1989,
s.25, might breach Article 5. The Court of Appeal, in *Re K (Secure
Accommodation Order: Right to Liberty)* [2001], a case heard shortly after
implementation, refused to find any breach, holding that the detention of a
child in secure accommodation came within the exception in Article 5(d).

The other exceptions include imprisonment 'after conviction by a
competent court'; arrest and detention of a person on reasonable suspicion of
having committed an offence; lawful detention in regard to the deportation or
extradition of immigrants.

Article 6

   1. In the determination of his civil rights and obligations or of any criminal charge
      against him, everyone is entitled to a fair and public hearing within a
      reasonable time by an independent and impartial tribunal established by law.
      Judgment shall be pronounced publicly but the press and public may be
      excluded from all or part of the trial in the interests of morals, public order or
      national security in a democratic society, where the interests of juveniles or the
      protection of the private life of the parties so require, or to the extent strictly
      necessary in the opinion of the court in special circumstances where publicity
      would prejudice the interests of justice.
   2. Everyone charged with a criminal offence shall be presumed innocent until
      proved guilty according to law.
   3. Everyone charged with a criminal offence has the following minimum rights:
      (a) to be informed promptly, in a language which he understands and in detail,
           of the nature and cause of the accusation against him;
      (b) to have adequate time and facilities for the preparation of his defence;
      (c) to defend himself in person or through legal assistance of his own
           choosing or, if he has not sufficient means to pay for legal assistance, to be
           given it free when the interests of justice so require;
      (d) to examine or have examined witnesses against him and to obtain the
           attendance and examination of witnesses on his behalf under the same
           conditions as witnesses against him;
      (e) to have the free assistance of an interpreter if he cannot understand or
           speak the language used in court.

Article 6 concerns the right to a fair trial in civil disputes as well as criminal
proceedings. In the latter this is relatively straightforward, and 'civil rights
and obligations' have been interpreted widely. There are many detailed
commentaries on the Act which provide helpful analyses of the complex and

developing Strasbourg jurisprudence (Swindells et al., 1999; Wadham and Mountfield, 1999). In terms of the law relevant to social workers, it is clear from decided cases that Article 6 applies to:

- family private law cases (*Airey* v. *Ireland* (1979));
- public law decisions (placing children in care (*Olsson* v. *Sweden* No. 1 (1988)); contact with children and fostering (*Eriksson* v. *Sweden* (1989)), adoption (*Keegan* v. *Ireland* (1994));
- domestic violence cases and secure accommodation applications (Swindells et al., 1999: ch. 13 and pp. 114–18);
- Detention under the Mental Health Act 1983 (*Winterwerp* v. *Netherlands* (1979)), and mental health review tribunals. Sections 72 and 73 of the Mental Health Act 1983 have had to be amended to reverse the burden of proof at tribunal hearings following the Court of Appeal's declaration of incompatibility in *R. (H)* v. *Mental Health Review Tribunal, North and East London Region, and Secretary of State for Health* [2001] (Feldman, 2002: ch.7).

Further reference is made to ECtHR decisions in relation to specific topics in subsequent chapters.

Article 8

1. Everyone has the right to respect for his private and family life, his home and his correspondence.
2. There shall be no interference by a public authority with the exercise of this right except such as in accordance with the law and is necessary in a democratic society in the interests of national security, public safety or the economic well-being of the country, for the prevention of disorder or crime, for the protection of health or morals or for the protection of the rights and freedoms of others.

The ECtHR has stated that the essential object of Article 8 is 'to protect the individual against arbitrary action by the public authorities' (*Kroon* v. *Netherlands* (1994)). In doing this the state is obliged to take action to ensure that the right is secured for the individual, and to ensure that that right is protected as against other individuals. In Article 8 cases there is very often a balance that has to be struck between the competing interests of the individual and the community. There is also often a difficult balance to be drawn between the rights of one individual and those of another.

Private life has been widely interpreted to include gender, sexual life, the physical and moral integrity of the person, personal information, paternity, and name – although a wide margin of appreciation has been allowed states in regard to restrictions on permissible changes of name. The case of *Gaskin* v. *United Kingdom* [1989] illustrates the positive obligations which arise from the right to respect for private life. The applicant, who had been in the care of Liverpool Social Services for almost the whole of his childhood, claimed that he had been abused whilst in care. When he was refused disclosure of the whole of his file, he complained to the ECtHR that the refusal was in breach of his right to respect for his private and family life. The court allowed the complaint on the grounds, *inter alia*, that refusal to disclose the files went beyond the margin of appreciation allowed between the competing interests of the individual and the child care system. UK law was subsequently changed to impose a duty to disclose personal files to the individual concerned, with safeguards for third party information.

Family life has also been widely interpreted by the ECtHR. It is not restricted to marriage-based relationships (*Keegan* v. *Ireland* (1994)), nor to heterosexual relationships (*Fitzpatrick* v. *Sterling Housing Association* [2000]). Its existence may depend on a number of factors such as whether the couple live together, the length of their relationship, and 'whether they have demonstrated their commitment to each other by having children together or by any other means...' (*X, Y, and Z* v. *United Kingdom* [1997]). If the existence of a family tie with a child is established, the state must act to safeguard and promote the integration of the child within his family. Although the central family relationships are husband and wife and parents and child, the members of 'illegitimate' families are equally entitled to Article 8 guarantees, as are near relatives such as grandparents, siblings and uncles and aunts (*Marckx* v. *Belgium* (1979), *Boyle* v. *United Kingdom* (1994)). The extent to which unmarried fathers may be treated differently from mothers and married fathers has been held not to breach Article 8 (*McMichael* v *United Kingdom* (1995)).

Once the applicant has established the fact of interference with a right under Article 8, it is for the state to show that the interference may be justified as being lawful, and necessary for the protection of one of the aims set out (Article 8(2) and see Swindells et al. (1999: pp. 52–4)).

Article 14

> The enjoyment of the rights and freedoms set forth in this Convention shall be secured without discrimination on any grounds such as sex, race, colour, language, religion, political or other opinion, national or social origin, association with a national minority, property, birth or other status.

Article 14 cannot be invoked on its own. It can only apply when the facts of the case fall within the terms of one or more of the substantive Articles. For Article 14 to apply, the applicant must therefore satisfy three requirements:

● that he is subject to difference in treatment from others in a similar situation (the status of illegitimate children in *Marckx* v. *Belgium*);
● in the enjoyment of one of the rights protected by the Convention; and,
● the difference cannot be justified, having regard to the concepts of legitimate aim, proportionality, and margin of appreciation.

First Protocol, Article 2

No person shall be denied the right to education. In the exercise of any of the functions which it assumes in relation to education and to teaching, the state shall respect the rights of parents to ensure such education and teaching are in conformity with their own religious and philosophical convictions.

The UK has reserved the right to only accept the principle in the second sentence in so far as it is compatible with the provision of efficient instruction and training and the avoidance of unreasonable expenditure. So far the negative framing of the Article has been reflected in fairly restrictive interpretation by the Court.

Conclusion

Interpretation of the Convention and Strasbourg jurisprudence by the domestic courts is at an early stage and the law will continue to develop. Prior to implementation, the Court of Appeal and judges in the Family Division made it clear that whilst they welcomed genuine applications under the Human Rights Act 1998, they would not countenance spurious points. Since October 2000, most applications on human rights issues that have reached the Court of Appeal have been unsuccessful. The right to make direct application to the ECtHR in Strasbourg still remains for applicants dissatisfied by the response of the UK courts to claims for breaches of the Convention.

Chapter 3
Discrimination

Discrimination exists in many forms. It is legislated against in the areas of race, sex and disability, though not all aspects of the Disability Discrimination Act 1995 are yet in force. The Race Relations Act 1976 and the Sex Discrimination Act 1975 are phrased in similar terms outlawing both direct and indirect discrimination and making overtly discriminatory behaviour a criminal offence. The Commission for Racial Equality and Equal Opportunities Commission monitor the effect of the legislation and encourage good practice. Following the Macpherson report into the killing of Stephen Lawrence, the Race Relations (Amendment) Act 2000 extended the application of legislation on race relations to the police. Sections 28–32 of the Crime and Disorder Act 1998 also create new offences of racially aggravated assault, criminal damage, public disorder and harassment which carry higher penalties. Section 82 of that Act also requires the court to take account of any racial element involved in the commission of any other offence when passing sentence. The Disability Discrimination Act 1995 covers direct, but not indirect, discrimination in the areas of employment and the provision of goods, facilities and services. People with a recognized form of mental disorder as well as people with physical disabilities and learning disabilities come within the Act. A Disability Rights Commission was belatedly created to support the implementation of the legislation.

Racial Discrimination

The Race Relations Act (RRA) makes it unlawful to discriminate either directly or indirectly on the grounds of race, colour, nationality or ethnic origin in the provision of housing, employment, education or the provision of goods, services or facilities to the public. A person discriminates against another (RRA 1976, s.1(1)(a)) if 'on racial grounds he treats that other less favourably than he treats or would treat other persons'. The phrase 'on racial grounds' has been interpreted as meaning any reason for an action based on race, including the dismissal of an employee who refused to carry out an instruction to exclude young black men from the amusement arcade in which he worked: *Showboat Entertainment Centre Ltd.* v. *Owen* [1984]. Discrimination on the basis of religion or language is not unlawful under the 1976 Act. There have been a number of cases brought on the definition of 'racial group' within section 3(1). In *Mandla and Anor* v. *Dowell Lee and*

Anor [1982], the House of Lords accepted that Sikhs were a racial group defined by their ethnic origins; the application of a 'no turban' rule therefore amounted, subject to its justifiability, to indirect discrimination against Sikhs. However, in *Dawkins* v. *Department of the Environment* [1993], the Court of Appeal held that Rastafarians did not comprise a racial group for the purpose of the Race Relations Act; not being a group with a 'long, shared history' defined by reference to their ethnic origins. It was accepted in *Commission for Racial Equality* v. *Dutton* [1989], that gypsies, but not travellers, were a racial group; only in Northern Ireland are members of the Irish Traveller Community expressly included as a racial group by virtue of the Race Relations (Northern Ireland) Order 1997. In *BBC Scotland* v. *Souster* [2001], it was decided that the cultural traditions of the English and the Scots were too broad for either to be considered a distinctive ethnic group.

The Race Relations Act, unlike the Sex Discrimination Act, does not apply to employment in private households. Although positive discrimination is not lawful under the Act, section 5(2)(d) enables appointments to be made based on race as a 'genuine occupational qualification'. In *Tottenham Green Under 5s Centre* v. *Marshall* [1989], the test was interpreted as being, can services be 'most effectively provided by that racial group', not can they *only* be provided by that racial group.

Evidential matters relating to complaints of discrimination were considered by the Court of Appeal in *Anya* v. *University of Oxford* [2001], a case in which a black candidate of whom one of the interview panel had a prior acquaintance, was turned down for appointment. The Court of Appeal acknowledged that discrimination might rarely be overt or deliberate, but could be unconscious or embedded. The whole history of the case as well as future developments therefore had to be considered as evidence of whether or not an ostensibly fair-minded decision was, or was not, affected by racial basis. The tribunal also had to give adequate reasons for their decisions.

Racist abuse and harassment are also forms of racial discrimination under the Act if the form of harassment used would not have been used against a person of a different racial group. Employers who do not protect their employees from racial abuse by a third party in circumstances in which the employer can control whether it happens or not, will be 'subjecting' the employee to racial harassment. So, in *Burton and Rhule* v. *De Vere Hotels* [1996], a manager's failure to ensure that two waitresses were not abused by a racist comedian was to 'subject' them to such abuse. The harasser himself could not be sanctioned by the tribunal; such behaviour might however now fall within the Protection from Harassment Act 1997, s. 1(1), which covers behaviour causing alarm or distress, and which attracts both criminal and civil sanctions. Such behaviour is not defined by reference specifically to sex or race (McColgan, 2000).

The Race Relations Act contains specific offences of instructing, inducing or attempting to induce another person or organization to discriminate. Only the Commission for Racial Equality (CRE) as the body set up to monitor the operation of the Act can take action with respect to these parts of the Act.

The Race Relations (Amendment) Act 2000 imposes specific duties upon public authorities, including local authorities, health authorities and the police, but excluding the courts to take action to eliminate unlawful discrimination, to promote equal opportunities and to promote good race relations. The CRE has developed a Code of Practice and four non-statutory guides on the Act. Public authorities will do this through the drawing up of Race Equality Schemes. In the employment sphere, public authorities are required to monitor by ethnic group their existing staff, and applicants for jobs, promotion and training. Schools must also publish and monitor the effect on pupils' achievement of their race equality policies. Chief Officers of Police are also made liable for all acts of discrimination carried out by any officer under their command when carrying out policing functions, which includes stop and search powers, arrest and charge, and controlling demonstrations. The decision to prosecute, which is taken by the Crown Prosecution Service, is not however subject to challenge under the Act. For social work agencies the Race Relations (Amendment) Act will require attention to race relations issues to be embedded in the organization and its policies and procedures.

Sex Discrimination

The Sex Discrimination Act 1995, s.1(1), provides that

> a person discriminates against a woman in any circumstances relevant for the purposes and provisions of this Act if –
>
> (a) on the grounds of her sex he treats her less favourably than he treats or would treat a man, or
> (b) he applies to her a requirement or condition which he applies or would equally apply to a man but –
> (i) which is such that the proportion of women who can comply with it is considerably smaller than the proportion of men who can comply with it, and
> (ii) which he cannot show to be justifiable irrespective of the sex of the person to whom it is applied, and
> (iii) which is to her detriment because she cannot comply with it.

Section 1 (above) relating to discrimination against women is applied equally to discrimination against men (s.2(1)). Less favourable treatment in respect of a person's marital status is also unlawful discrimination under the Act (s.3(1)), but only in relation to employment.

Transsexuals were brought within the ambit of the Sex Discrimination Act for the first time, following the decision of the European Court of Justice in

P v. *S and Cornwall County Council* [1996] that discrimination on the grounds of gender reassignment amounted to sex discrimination contrary to the Equal Treatment Directive. The Sex Discrimination (Gender Reassignment) Regulations 1999 (SI 1999 No. 1102) introduced a new section 2A into the Sex Discrimination Act prohibiting direct discrimination though only in relation to employment and training. It remains the case under English law that persons who have undergone gender reassignment are regarded, for the purposes of marriage, imprisonment and so on, as retaining the biological sex of their birth (McColgan, 2000).

Under the Sex Discrimination Act, unlike the Equal Pay Act, there is no need to identify an individual who has been more favourably treated on the grounds of sex. Treating women differently from men because of stereotypical assumptions, for example that they will not be the chief bread-winner, amounts to sex discrimination: *Coleman* v. *Skyrail Oceanic* [1981]. There must be a causal link between the discrimination and membership of a particular group (as with racial discrimination). This is sometimes called the 'but for' test, as applied in *Jones* v. *Eastleigh Borough Council* [1990] where the House of Lords held that it was unlawful discrimination to apply a criterion, namely reaching pensionable age, which discriminated between men and women in respect of free entrance to the local swimming pool. Mr. Jones, aged 61, would have been admitted free of charge 'but for' the fact that he was a man and the pensionable age for men was 65, as opposed to 60 for women. The *Jones* case established the general principle that in such cases of direct discrimination, justification is not a defence and, in any case of discrimination, motive or intention is irrelevant.

The concept of indirect discrimination, as in the race relations arena, seeks to capture those 'Practices that are fair in form, but discriminatory in operation' (McColgan, 2000: 67). A successful claim of indirect discrimination requires the applicant to establish the existence of (a) a requirement or condition, with which (b) a considerably smaller proportion of his/her sex or racial group can comply, and with which (c) the applicant himself cannot comply. The employer's defence to a claim of indirect discrimination is that the application of the requirement or condition was justifiable. The choice of the 'pool' against which the potentially discriminatory impact of the requirement or the condition can be tested is therefore crucial. Employment Tribunal members will take account of their members' local knowledge and expertise in selecting the 'pool', but what properly constitutes a pool is a matter of law. So in *University of Manchester* v. *Jones* [1992], a 44-year-old woman who was rejected for a job limited to graduates aged 27–35 could compare herself only with other graduates with relevant experience, whether male or female; the fact that fewer women were able to obtain degrees as mature students under the age of 35 was irrelevant; age discrimination could not be argued, as this in itself is not unlawful.

The burden of proof in a claim of sex discrimination was considered by the Court of Appeal in *Whiffen* v. *Milham Ford Girls' School* [2001]. The case was brought by a female teacher on one of a number of short-term contracts. The school had chosen not to renew short-term contacts and also had a number of permanent staff who would potentially be subject to a redundancy selection procedure. The tribunal had found that there was indirect discrimination under section 1(1)(b) of the Act as more women than men were on short-term contracts. That having been proved, the onus then shifted to the employer to show that the discriminatory requirement was justifiable irrespective of the sex of the employee. It could not however do that by reference to an *apparently* gender neutral section policy (contract staff should go first), because that policy had already been shown to be indirectly discriminatory. Instead the justification had to relate to the employer's general policy that only the permanent employees who remained would be subject to a redundancy selection procedure.

Protection from discrimination on the ground of gender under the Sex Discrimination Act may not also offer protection from discrimination on the grounds of sexual orientation, unless it can be shown that men and women would have been treated differently in this respect. So, in *Pearce* v. *Governing Body of Mayfield Secondary School* [2001], a lesbian teacher who had been subject to homophobic taunts by pupils could only be compared with a homosexual man in the same situation. The Court of Appeal found that because a homosexual man would have received the same treatment, there was no evidence of less favourable treatment on the grounds of sex. The impact of the Human Rights Act was considered in *Security of State for Defence* v. *Macdonald* [2001]. The applicant was dismissed from the RAF because of his homosexuality, and the Employment Appeal tribunal found that this was direct discrimination, interpreting the Sex Discrimination Act to be compatible with Art. 8 of the ECHR, and consistent with the decision of the European Court of Human Rights in the 'gays in the military case' of *Lustig-Prean and Beckett* v. *United Kingdom* (2000).

The position of women in relation to pregnancy and maternity leave and also requests for family-friendly working policies has created particular challenges to the interpretation of the Sex Discrimination Act. This is because discrimination under the Act is defined in terms of 'less favourable treatment' and there is no male counterpart with which to compare. In *Hayes* v. *Malleable Working Men's Club and Institute* [1985], a solution was found in comparing the treatment experienced by a pregnant woman with that of a male employee who was unavailable for work through sickness; though their circumstances could never be called the same, the tribunal came up with the useful phrase, that they were 'not materially different'. European law is relevant here: in *Dekker* v. *Stichting Vormingsentrum voor Jonge Volwassen Plus* [1994], the European Court of Justice held that dismissal, by reason of pregnancy, of a woman from indefinite employment breached the Equal Treatment Directive 76/207, on which national laws regarding sex discrimination are based. The House of Lords in *WDB* v. *EMO Air Cargo (UK) Ltd (No. 2)* [1994], accepted that the only way to reconcile the Directive with the more precise test of unlawful discrimination set out in section 1(1)(a) of the Sex Discrimination Act was to abandon the comparison with the hypothetical man and to regard pregnancy solely as a relevant circumstance in relation to unavailability for work. It is clear therefore that dismissal by reason of pregnancy is unlawful sex discrimination, though this principle will not necessarily apply to short-term contracts, or time-limited vocational training where actual availability is necessary for performance of the contract.

In respect of employment law, the Employment Relations Act 1996, s.99(1) makes the position clear: dismissal where the reason is pregnancy or any other reason connected with pregnancy, is automatically unfair, irrespective of the employee's length of service or hours worked. Entitlement to maternity leave, time off for antenatal care and protection against detrimental treatments, for example refusing overtime, is contained in the Maternity and Parental Leave etc. Regulations 1999. There are however some advantages in arguing a case based on the Sex Discrimination Act; in sex discrimination cases there is no limit on the amount of damages recoverable (the same is true under the Race Relations Act), and qualifying periods in terms of continuous employment do not apply.

Opportunities to change one's working pattern or reduce working hours to accommodate family commitments many also be discussed in the context of the Sex Discrimination Act. In *London Underground* v. *Edwards* [1995] the complainant's employers had failed to justify a shift system with which women were less able to comply than men. There was no justification for such a system under s.5(3) as amendment was a reasonable step which would have involved little difficulty and expense. Though there is no entitlement to reduced working hours to fit in with child-care commitments, the obligation is on employers to consider such a request and to justify its refusal. Discrimination against mothers or fathers, based on gender, will also be unlawful sex discrimination.

In *Coker* v. *Lord Chancellor*; *Osamor* v. *Lord Chancellor* [2001], there were two separate applicants; one alleging sex discrimination and the other racial discrimination in respect of the appointment by the Lord Chancellor of a white male from within his circle of acquaintances to the post of special adviser. It was held that the Lord Chancellor's decision to appoint a person known to him to that particular post without advertising the vacancy did not constitute indirect sex or racial discrimination since the requirement that the appointee be personally known to the Lord Chancellor had the effect of excluding almost the entirety of the appropriate pool of persons used to determine whether the requirement has a disproportionate effect on women or on a particular racial group.

Disability Discrimination

Legislation concerning discrimination on the grounds of disability was not enacted until 1995. The Disability Discrimination Act of that year is being brought into force in stages. The Disability Discrimination Act 1995 covers only direct discrimination against people with disabilities, and not indirect discrimination 'on the grounds of disability'. Despite the development of the social model of disability (Oliver, 1996), the definition of 'disability' in s.1(1) of the Act is based on a medical and functional model:

> A person has a disability for the purposes of this Act if he has a physical or mental impairment which has a substantial and long-term adverse effect on his ability to carry out normal day to day activities.

Schedule 14 describes 'day to day activities' in terms of 'mobility; manual dexterity; physical co-ordination; continence; ability to lift, carry or otherwise move everyday objects; speech, hearing or eyesight; memory or ability to concentrate, learn or understand; or perception of the risk of physical danger'. Asymptomatic conditions are thus excluded from the definition of disability; severe disfigurement (Schedule 1, para. 3(1)) is to be treated as having a substantial adverse effect on the ability of the person concerned to carry out normal day to day activities; but 'mental impairment' includes an impairment resulting from or consisting of a mental illness only if the illness is a clinically well recognised illness (Schedule 1, para. 1(1)). The effect of an impairment is a 'long term' effect only if it has lasted for at least 12 months, or is likely to last for at least 12 months, or is likely to last for the rest of the life of the person affected (Schedule 1, para. 2(1)).

There are three areas in which discrimination is unlawful; in respect of employment, the provision of goods, facilities and services, and in the disposal or management of premises.

Employment

Discrimination in employment is less favourable treatment 'for a reason which relates to the disabled person's disability' (s.5(1)(a)), but this is subject to a statutory defence of 'justification' (s.5(3)). There is, however, a duty upon the employer where there would otherwise be substantial disadvantage to a disabled person to make reasonable adjustments; the initiative is not with the employee to suggest what adjustments would need to be made to the working environment or terms and conditions of employment in response to their disability: *Cosgrove* v. *Casear and Howie* [2001]. The reason put forward by the employer for the less favourable treatment of a disabled employee has to be both material and substantial. However, when a properly conducted risk assessment has taken place, an employment tribunal hearing a claim of disability discrimination cannot substitute its own appraisal for that of the employer; *Jones* v. *Post Office* [2001], where the Court of Appeal held that restrictions on the driving duties of an employee who had suffered a heart attack and who had diabetes was not irrational. Statistics (DfEE, 1999) show that disabled people are substantially disadvantaged in the employment market; disabled people account for nearly a fifth of the working age population in Great Britain, but for only about one-eighth of all in employment, and are over six times more likely than non-disabled people to be dependent upon benefits. The largest group (19 per cent) of people who are long-term disabled have back or neck problems, 8 per cent have a mental disorder and 2 per cent have learning difficulties.

The Provision of Goods and Services

In respect of the provision of goods, facilities and services, s.19(1)(a) makes it unlawful for a provider of services to discriminate against a disabled person in refusing to provide or deliberately not providing, to the disabled person any service which he provides, or is prepared to provide to members of the public. Such services include (s.19(3)) access to and use of any public places; accommodation in hotels, and so on; facilities by way of banking or insurance or credit; facilities for entertainment, recreation or refreshment, and the services of any profession or trade or any local or other public authority. Section 21 further provides that where the provider has a practice, policy or procedure which makes it impossible or unreasonably difficult for disabled persons to make use of a service, there is a duty upon the provider to take reasonable steps to change that practice, policy or procedure so that it no longer has that effect.

Accommodation

Except in cases where the occupier shares accommodation, s.22(1) makes it unlawful for a person with power to dispose of any premises to discriminate against a disabled person, either in the terms on which he offers to dispose of the premises, or by refusing to dispose of the premises to the disabled person or in his treatment of the disabled person in relation to others who are on a list (such as a housing allocation register) as in need of accommodation.

Discrimination in Other Areas

The Secretary of State is given powers under Part V of the Disability Discrimination Act to make regulations in respect of access to taxis, public service vehicles and rail vehicles. Although discrimination in the provision of education, whether in schools, colleges or institutions of higher education, is not included in the definition of 'goods, facilities and services' under Part III of the Disability Discrimination Act, the Special Education Needs and Disability Act 2001 (see page 177) will extend the concept of disability discrimination into the field of education.

There is a timetable for the implementation of the Disability Discrimination Act 1995. The employment provisions of the Act have been in force since December 1996, as has the prohibition on direct discrimination in relation to goods and services, though the duty to make reasonable adjustments in this sphere was not introduced until October 1999. From 2004 there will be a duty to remove or alter physical features that make access to services impossible or unreasonably difficult for people with disabilities.

Conclusion

Anti-discriminatory legislation in the UK outlaws differences in the treatment of individuals on the basis of gender or race, and direct discrimination against disabled people. It does not focus upon disadvantage or inequality of opportunity, and extends its protection only to narrowly defined groups. The impact of Art. 14 of the European Convention on Human Rights is yet to be seen. Article 14 regulates discrimination in categories wider than those existing in domestic law, covering as it does, sex, race, colour, language, religion, political or other opinion, national or social origin, association with a national minority, property, birth or other status. Article 14 does not give rise to free-standing rights against discrimination in any context, but only in the exercise of the other rights and freedoms guaranteed by the European Convention. However, this will operate in areas where domestic law has given no protection, for example discrimination against individuals on the basis of their sexual orientation regardless of gender. Thus in *Lustig-Prean and Beckett* v. *UK* and *Smith and Grady* v. *UK* (2000), the European Court of Human Rights held that the United Kingdom's ban on homosexual activity in the armed services was contrary to their right to respect for private life under Article 8. A change in domestic law is awaited, as the law of the European Community is also operational in this field. The European Union Article 13 Directive of October 2000 extends the scope of anti-discriminatory policies in the workplace by requiring governments to outlaw discrimination in the field of employment on the grounds of sexual orientation and religion by 2003, and on the grounds of age by 2006.

Chapter 4

Challenging Local Authority Decisions

Decision-making in local authorities is founded on powers and duties set out in statute and regulations and elaborated in departmental directions and guidance. Local authorities have to act within the law and guidance, and can be held accountable for failure to do so. There are a variety of ways in which adult or child clients (or adults on their behalf) who are dissatisfied with a service provided or denied may dispute decisions taken by the local authority. These include using statutory complaints procedures; having recourse to the local government Ombudsman; invoking the Secretary of State's default powers; seeking judicial review of the decision-making process; and, actions for damages for injury suffered as a consequence of breach of statutory duty or negligence.

Local Authority Complaints Procedures

Prior to 1991, there was a very patchy provision of access to internal procedures whereby dissatisfied clients of social services departments could challenge decisions made about them. Where procedures existed, they were invariably internal, lacking any element of independence from the local authority. Within the policy climate of 'consumers' rights', the Citizen's Charter, and other moves towards increasing the accountability by public bodies, the Children Act 1989 and the National Health Service and Community Care Act 1990 required local authorities to set up complaints procedures with an independent element.

The procedures under both Acts for dealing with representations and complaints made by adult or child clients of social services departments, or by adults on behalf of children, are similar though not identical. Every authority had to appoint a designated officer (DCO) to receive and deal with complaints under both Acts through a three-stage procedure. At the first stage, informal resolution is sought with the relevant worker or manager. If the client remains dissatisfied he or she must complain in writing to the DCO who has to arrange for a formal investigation of the complaint within a tight time scale. Initially only in Children Act complaints but, shortly for community care complaints as well, an independent person (IP) is appointed to scrutinize the work of the investigating officer (IO). The IO reports in writing to the

DCO on his or her findings in relation to the complaint(s), on which the IP may comment. If dissatisfied with the outcome of the second stage, the complainant may request that the investigation of the complaint be referred to a hearing before a panel of three people of whom one must be independent (neither an officer nor an elected member of the local authority). In line with previous practice in many authorities, the reforms due to be introduced require that the panel should be chaired by the independent person.

The panel hearing the complaint, at which the complainant may be accompanied by a friend or supporter, but not formally legally represented, has all correspondence and the IO's report and IP's comments available to it. It also hears any additional representations regarding the investigation of the complaint(s) the complainant wishes to put before it, to which the IO or social worker or manager may respond. Following the hearing, the panel has to report on their findings within 24 hours and may make recommendations to the director of social services and the social services committee, who have discretion as to whether they accept the recommendations. If they do not do so, this may provide grounds for judicial review of the decision complained of (see below). A complainant who is not satisfied with the panel's decision can take their case to the Ombudsman (see below).

Since statutory complaints procedures were introduced in 1991, the Social Services Inspectorate (SSI) have produced three overview reports on inspections of complaints procedures in a number of local authorities (SSI, 1993, 1994, and 1996). Researchers from the University of Sheffield undertook a comparative study of the procedures in six local authorities (Jordan and Williams, 1996) and several pressure groups working with children have produced reports on single-issue studies (Children's Society, 1998; Voice of the Child in Care, 1998). In 2000, the Department of Health convened an advisory group to consider whether, having regard to such research as there was, and anecdotal evidence, the procedures under both Acts were in need of any amendment. Various proposals were circulated for discussion (Department of Health (2000a), *Listening to People*). The proposals, which received widespread support, required minor amendments to the Children Act 1989, introduced in the Adoption and Children Act 2002, s.112, and new regulations and guidance. The main changes are

- to add an informal resolution stage, to be completed within 14 days, to Children Act 1989 complaints;
- to require the appointment of IPs at the second stage of all complaints, except where regulations provide for attempts at an informal resolution;
- to extend the second stage time limit for complaints by adults on behalf of children (but not those by children which still have to be dealt with within 28 days) to three months;
- to require that panel hearings are chaired by an independent person; and,
- to introduce (with some flexibility) a time limit for making complaints.

Local Government Ombudsman

The office of local government Ombudsman developed from the appointment in 1967 of a Parliamentary Commissioner for Administration with responsibility for investigating complaints and allegations of maladministration in central government departments, leading to injustice to individuals. The classic formulation of maladministration is the so-called 'Crossman catalogue' of 'bias, neglect, inattention, delay, incompetence, ineptitude and arbitrariness' (McDonald, 1997: 45).

In 1974, maladministration in local authorities became subject to similar scrutiny. There are now three local government commissioners (Ombudsmen) covering all local authorities in England, as well as one each for Scotland and Wales. They investigate, free of charge, individuals' allegations of injustice suffered as a result of maladministration by local authorities and may result in a recommendation for the payment of compensation. Complaints must be made within three months and alternative remedies, including the statutory complaints procedure, must usually already have been exhausted unless the Ombudsman feels that it is not reasonable to use those remedies. Social services' clients, dissatisfied with the outcome of recourse to the complaints procedure, may go on to take their case to the Ombudsman. It is not unusual for the length of time taken by a local authority to respond to a complaint to be the subject of allegations to the Ombudsman that an individual has suffered injustice through maladministration (Department of Health, 2000: para. 5.1).

The Ombudsman has access to all relevant files and records and has the same powers as a High Court judge to order the production of documents or the attendance of witnesses, although hearings are rare. Ombudsman's reports are public documents; the parties receive copies and if local authorities fail to comply with recommendations there are mechanisms for publicizing that fact and seeking compliance (McDonald, 1997: 46).

Powers of the Secretary of State

If a local authority fails without reasonable excuse to carry out any of its social services duties (not powers), the Secretary of State can under the Children Act 1989, s.84 or the Local Authority Social Services Act 1970, s.7D, inserted by section 50 of the National Health Service and Community Care Act 1990, declare the local authority to be in default. He or she can then issue directions to ensure that the duties are complied with within a specified period, and enforce that direction through judicial review in the Administrative Court (see below). In addition, where a local authority is not meeting the government's 'best value' requirements, the Secretary of State has power under the Local Government Act 1999 to 'take over' its functions.

Although these draconian default powers exist, their exercise is discretionary and there is no recorded instance of their having been used, nor are any records kept of the number of applications made. The powers appear to serve little practical purpose. The political purpose is to provide a mechanism whereby if an intransigent local authority was in conflict with the Secretary of State 'the default power could be used to assert the authority of the latter' (McDonald, 1997: 44).

Judicial Review

Judicial review is a remedy in public law, located within the Administrative Court (formerly the Divisional Court, see page 5) which allows individuals to challenge the legality and adherence to due process of public bodies' decision making. Access to judicial review is usually dependent upon other remedies, such as recourse to statutory complaints procedures, having been exhausted. The court does not, as in an appeal, substitute its view for that of the authority. It may make an authoritative declaration of what the law is (as in *Gillick* v. *West Norfolk and Wisbech Area Health Authority* [1986]) or may order the authority to reconsider its decision, if necessary through the use of the prerogative powers of:

- mandatory order, ordering a court or public body to carry out a duty;
- prohibitory order, which operates to prevent a public authority taking invalid decisions; and
- quashing order where the invalid decisions of public bodies may be set aside.

For more detail see, for instance, Slapper and Kelly (2001: 232–4). Judicial review is a complex and fast growing area of law, and has been substantially affected by implementation of the Human Rights Act 1998.

Judicial review is not concerned with the merits of the decision but with whether the process by which it was reached was so flawed as to warrant one of the actions described above by the court. A decision may be reviewable because it is *ultra vires*, that is to say beyond the statutory powers of the body making the decision. Or it may be based on a misinterpretation of the law, or be contrary to the principles of natural justice in that the decision-makers could be shown to be biased or reached a decision based on only hearing one side. Finally, even if the decision-making could be shown to be legally and procedurally satisfactory, the actual decision might be considered so irrational or unreasonable that no reasonable body could have reached that decision. This principle is referred to as 'Wednesbury unreasonableness' after the judgment of Lord Green MR in *Associated Provincial Picture Houses Ltd.* v. *Wednesbury Corporation* [1948].

Recently, the ECtHR principle of proportionality (see page 17, above) has replaced the more than 50-year reign of the 'Wednesbury principle'. Prior to implementation of the Human Rights Act 1998 there was considerable debate amongst lawyers as to whether, since the only justification for interference with a basic human right is that permitted by the Convention, the very restrictive test of unreasonableness could survive (Supperstone and Coppel, 1999). It was soon apparent that it would not. The decision in the ECtHR in *Smith* v. *United Kingdom* [1998], where it was found that gays in the armed forces had been denied an effective remedy (Article 13) because of the limitations of the 'reasonableness' test, made it clear that once decisions by public bodies had to be Convention compliant, the courts would have to change their approach.

In *R* v. *Secretary of State for the Home Department, ex p Daly* [2001], a case which concerned the policy of searching prisoners' cells and all their correspondence including that with their solicitors, the House of Lords confirmed that the proportionality of any interference will now be an issue in any review by the courts of the decision of a public authority. The present position appears to be as follows.

> [T]he court will now undertake a more stringent review of the decision-making of public authorities, at least where Convention rights are in play; however, while the public authority will need to show that any interference is legitimate (rather than simply that it is reasonable or not reasonable), the decision remains that of the public authority – the court's power is one of review. In short, the court will not ask itself whether the decision is one that it would have made (a merits based approach); nor will it ask itself whether the decision was so unreasonable that it cannot be sustained (*Wednesbury*). Rather the court will require the decision-maker to show that a decision which interferes with the human rights of any individual is one that is for a permissible reason and one that is necessary in a democratic society. (Plowden and Kerrigan, 2001: 1292)

Civil Actions

A successful action for breach of statutory duty or negligence at common law provides the only means whereby an individual can obtain significant compensation for a wrong done by a local authority. Until recently the courts were markedly reluctant to allow actions against local authorities in breach of a duty of care (*X (Minors)* v. *Bedfordshire County Council* [1995]). However, this is another area of the law which following implementation of the Human Rights Act, with its requirement that domestic courts take into account ECtHR jurisprudence, is changing, in a way that makes it likely that there will be many more successful claims in the future (*Barrett* v. *Enfield London Borough Council* [1999]; *Phelps* v. *Hillingdon London Borough Council* [2000]). These decisions of the House of Lords not only make it much less likely that claims will be struck out as in the past as being non-justiciable, but that, as in *Phelps*, they may be successful at trial.

Whilst many welcome the justice of those who have clearly suffered profoundly into adulthood as a direct consequence of the negligent practice of professionals who owed them a duty of care, receiving compensation, the way in which the law appears to be developing is by no means unproblematic. It may well encourage very defensive social work practice, and has significant resource implications for local authorities (Mullis, 2000; 2001).

PART II
CHILDREN AND FAMILIES

Chapter 5

Child and Family Social Work: The Evolving Legal Framework

At the beginning of the twenty-first century, the Children Act 1989 has been in force for over a decade, the long overdue reform of adoption law is finally on the Statute Book, and the three services previously providing support and reports to court on children in family proceedings have been unified to form the Child and Family Court Advisory and Support Service (CAFCASS).

Children Act 1989: Origins, Principles and Proceedings

The Children Act 1989 which regulates most of the private and public law relating to children, with the exception of adoption, has been implemented for a decade with as yet, given the societal and child care policy shifts that occurred during the 1990s, extraordinarily little amendment. In part that has to be attributed to the long and careful gestation of the Act. A process of parallel, if very different, review and proposals for reform of the public and the private law lasted from the mid 1970s to introduction of the Children Bill in 1988 (Ball, 1991).

The result was a major reforming and consolidating statute, underpinned by research and 'involving debate between local authorities, voluntary organisations, academics, lawyers and civil servants with widely different perspectives and experiences' (Masson, 2000: 580). Importantly, the Act brought together the previously separate strands of the law within a uniform set of principles administered within three tiers of courts with concurrent jurisdiction.

The Children Act 1989 is predicated on the belief that children are generally best brought up within their own families, with the state and the courts only intervening where necessary. The private law provisions in Part II, although they contain no presumption of continued contact with the absent parent, seek to encourage the continued involvement of both parents with their children's upbringing regardless of the ending of the relationship with each other. In a symbolic move, the previous concept of 'parental rights and duties' was replaced with that of 'parental responsibilities'; more substantially, that responsibility survives parental separation. At the same time the growing recognition of children as individuals with rights of their own, separate from those of their parents, were for the first time given statutory recognition. This was manifested through requirements to consult children's wishes and feelings whenever decisions are made about their future, and a right for children of sufficient age and understanding to refuse medical examination or assessment in certain circumstances. The latter has been somewhat diminished by the courts (*South Glamorgan County Council* v. *W and B* [1993]).

The public law provisions of the Act were drafted with the intention of securing a better balance between the rights of parents to bring up their children without interference; the rights of children to have their voice heard and listened to; and, the duty of the state, through local authorities and the courts, to intervene to protect children at risk of neglect or abuse within their families. History shows that most reforming legislation, by overreacting to perceived imbalances, results in a swing too far in the other direction (Fox-Harding, 1991; Parton, Thorpe and Wattam, 1997). As yet, despite some robust research-based critiques of child-care practice under the Act (Department of Health, 1995; 2001) and important revisions of guidance on planning, child protection and child assessment (Department of Health and Department for Education and Employment, 1996; 2000b; Department of Health, Home Office and Department for Education and Employment, 1999; National Assembly for Wales, 2000; Department of Health, Department for Education and Employment and Home Office, 2000), there does not appear to be any clamour to redress the balance set over a decade ago.

Principles and Orders

The principles that underpin the Act are that:

- children are generally best looked after within the family, with both parents playing a full part in their upbringing, helped, when necessary, by the local authority providing services on a voluntary basis in partnership with parents;
- children's voices should be listened to;
- court proceedings should be a last resort;
- in any court proceedings concerning the child's upbringing or property, the child's welfare is the court's paramount consideration;
- delay by courts in reaching decisions is likely to be damaging to the child;
- in most proceedings, courts should consider the whole range of available orders and not only those applied for;
- courts should only make orders which are likely to be of positive benefit to the child.

The range of orders available in family proceedings under the Children Act 1989 give the courts a flexibility which could previously only be exercised under the inherent jurisdiction in the High Court (see page 70). This flexibility is achieved both through the enhanced range of orders and through the availability of private law orders (see Chapter 6) in care and other public law proceedings, whether or not they are applied for. For instance, a court considering a local authority application for a care order, may, if that is what is decided to be in the child's best interests, make a residence order (see page 62) to a relative or friend instead, possibly, provided the threshold conditions for the making of a care or supervision order were satisfied (see Chapter 10), accompanied by a supervision order as well.

The Welfare Criteria

In almost all proceedings under the Act, courts making decisions regarding the care and upbringing of children and the administration of their property must reach their decisions having regard to the principle set out in section 1(1) of the Act: 'the child's welfare shall be the court's paramount consideration'.

In order to direct attention to the issues to be considered, the Act contains a checklist of key factors for courts to consider in order to make an informed decision. Section 1(3) requires the court to have regard in particular to:

1   the ascertainable wishes and feelings of the child concerned (considered in the light of his age and understanding);
2   his physical, educational and emotional needs;
3   the likely effect on him of any change in his circumstances;
4   his age, sex, background and any characteristics of his which the court considers relevant;
5   any harm which he has suffered or is at risk of suffering;
6   how capable each of his parents, and any other person in relation to whom the court considers the question to be relevant, is of meeting his needs;
7   the range of powers available to the court under this Act in the proceedings in question.

The items are not set out in any order of priority, and each will be of more or less relevance in individual cases.

In addition to the welfare principle, there are two other general principles set out in section 1. The first recognizes that delay, unless purposeful, is likely to 'prejudice the welfare of the child' (s.1(2)), and the second (s.1(5)) requires that courts shall not make any orders unless it considers that 'doing so would be better for the child than making no order at all'.

Human Rights Act 1998

Since its implementation in 1991, provisions of the Children Act 1989 have been interpreted and defined by a growing body of case law, and more recently they are being scrutinized for their compatibility with the ECHR (see

Chapter 2). Very few lacunae have been identified during this process and as yet few substantial amendments made. Those there have been include: provisions relating courts' powers when making emergency protection and interim care orders where a child is at risk from domestic violence (Family Law Act 1996, Part IV), and in relation to children leaving care under the Children (Leaving Care) Act 2000. Further amendments are likely to be introduced by the Adoption and Children Act 2002 (see Chapters 6 and 11). Otherwise, the provisions remain much as enacted.

In *Re S (Minors) (Care Order: Implementation of Care Plan); Re W (Minors) (Care Order: Adequacy of Care Plan)* [2002], the House of Lords overturned the Court of Appeal's Human Rights Act attempt to challenge the intention of Parliament by introducing external scrutiny of local authorities' adherence to care plans following the making of a care order. Their Lordships' support for the Court of Appeal's reasoning resulted in amendments to the 1989 Act (see page 90).

Messages from Research

Just as the provisions of the Children Act 1989 were substantially informed by research into all aspects of child care practice under previous legislation (Department of Health and Social Security, 1985), so throughout the 1990s, the Department of Health commissioned research into all aspects of the working of the 1989 Act. A comprehensive overview of this research, identifying key themes and trends was published in 2001 (Aldgate and Statham). Earlier, the Department had published an overview of 16 studies relating to the organizational and practice context of child protection under the Children Act 1989 (Department of Health, 1995) and of studies of the care of children in residential homes (Department of Health, 1998). These studies into all aspects of the 1989 Act are complementary to each other. There have also been a number of studies into process and outcome in regard to adoption, the one major area of child law outside the Act, which have also been drawn together in an overview report (Department of Health, 1999).

The breadth of the research and the identification of themes and trends through the overview reports provide a wealth of information for policy-makers and practitioners. Further research will, of course, be needed to determine whether the lessons from research have been learned.

Reform of Adoption Law

The reform of adoption law, which by the late 1980s was recognized as being needed as a matter of urgency to provide for the radically changed nature of the adoptive population (Department of Health, 1999; Lowe, 2000), has lagged badly behind. At the time of implementation of the Children Act in

1991, work was already under way on the major review of adoption law which was published for discussion as the report of an interdepartmental working group in 1992 (Department of Health and the Welsh Office, 1992). Governmental ambivalence in the 1992–97 Conservative and first Labour administrations have resulted, despite a White Paper in 1993, two subsequent consultation papers in 1994 and a draft bill in 1996, in delay that only came to an end with a flurry of Prime Ministerial activity in 2000. This was followed by a White Paper at the end of the year, and the introduction of the Adoption and Children Bill in March 2001, a time when it was inevitable that the bill would fall on the calling of the general election.

A revised Adoption and Children Bill had its first reading in the House of Commons in October 2001, and will be enacted in 2002 and probably implemented in 2004 (see Chapter 11).

Children and Family Court Advisory and Support Service

Until recently, for historical reasons, the welfare interests of children in court proceedings have been represented very differently depending on the nature of the proceedings. Probation officers, generally without any child-care training, acted as welfare officers producing reports concerning children within families for the courts in private law proceedings (Children Act 1989, s.7). Guardians *ad litem*, for the most part fee-attracting, though also some local authority employed, 'safeguarded the welfare of the child' and produced reports in public law and some adoption proceedings. The Official Solicitor, an officer of the Supreme Court with a primary responsibility for the interests of children and mentally disordered patients, represented children in wardship and other particularly complex cases in the High Court. The variability in the service provided has not only been in regard to the task of the report writer, but also in relation to their level of specialist expertise (Timmis, 2001). There has long been agreement that unification of the three strands, to provide a service of the quality of the best, was a legitimate objective. Unfortunately, the process of reform appears to have been expedited for resource reasons and the new service has got off to a bad start.

In April 2001 the CAFCASS, established under the provisions of the Criminal Justice and Court Services Act 2000, replaced the previous arrangements for representing and reporting on children in family proceedings. Three very different organizations, working in discrete though overlapping areas, were brought together in great haste and with publicly aired acrimony. This is especially the case in regard to the terms and conditions for the previously fee-attracting members of local authority panels of guardians *ad litem* and reporting officers. Probably the repository of the greatest level of child-care expertise in the ingredient services, but who had also arguably had exceptionally favourable, relatively autonomous, working conditions.

Table 5.1   CAFCASS functions and titles

Function	Old title	New title
Report by probation officer (Children Act 1989, s.7(1)(a))	Court Welfare Officer	Children and Family Reporter
Report by local authority (Children Act 1989, s.7(1)(b))	Officer of local authority	Welfare Officer
Representation of subject child in public law case (Children Act 1989, s.41)	Guardian *ad litem*	Children's Guardian
Representation of non-subject child as a party (Family Proceedings Rules 1991, (SI 1991/1247) rr2.57, 9.2 and 9.5)	Guardian *ad litem*	Guardian *ad litem*
Representation of child subject in adoption case	Guardian *ad litem*	Children's Guardian
Collecting parental consent in adoption case	Reporting Officer	Reporting Officer
Representation of child in Human Fertilization and Embryology Act 1990 case	Guardian *ad litem*	Parental Order Reporter
Representation of child in inherent jurisdiction cases (Civil Procedure Rules 1998 (SI 1998/3132) Part 21)	Litigation Friend	Litigation Friend

Source: Family Law, 2001: 572.

The swift development of an effective, homogenous, child-centred service to represent the interests of children across the range of family proceedings is a legitimate aim for the new service. As an experienced former member of a guardian *ad litem* panel says:

Children do not care how we organise ourselves; they do not care what we call ourselves; children do not mind how much we get paid. Children simply want a good, reliable service, adaptable to their individual needs, supplied by a sensitive, effective and suitably qualified professional. (Timmis, 2001: 280)

Unfortunately all the indications are that, at least in the short term, poor planning and over hasty implementation of the new arrangements are likely to result in a diminished and impoverished service for children (White, 2001; Gerlis, 2002).

The Renaming of Report Writers and Children's Representatives

On 1 April 2001 when CAFCASS came into existence, the names of most of those with previous reporting and representation functions in family proceedings changed. Table 5.1 provides a guide to the functions and the old and new titles.

Chapter 6

Parents, Guardians and Parental Responsibility

In this Act 'parental responsibility means all the rights, duties, powers, responsibilities and authority which by law a parent of a child has in relation to the child and his property' (Children Act 1989, s.3(1)).

In contrast to earlier provisions, the Act provides consistent rules about the acquisition, exercise, and extent of parental responsibility, both as regards the child's parents and other people. As a consequence of societal changes and following a lengthy consultation process, the law relating to parental responsibility will be substantially reformed on implementation of the Adoption and Children Act 2002.

Parents and Parental Responsibility

The current law provides that the mother of the child and the father, if he was married to the mother at the time of the birth or subsequently, have full parental responsibility. This also applies where the child was born within a marriage as a result of assisted reproduction (artificial insemination by donor – AID) (Family Law Reform Act 1987, s.27). Similar provision is made for the parents of children born as a result of egg or embryo donation under the Human Fertilization and Embryology Act 1990, ss.27 and 28.

At present when the father is not married to the mother of the child, as a parent he has a restricted legal status in relation to the child unless he acquires parental responsibility. Full parental responsibility can only be acquired by an unmarried father either by formal written agreement with the mother or by court order. A mother's agreement to share parental responsibility with the child's father has to be made in the form prescribed in regulations and registered with the court. As a result of some evidence of fraud the regulations require that the agreement is witnessed by a justice of the peace or an officer of the court (Parental Responsibility Agreement (Amendment) Regulations 1994). Only a very small proportion of births outside marriage each year registered by both parents are followed by an agreement and even fewer by a court order.

Where an unmarried father applies for a parental responsibility order, the courts seem to have taken, as their starting point, the principle – already well established under section 4 of the Family Law Reform Act 1987 that, all else being equal, it is in the interests of a child's welfare to know his or her genetic identity, even if there is little or no continuing contact with the absent father. This applies even if the child is in the care of the local authority whose long-term plans for the child may not include the father. In *Re H (Minors) (Local Authority: Parental Rights) (No. 3)* [1991], Balcombe LJ suggested that the factors which should be taken into account when considering whether or not to make a parental responsibility order were:

(1)   the degree of commitment which the father had shown to the child;
(2)   the degree of attachment which exists between the father and the child;
(3)   the reasons for the father applying for the order. (Ibid.: 216c)

In *Re G (A Minor) (Parental Responsibility Order)* [1994] the Court of Appeal held that, even where a child was the subject of a care order and the father was 'awkward, difficult and thoroughly unresponsive to the approaches of social workers who have the interests of his child at heart', that would not, where he had shown considerable commitment and where there was a degree of attachment between father and daughter, 'unfit him to have the order which gives him a locus standi in the life of his child' provided that he would not use his increased legal status in a way that was damaging to the child's interests. In contrast, in *Re H (Parental Responsibility)* [1998], although the father had fulfilled the three conditions, the Court of Appeal considered that there were other factors adverse to the father which were sufficient to deny him parental responsibility.

Once made, parental responsibility orders or agreements may only be brought to an end on the application of anyone with parental responsibility for the child or, with the leave of the court, the child. Clearly, given courts' attitudes to the making of parental responsibility orders there will be a reluctance to terminate them, although the decision will be solely guided by consideration of the child's welfare. In a case in which it could be shown that the continued involvement of an abusive father in the child's life was likely to be damaging, the court decided that the child's welfare would be better served by termination of an agreement made between the mother and father when the child was nine weeks old (*Re P (Terminating Parental Responsibility)* [1995]).

Reform of the Law Relating to Parental Responsibility

The number of children born to parents who are not married to each other, but who jointly register the child's birth and reside at the same address continues to rise. In a consultation paper (Lord Chancellor's Department, 1998), the Lord Chancellor's Department identified the key issues that made the present law unsatisfactory. They included:

● widespread ignorance of their lesser parental status amongst fathers who had jointly registered the child's birth with the mother;

- the low incidence of parental responsibility agreements and court orders;
- the sense of injustice of fathers required to pay to support their children, but denied the legal status of parental responsibility.

Responses to the consultation paper overwhelmingly supported amendment of section 4 of the Children Act 1989 to give parental responsibility, which can only be terminated with the agreement of all with parental responsibility or by court order on the application of either parent or (with leave) the child, to unmarried fathers who register the child's birth jointly with the mother. The Adoption and Children Act 2002, enacts this reform. The changes are not uncontentious. There is a view that women who are not in a stable relationship will be well advised to continue to register children in their sole name, in order to avoid subsequent duties to consult an absent father about important decisions relating to the child (Eekelaar, 2001).

Guardians

The legal guardian of a child has full parental responsibility in the place of a parent. Anyone may apply to the court to become the guardian of an orphan child, or a child in respect of whom a residence order was made to a parent who died whilst the order was in force. The power to appoint a guardian to assume the place of the parent in the event of his or her death is one which can only be exercised by a parent with parental responsibility. If such a parent dies, his or her appointment in writing of a guardian will only take immediate effect if the child has no other parent with parental responsibility living, or if the parent who died had a residence order in regard to the child at the time of death. Otherwise the appointment will not take effect unless the other parent dies whilst the child is still a minor (Children Act 1989, s.5).

Acquisition of Parental Responsibility by Other People

More than two people may have parental responsibility for a child at the same time. Parents, including adoptive parents and those with a parental order under the Human Fertilization and Embryology Act 1990, s.30, do not lose parental responsibility, except through adoption of the child (see Chapter 11). They may share it with:

- Any person who has a residence order in their favour has parental responsibility for the child as long as the order lasts.
- A local authority has parental responsibility when the child is the subject of a care order, or for the duration of an emergency protection order.
- The Adoption and Children Act 2002 (ACA 2002) amends the Children Act 1989, s.4, by inserting section 4A which provides that a step-parent

may acquire parental responsibility with the agreement of the parent(s) with parental responsibility or by court order. Such an order may only be brought to an end by a court order on the application of any other person with parental responsibility or, with leave, the child.

- The 2002 Act also introduces the new legal status of special guardianship which effectively transfers parental responsibility for a child to the special guardian(s), but without the final legal severance from the birth family effected by adoption (see below).
- Under the ACA 2002, when a placement order is made, the adoption agency and the people with whom the child is placed acquire parental responsibility while the child is placed with them.

The Exercise of Parental Responsibility

No order, apart from an adoption order (see Chapter 11) can deprive parents of their parental responsibility, but the power to exercise it may be curtailed. Parents may through court orders lose the capacity to exercise most aspects of the legal status but it continues, subject to section 2(8) of the Children Act which provides that the possession of parental responsibility does not entitle the holder to act inconsistently with an order made under the Act.

Parents who both have parental responsibility share equally and independently the right to make decisions regarding where a child shall live, how (subject to the Education Acts) they shall be educated and with whom they shall have contact, although one parent, unless they have sole parental responsibility, cannot unilaterally change the child's name or habitual residence (*Re A (Wardship: Jurisdiction)* [1995]). The rights and powers which parents exercise in regard to their children are exercised on the child's behalf. The corollary of this is that as children mature they become more able to make their own decisions (*Gillick* v. *West Norfolk and Wisbech Health Authority* [1986]). When the wishes of older children conflict with the rights of parents to make decisions on their behalf, the law can be both complex and contradictory (see page 58).

Special Guardianship

In the early 1990s, the members of the interdepartmental working group reviewing adoption law, recognized the fact that for some children in need of permanent, secure placement outside their birth family the absolute termination of the legal relationship effected by adoption was not appropriate. For these children an order of greater permanence than that achieved by a residence order (see Chapter 7), but without irrevocable legal severance from the birth family, was needed. The term *inter vivos* guardianship was proposed. Although not taken up by the Conservative government when the

Adoption Bill 1996 was published for consultation, the order, renamed 'special guardianship' was proposed in the White Paper, *Adoption: A New Approach* (2000), and included in Part II of the Adoption and Children Act 2002 which amends the Children Act 1989 by the insertion of new sections 14A–14G. Special guardianship orders may be applied for as of right or with leave, or by the court on its own motion.

The following are entitled to apply for special guardianship orders either individually or jointly with another person, to whom they do not have to be married.

- any guardian of the child;
- anyone who holds a residence order, or has the consent of anyone in whose favour a residence order is made;
- anyone with whom the child has lived for three out of the past five years (with the consent of the local authority, foster parents may apply after one year);
- if the child is in care, anyone applying with the consent of the local authority;
- in any other case, anyone who has the agreement of all those with parental responsibility for the child.

Anyone else, including the child, may apply with leave of the court. The court may also make a special guardianship order in any family proceedings concerning the care or upbringing of a child, even if no application has been made.

Applications for Special Guardianship

Anyone wanting to apply for a special guardianship order must give three months' written notice of their intention. The local authority must investigate and prepare a report (the content of which may be prescribed in regulations) for the court about the suitability of the applicants and any other relevant matters. The court may not make a special guardianship order without considering such a report, and it appears likely that there will be provision for the appointment of a CAFCASS officer in appropriate special guardianship proceedings. The court hearing the application must apply the paramountcy principle in section 1(1) of the 1989 Act and the welfare checklist (s.1(3)).

The Effect of a Special Guardianship Order

The intention is that the special guardian has sole responsibility for day-to-day decisions in the child's life and in relation to his upbringing. However, unlike adoption, the birth parents remain legally the child's parents although they retain minimal power to exercise parental responsibility. The special guardian may exercise parental responsibility for the child to the exclusion of parents or guardians, except where consent is required for the child's adoption, or the law requires the consent of more than one person with parental responsibility, for instance for sterilization (s.14C). Section 5 of the Children Act is amended to allow a special guardian to appoint another person to be the child's guardian in the event of his death (s.14G(4)).

Special guardians may take the child out of the jurisdiction for up to three months, but may not change the child's surname or take the child out of the jurisdiction for longer than three months without the consent of anyone else with parental responsibility or leave of the court (s.14C(3)). The court may give such leave when making the special guardianship order, and must at the same time consider whether any contact order should be made (s.14B).

A special guardianship order when made discharges any existing care order, related contact order (see Chapter 10), and any order made under section 8 of the Children Act 1989 (see Chapter 7).

Discharge or Variation of Special Guardianship Orders (s.14D)

In contrast to adoption orders (Chapter 11), special guardianship orders can be discharged or varied by a court. This may be on the application of a special guardian, any parent or guardian of the child, a local authority with a care order in respect of the child, and anyone with a residence order. The child may apply with the leave of the court. Although parents and guardians may apply they may not do so during the first year after the making of the order, and after that only if there has been 'a significant change of circumstances' since the order was made (s.14D(5)).

Special Guardianship Support Services

Local authorities have a duty to make arrangements for the provision of special guardianship support services, and the assessment of the need of children who are the subject of special guardianship, or special guardians, for the need for services, and determine whether to make provision. There will be detailed and prescriptive regulations which seem likely to mirror post adoption services for adopted children and adoptive families.

Schedule 3 to the ACA 2002 amends provisions added to the Children Act 1989 by the Children (Leaving Care) Act 2000, to place on local authorities a duty to consider whether to provide advice and assistance to former looked after children aged between 16 and 21 who are subject to special guardianship orders. Where the authority decides that the young person is in need of advice and assistance that the special guardian is unable to provide, the authority is under a duty to advise and befriend him or her, and may provide him or her with assistance.

The Rights and Responsibilities of Parents

Parents have some rights and responsibilities regardless of whether they have parental responsibility, and some only when they do. Other people who are not parents and do not have legal parental responsibility, may have responsibilities which are the same as those of parents simply because they care for the child without any legal relationship.

Registering the Birth and Naming a Child

It is the responsibility of a parent with parental responsibility to register the birth of a child within five weeks, and their right to choose the child's names. After that the child's surname can only be changed with the consent of everyone with parental responsibility, or by order of the court.

Custody of the Child

Unless a court has ordered to the contrary (see Chapter 7), anyone with parental responsibility has the right of custody of a child, and it is a criminal offence under the Child Abduction Act 1984 for anyone else to remove or keep the child away from the parents. It is also an offence for a parent to remove a child from the United Kingdom without the consent of every person with parental responsibility or a court order. The Hague Convention on the Civil Aspects of International Child Abduction, incorporated into UK law by the Child Abduction and Custody Act 1985, regulates the return of abducted children to their place of habitual residence (see further: Lowe and Douglas, 1998; Cretney and Masson, 2002; Hayes and Williams, 1999).

Day-to-day Care

Any person over the age of 16 who has day-to-day care of a child may be regarded as responsible under criminal law if the child is neglected or abused (Children and Young Persons Act 1933, s.1). In the same circumstances, the local authority is under a duty to investigate and support the family with services, or seek to find a relative able and willing to assume care of the child. If they fail to find anyone prepared to act on a voluntary basis, or the parents resist help, the authority may need to secure a care order in order to acquire parental responsibility (see Chapter 9).

Education

Any person with whom a child lives has a duty to ensure that a child of school age attends school (see Chapter 17).

Consent to Medical Treatment

If a doctor provides medical treatment without consent, which in the case of a child below the age of 16 and not 'Gillick-competent' must be given by a person with parental responsibility, he or she may be charged with assault. The Family Law Reform Act 1969, s.8, gives children aged 16 or over the right to consent to medical treatment, and the House of Lords' decision in *Gillick* v. *West Norfolk and Wisbech Health Authority* [1986] extends that right to a child 'of sufficient intelligence and understanding' under the age of 16. Where, rather than giving consent, a 16–17-year-old or a 'Gillick competent' child is refusing life saving treatment, the situation is less straightforward. The law has developed in a way that protects doctors and avoids constant applications to court (Eekelaar, 1993). In most circumstances, faced with a mature child or young person who is refusing to consent to treatment, doctors may seek to persuade them to change their mind, but will accept the decision. However, in (generally) life-threatening situations, where children, including those with a statutory right to give their own consent, cannot be persuaded, either anyone with parental responsibility or the High Court through use of the inherent jurisdiction or a specific issues order can give valid consent (*Re R (A Minor) (Wardship: Medical Treatment)* [1991]; *Re W (A Minor) (Medical Treatment)* [1992]; for a general discussion see Bainham, 1998: ch. 8; Fortin, 1998: ch. 5).

Where parents of a child, generally on religious grounds, are refusing consent to essential medical treatment an application may be made to the High Court, which may or may not over-rule the parents' wishes (Cf. *Re T (Wardship: Medical Treatment)* [1997] and *Re A (Conjoined Twins: Medical Treatment)* [2001]). In an emergency the application can be made *ex parte*.

If treatment, such as an immediate blood transfusion, is essential to save a child's life and there is no one immediately available to give consent, doctors have been advised by the Department of Health that they are unlikely to be held liable for assault and should treat without waiting for a court order (Ministry of Health, 1967).

Appointing a Guardian or Consenting to the Child's Adoption

Only a parent with parental responsibility can appoint another person to become the child's guardian in the event of their death (see above, page 53) or consent to the child's adoption (Chapter 11).

Chapter 7

Family Breakdown

When a relationship involving children breaks down, arrangements regarding the children will to a large extent depend on whether or not the parties were married to each other. Permanent dissolution of a valid marriage, when both parties are still living, can be achieved only by divorce, although a marriage suffering from a fundamental defect, such as non-consummation, may be annulled. In other proceedings orders may be made which relate to the parties or children of a marriage or, in some circumstances, to cohabitees. The law relating to marriage and the family is both wide in its scope and complex in nature; this chapter gives only a brief introduction; for further detail it will be necessary to consult a specialist textbook (see, for example, Hayes and Williams, 2000; Cretney, 2001; Cretney and Masson, 2002).

Divorce

A marriage can be terminated only by death or by a decree of divorce or nullity. All suits for divorce are commenced by a petition presented to a divorce county court, and almost all will be concluded there; cases may be transferred to the High Court if their complexity, difficulty or gravity justify the move.

Until 2001 it was thought that the law relating to divorce would be radically altered upon implementation of Part II of the Family Law Act 1996 which enacted many of the proposals for reform set out in the White Paper, *Looking to the Future: Mediation and the Grounds for Divorce* (HMSO, 1995). That Act provided that the sole ground for divorce would, as at present, be the irretrievable breakdown of the marriage but that the five fault grounds – set out below – would be replaced by a 'no fault' requirement of evidence of the passing of a year – the minimum time within which a divorce could be obtained – and satisfactory compliance with procedural requirements. Anyone wishing to start the divorce process would have been required to attend an information-giving session covering separation, divorce and their effects on children, the availability of family mediation, marriage guidance and other services. Much greater use would have been made of mediation services, set up and funded alongside community legal services.

In January 2001 the Lord Chancellor announced, to no great surprise, that in the light of the unsatisfactory findings of evaluations of trial mediation schemes, Part II of the 1996 Act would not be implemented, and that further thought would be given to the reform of divorce law.

Under the present law no petition may be presented within the first year of marriage, although one presented after that may be based on events which occurred during the first year. Currently, the sole ground for divorce is that the marriage has irretrievably broken down; this can only be established by proving one of the five grounds set out in section 1 of the Act:

1   that the respondent has committed adultery and that the petitioner finds it intolerable to live with the respondent;
2   that the respondent has behaved in such a way that the petitioner cannot be expected to live with the respondent;
3   that the respondent has deserted the petitioner; and that this has been for a continuous period of two years;
4   that the parties have lived apart for a continuous period of at least two years, and that the respondent consents to the decree being granted;
5   that the parties have lived apart for a continuous period of at least five years immediately preceding the presentation of the petition.

Although the consent of the respondent is not required, the decree may be withheld if it can be shown that to grant it would cause grave financial or other hardship.

When the petition is served on the respondent, it must be accompanied by two forms – one setting out the steps to be taken and the consequences of a decree and the other being a form of acknowledgement of service which asks the respondent whether the proceedings are going to be defended. If the respondent wishes to defend the proceedings, he or she must file an answer within 29 days of receiving the petition, and then the case will be heard in open court.

Under what is called the 'special procedure' – in fact the normal procedure in undefended cases – neither party needs to attend court. The petitioner has to make a written application for directions for trial accompanied by an affidavit verifying the facts set out in the petition, any corroborative evidence relied on and certain other information. The district judge enters the cause in the special procedure list and, provided that he is satisfied that the petitioner has proved his or her case and is entitled to a decree, this will be certified and a date fixed on which the judge will announce the decree nisi in open court.

Unless the court orders to the contrary the petitioner may apply after six weeks (or any shorter time fixed by the court) for the decree to be made absolute. If the petitioner does not apply, the respondent may do so after three months from the earliest date on which the petitioner could have applied. Once the decree is absolute (but not before), the marriage is at an end and either party may remarry.

In addition to granting the divorce decree, the court may make a wide range of orders regarding finance, property and, where necessary, children. The court no longer has to certify that it is satisfied with the arrangements made for the children of the family. Instead the new section 41 of the Matrimonial Causes Act 1973 (Children Act 1989, Schedule 12, para. 31) provides that the court shall consider whether it should exercise any of its powers under the Act. If it considers that an order may be necessary, but is not in a position to decide, it must declare that the decree may not be made absolute until the court so orders.

The replacement of legal aid with Community Legal Services (see page 10) has effectively brought the provision of legal services for other proceedings more in line with those in place since 1977 in undefended divorce proceedings, although with an enhanced requirement to make use of mediation.

Children and Divorce

The whole principle and nature of orders regarding the children of the family following the breakdown of a marriage were profoundly altered by the Children Act 1989. Under the private law provisions of that Act both parents continue to have parental responsibility for their children regardless of the breakdown of their relationship. If they are able to agree, it is assumed that they will both have an equal say in their children's future and that there is no need for any court order. Each parent will continue to exercise 'all the rights, duties, powers, responsibilities and authority which by law a parent of a child has in relation to the child and his property' (Children Act 1989, s.3(1)).

Private Law Orders

Where parents are not able to agree, or others wish to be involved either by caring for or having contact with the child, the Act provides, in section 8, a menu of orders none of which remove parental responsibility although they may to greater or lesser extent restrict its exercise. A parent, including an unmarried father, or guardian of a child, or anyone with a residence order in their favour, may apply for any order under section 8 in relation to the child as of right. Anyone else, including the child, may seek leave of the court to make an application, subject to certain restrictions. Where a child is the subject of a care order applications are restricted to residence orders, which if made bring the care order to an end (contact with a child in care is regulated under section 34, not section 8, see page 92). Local authorities may only apply for prohibited steps or specific issues orders, they may not apply for residence or contact orders in favour of the authority. A local authority foster parent with whom the child has lived within the previous six months may not seek leave to apply for a section 8 order unless he or she has the consent of the local authority, is a relative of the child, or the child has lived with her for a total of three out of the previous five years. When the Adoption and Children Act 2002 is implemented, the period will be reduced to one whole year.

When deciding whether to grant leave, courts have to have regard to the nature of the proposed application, the applicant's connection with the child, and the likely effect, in terms of disruption to the child's life, of the application (s.10(9)). At the leave stage the welfare test does not have to be applied; nor does the court have to consider the child's wishes and feelings or the other 'checklist' items (*Re A (Minors) (Residence Orders: Leave to Apply)* [1992]; *Re SC (A Minor) (Leave to Seek a Residence Order)* [1994]).

Residence Order

Residence orders settle the arrangements as to the person with whom the child is to live (Children Act 1989, s.8).

Where a residence order is made in favour of an unmarried father, the court must at the same time make a parental responsibility order under section 4. This gives the father full parental responsibility, whereas non-parents with residence orders acquire parental responsibility which is effectively limited to day-to-day decision-making in that it excludes the power to consent to the child's adoption (see Chapter 11), or appoint a guardian for the child, and it comes to an end with the residence order on the child reaching 16 years or the order being discharged. Where a parent with a residence order appoints a guardian for the child the appointment takes effect on that parent's death, regardless of whether the other parent is still alive, unless the residence order was made jointly with the surviving parent. Shared residence orders may be made, but the courts appear reluctant to give clear guidance regarding their use (*A v. A (Minors) (Shared Residence)* [1994]).

The making of a residence order automatically restricts anyone from changing the child's surname or removing him or her from the United Kingdom for more than one month without the consent of every person with parental responsibility, or of the court (rules which apply in regard to parents with parental responsibility whether or not there is a residence order in place). In addition, a wide variety of directions and conditions may be attached to the order – for instance to restrict *any* removal from the United Kingdom, in cases in which the non-residential parent has a concern that if children were to be taken out of the jurisdiction they might not be returned.

Special guardianship which will provide a legal status between that of a person with a residence order and an adoptive parent will become available when the Adoption and Children Act 2002 comes into force (see pages 54–56).

Contact Order

A contact order means an order requiring the person with whom a child lives, or is to live, to allow the child to visit or stay with the person named in the order, or for that person and the child otherwise to have contact with each other (Children Act 1989, s.8).

Contact orders are only needed where the child's carer is restricting or prohibiting contact and an agreed arrangement cannot be reached. Orders may be for 'reasonable' contact where this can be agreed or may be precisely defined as to nature and duration. As with residence orders, a wide variety of conditions may be attached to contact orders provided that their primary purpose is directed towards the child's welfare.

The benefit to the child of maintaining contact with both parents after their relationship with each other breaks down has been developed into a judicial presumption in favour of contact, even where it is being determinedly resisted by the parent with whom the child lives. The Court of Appeal has held that the right is a fundamental one belonging to the child, which should only be denied if there are cogent reasons why contact should be denied (*Re H (Minors) (Access)* [1992]). Mothers who disobeyed contact orders were labelled as 'implacably hostile', regardless of the reason for their disobedience (Bailey-Harris et al., 1999). It is only in the last few years that judges in the High Court and Court of Appeal have, on the basis of research demonstrating the harm caused to children involved in domestic violence, recognized that some women have good reason to resist any contact between children and their violent fathers (Kaganas and Day Sclater, 2000; Sturge and Glaser, 2000). The general principle that it will generally be in the interests of a child's welfare to maintain contact with an absent parent remains unchanged, but the President of the Family Division, Dame Elizabeth Butler-Sloss, has made it clear that courts dealing with family matters should be more aware of the existence and consequences of domestic violence. In four linked judgments she set out the way in which courts should approach contact cases where there are allegations of violence that might affect the outcome (*Re L (Contact: Domestic Violence)*; *Re V (Contact: Domestic Violence)*; *Re M (Contact: Domestic Violence)*; *Re H (Contact: Domestic Violence)* [2000]).

Prohibited Steps Order

'A prohibited steps order' means an order that no step which could be taken by a parent in meeting his parental responsibility for a child, and which is of a kind specified in the order, shall be taken by a person without the consent of the court (Children Act 1989, s.8).

This order allows all courts in family proceedings access to powers once only available in wardship. Prohibited steps and specific issues orders (see below) may not be used 'with a view to achieving a result that could be achieved by making a residence order to contact order' (s.9(5)) and, as was envisaged prior to implementation of the Act, it appears, given the low incidence of the making of such orders, that the circumstances in which a prohibited steps order, rather than a condition in a residence or contact order, would be needed are rare (see Table 7.1). This does not, however, mean that they do not add important flexibility to courts' powers in family proceedings.

Table 7.1   The incidence of section 8 orders made in private law proceedings in all levels of court, 2000

Residence orders	25,809
Contact orders	46,070
Specific issues orders	2457
Prohibited steps orders	5345

Source: Lord Chancellor's Department, *Judicial Statistics* (2001)

A prohibited steps order may not be used as an alternative means of protecting children, where a local authority refuses, in circumstances in which the judge believes children to be at risk of significant harm, to apply for a care or supervision order under Part IV of the Act (see below, Chapter 8) (*Nottinghamshire County Council v. P* [1993]). However, in *Re H (Prohibited Steps Order)* [1995], it was held that a prohibited steps order could properly be made against a person who was not a party in the proceedings, or even present in court, to prohibit contact between him and a child he was alleged to have abused and her siblings.

Specific Issues Order

'A specific issues order' means an order giving direction for the purpose of determining a specific question which has arisen in connection with any aspect of parental responsibility (Children Act 1989, s.8).

This order, together with the prohibited steps order, gave courts orders with much of the flexibility previously only available through use of the cumbersome and expensive, albeit infinitely flexible, wardship jurisdiction. Specific issues orders have been used to determine a wide range of different matters, including, for instance, where parents disagreed, where a child should be educated (*Re A (Specific Issue Order: Parental Dispute)* [2001]). Possibly, the main use of specific issues orders is to obtain consent for medical treatment in circumstances in which parents are refusing to give their consent. See, for instance, the case of *Re R (A Minor: Blood Transfusion)* [1993], in which two Jehovah's Witnesses were refusing consent to a blood transfusion for their child. Rather than make the child the subject of a care order, the local authority applied for, and was granted, a specific issues order authorizing the transfusion.

Children's Applications

Section 10(8) of the Children Act 1989 allows children to make applications for leave to apply for a section 8 order. Following a few highly publicized early cases in which children applied for leave to apply for residence orders to allow them to live away from their parents, when a rush of applications from temporarily disaffected teenagers was anticipated, a Practice Direction was issued restricting the hearing of children's applications for leave to the High Court (Practice Direction (Family Proceedings Orders: Applications by Children) [1993]).

Early cases established that leave would only be granted if the issues were grave and not capable of resolution by the family, and that at the leave stage, the likelihood of the application being successful rather than the welfare of the child should be the court's concern (*Re C (A Minor) (Leave to Seek a Section 8 Order)* [1994]; *Re SC (A Minor) (Leave to Seek a Residence Order)* [1994]).

Family Assistance Order

Under section 16 of the Children Act 1989 with the consent of the parties, courts may make a family assistance order for up to six months in any family proceedings. This order is intended to provide short-term help from a Child and Family Court and Support Services (CAFCASS, see Chapter 5) family court reporter or a local authority social worker to 'advise and assist and (where appropriate) befriend members of a family'. The main purpose of the order, to which all parties have to consent, is to provide help in the immediate aftermath of family breakdown – in particular help over contact arrangements and so on. Unless there is a concurrent section 8 order, the supervisor has no power to bring the section 16 order back to court for a variation (DoH, 1991a, vol. 1, para. 2.50). A local authority is not bound to implement a family assistance order if it does not have the resources to do so (*Re C (A Minor) (Family Assistance Order)* [1996]).

Financial Provision

Absent parents are expected to pay towards the maintenance of their children until they reach the age of 16, or beyond if they are in full-time education. Many do so by agreement, otherwise payment may be enforced either through the courts or by the Child Support Agency (CSA). Implementation of the Child Support Act 1991 in 1993 effectively removed from the courts, to the CSA, powers to order absent parents to make payments for the benefit of their children in most circumstances. Under the 1991 Act, provided that a parent or any other person with the care of a child takes appropriate steps to obtain child support maintenance, the law requires the absent parent to make regular payments. This applies regardless of whether the parents were married to each other or in an unmarried or casual relationship.

Since the implementation of the Child Support Act 1991 as amended in 1995, new claims for child maintenance are handled by the CSA which is part of the Department of Social Security. The role of the agency is to make a maintenance assessment and to collect and enforce maintenance for 'qualifying' children. The terms used in the Act have specific meanings: section 3 provides:

(1) A child is a 'qualifying child' if –
   (a) one of his parents is, in relation to him, an absent parent; or
   (b) both of his parents are, in relation to him, absent parents.
(2) The parent of any child is an 'absent parent', in relation to him, if –
   (a) that parent is not living in the same household with the child; and
   (b) the child has his home with a person who is, in relation to him, a person with care.
(3) A person is a 'person with care', in relation to any child, if he is a person –
   (a) with whom the child has his home;
   (b) who usually provides day to day care for the child (whether exclusively or in conjunction with any other person); and
   (c) who does not fall within a prescribed category of person.

Child support officers calculate maintenance by applying rules and using a formula to arrive at the amount payable. The calculations are immensely complex. Where a 'person with care' does not rely on state benefits they can make their own decision as to whether to apply to the court for lump sum payments for the benefit of the child and/or the transfer of property for the benefit of the child under section 15 of, and Schedule 1 to, the Children Act 1989. Where, however, a parent with care of children has no income or an inadequate income and is in receipt of income support, working families' tax credit or disabled persons tax credit, the Act requires him or her to authorize the CSA to take action to recover child support from the absent parent. If a parent in this situation refuses to give authority, or to provide information required by the agency to enable the absent parent to be traced and a means assessment made, his or her benefit may be reduced.

There are some exceptions to these draconian provisions, in that a parent with care who is supported by state benefits will not be required to authorize the agency to recover maintenance where there are reasonable grounds for believing that it would result in 'a risk to her, or any child living with her, suffering harm or undue distress as a result' (s.6(2)). No guidance is given in the Act as to the meaning of 'harm or undue distress' and, in practice, interpretation appears to be restricted to risk of physical harm (CSA guidelines). More detailed accounts of the Child Support Acts 1991 and 1995, and helpful discussion of the issues involved, can be found in leading family law texts (Hayes and Williams, 2000; Lowe and Douglas, 1998; Cretney and Masson, 2002; Black, Bridge and Bond, 2000), and updated information, including application forms are available on the CSA website: http://www.dss.gov.uk/lifeevents/ benefits/child_support_maintenance.htm

Jurisdiction in Private Law Proceedings

The magistrates' family proceedings court has a concurrent jurisdiction with the county court and the High Court in most private law proceedings relating to family breakdown under the Children Act 1989, and sole jurisdiction in what remains of the Domestic Proceedings and Magistrates' Courts Act 1978. Magistrates have no jurisdiction in divorce or inherent jurisdiction proceedings.

The Matrimonial Home

Ownership

Ownership and rights on dissolution of a marriage are technical, complex and beyond the scope of this book; for lucid explanations, see Hayes and Williams, 2000; Black, Bridge and Bond, 2000; Cretney and Masson, 2002.

Occupation

The right to occupy the matrimonial or joint home is generally critical at the time of divorce or separation. The law relating to the occupation of the family home was substantially altered when most of Part IV of the Family Law Act 1996 came into force in 1997. Various occupation orders are available, depending on the status and circumstances of the applicant and the respondent. The Act gives greater protection to married couples and property owners. This is reflected in the range of orders that may be made under section 33 to 38 of the 1996 Act. Occupation orders may be applied for in other family proceedings or may be free-standing applications. (For a full account of rights of occupation see, for example, Hayes and Williams, 2000: ch. 8; Lowe and Douglas, 1998: ch. 5; Black, Bridge and Bond, Part V.)

Domestic Violence

Domestic assaults are criminal offences for which the attacker can be charged with one or more of the various offences against the person, including, since the House of Lords ruling in *R* v. *R* (*Rape: Marital Exemption*) [1994], that of rape of a spouse. A victim of domestic violence may be entitled to make a claim under the Criminal Injuries Compensation Scheme although, as a member of the same household as the perpetrator, certain conditions have to be satisfied before compensation can be claimed. In civil law, where the main issues are accommodation and personal protection, remedies for victims of domestic violence – whether adults or children – are available under Part IV of the Family Law Act 1996 which replaced the earlier confusing jumble of provisions. Victims of domestic violence may seek orders to secure their personal protection (non-molestation orders), and possibly secure the temporary removal of the violent partner from the family home (occupation orders).

Non-molestation Orders

On the application of a victim of domestic violence or other behaviour amounting to molestation, the court may make orders prohibiting the respondent from molesting another person associated with the respondent, or a relevant child. 'Molestation' has been widely interpreted in decisions under existing legislation to cover not only physical violence but also telephone calls, and even persistently following the applicant. The test set out in the Act is 'the need to secure the health, safety and well-being' of the applicant or any other person whom the court considers in need of protection, and any relevant child (s.42(5)). Both occupation and non-molestation orders may be made either within other family proceedings or without other family proceedings being instituted. Children under the age of 16 will require the leave of the court to make an application for either order. Both orders may be made *ex parte* in an emergency.

Such orders only provide protection if backed up with strong enforcement powers which the courts are prepared to use and the police to act on. The enforcement of orders under the 1996 Act are subject to the general law of contempt through the attachment of powers of arrest to all or part of the order. As under previous legislation, undertakings may be accepted by the court and are otherwise enforceable as if they were orders of the court, the main difference between an order and an undertaking being that a power of arrest may only be attached to an order, not to an undertaking.

Occupation Orders

The Family Law Act 1996 provisions considerably extend the categories of persons who may apply for occupation orders, although where the applicant is a cohabitant or former cohabitant rather than a spouse, the court is required, unless the likelihood of significant harm to children is an issue, 'to have regard to the fact that the parties have not given each other the commitment required in marriage'. For cohabitants and former cohabitants the order can only be made initially for a maximum of six months, with a possible extension of up to six months.

One of the principal features of the Act, implementing the Law Commission's recommendations, is the extension of the categories of 'associated persons' who may apply for non-molestation orders. For the purposes of the legislation a person is associated with another person if:

1 they are, or have been, married to each other;
2 they are cohabitants or former cohabitants;
3 they live, or have lived, in the same household, otherwise than merely by reason of one of them being the other's employee, tenant, lodger or boarder;
4 they are relatives;
5 they have agreed to marry one another (whether or not that agreement has been terminated);
6 in relation to any child, they are both persons who are parents of the child, or have or have had parental responsibility for the child; or
7 they are parties to the same family proceedings.

The persons protected under the new provisions include 'relevant children', defined to include:

1 any child who is living with or might reasonably be expected to live with either party to the proceedings;
2 any child in relation to whom an order under the Adoption Act 1976 or the Children Act 1989 is in question in the proceedings; and
3 any other child whose interests the court considers relevant.

Amendments to the Children Act 1989

The lack of powers for courts to remove alleged abusers, in order to allow the child to remain safely in the family home, had long been a matter of concern. The 1996 Act amended the Children Act 1989 so that alleged abusers can be ordered to leave the family home for the duration of an emergency protection order (s.44A) or during an interim care order (s.38A). For the exclusion requirement to be included in an interim care order,

> The conditions are –
> (a)   ... there is reasonable cause to believe that, if a person ('the relevant person') is excluded from a dwelling-house in which the child lives, the child will cease to suffer, or cease to be likely to suffer, significant harm, and
> (b)   that another person living in the dwelling-house (whether a parent of the child or some other person) –
>   (i)   is able and willing to give to the child the care which it would be reasonable to expect a parent to give him, and
>   (ii)   consents to the inclusion of the exclusion requirement.
> (Children Act 1989, s.S38A(2))

The conditions in regard to emergency protection orders are similar though differently worded.

The exclusion requirement may require the relevant person to leave the premises where he is living with the child, and/or refrain from visiting, and/ or exclude him from a defined area around the premises.

In practice the critical factor will be the willingness of the mother or another person to protect the child. For this reason the order can only be made with their consent.

The Inherent Jurisdiction and Wardship

Prior to implementation of the Children Act 1989, the development of the inherent jurisdiction of the High Court exercising the powers of the Crown as *parens patriae* (the King as father of his people), was almost exclusively through exercise of the wardship jurisdiction. Since 1991, use of the inherent jurisdiction, which unlike wardship extends to adults as well as children, has developed considerably, so that Lowe and Douglas (1998, ch. 16) suggest that it should now be regarded as a separate jurisdiction.

The main difference between the two jurisdictions is that unlike wardship, the inherent jurisdiction does not place the child under the ultimate responsibility of the court. The High Court exercising the inherent jurisdiction outside wardship has the same wide-ranging and flexible powers to make orders in regard to the child's welfare, but it does not, as in wardship, have a continuing supervisory role; there is no requirement that the court should sanction any important steps in the child's life.

Wardship

Despite its being a common law rather than a statutory jurisdiction, procedure in wardship cases is governed by the Supreme Court Act 1981 and the Rules of the Supreme Court (Order 90, Rules 3–11). Under these Rules, anyone with a declared personal or professional interest can make a child a ward of court by taking out an originating summons with immediate effect. 'A ward of court is a child whose guardian is the High Court' (Law Commission, 1987b). The effect of this is that, whoever had day-to-day care and control of a ward, no important decision may be taken in his or her life without reference to the court, and the judge has the power to make infinitely flexible arrangements within the constraints of the criteria that all decisions have to recognize that the welfare of the child is paramount. Unless an appointment for a hearing is made within 21 days, wardship lapses. If an appointment is made, the child continues to be a ward until the full hearing unless there is a successful interim application to de-ward (1981 Act, s.41).

The High Court has exclusive jurisdiction to make a child a ward and to de-ward, but all intermediate decisions may be transferred to and from the county court in accordance with a Practice Direction [1986] of the President of the Family Division.

The use of wardship rose dramatically during the 1970s and 1980s. Almost all of the considerable rise in the numbers of originating summons were accounted for by applications made by, or with the agreement of, local authorities whose applications by 1990 made up more than 60 per cent of the total. This increase in the use of wardship led to long delays and very considerable expense. It was also perceived to be biased against parents, both because of the delays in trial of the substantive issues, and because for complex legal reasons they could only make children wards of court with the agreement of local authorities (Morton and Masson, 1989).

The range and flexibility of orders available under the Children Act 1989, particularly the introduction of specific issues and prohibited steps orders, deliberately rendered use of wardship unnecessary in most cases and it is no longer available to local authorities as a route by which to secure care or supervision orders (s.100). As a result the number of wardship cases has dropped dramatically from the high of the late 1980s to a number that is too insignificant to be reported in the annual judicial statistics. The jurisdiction still remains for private law proceedings and other issues relating to children in which there appears to be a lacuna in the law, and where there is the need for the court to maintain continued supervision over the child's life.

Chapter 8
Local Authorities' Powers and Duties

Services for Children in Need

The presumption under the Children Act 1989 is that social work intervention, when needed, will wherever possible be in the form of the provision of supportive services to children and their families on a partnership basis. Part III can be seen as the cornerstone of the Act so far as child-care work is concerned. Under section 17 local authorities have a positive duty to:

> safeguard and promote the welfare of children within their area who are in need; and so far is consistent with that duty promote the upbringing of such children by their families, by providing a range and level of services appropriate to those children's needs.

A child 'in need' is defined under section 17(10) as one who is unlikely 'to achieve or maintain, or to have the opportunity of achieving or maintaining, a reasonable standard of health or development without the provision to him of services by a local authority', or his health or development is likely to be significantly impaired, or further impaired, without the provision of such services; or he is disabled. 'Development' means physical, intellectual, emotional, social or behavioural development, and 'health' means physical or mental health (s.17(11)). Local authorities also have preventive and investigative duties under the Act which relate to all children. These include the duty to 'take reasonable steps' through the provision of services detailed in Schedule 2, Part I, 'to prevent children within their area suffering ill-treatment or neglect' (para. 4); and to 'take reasonable steps' designed to reduce the need to bring care, criminal or other family proceedings relating to them.

The whole range of services which local authorities must or may provide in order to carry out their preventative role are set out in Part III and Schedule 2, Part I (DoH, 1991a, vol. 2). These include day care, accommodation, aftercare, services for families and co-operation between authorities, as detailed below. Where there is a duty to provide services, local authorities cannot decide arbitrarily which category of children they will or will not provide services for (ibid., vol 2: 137). It is, however, a proper exercise of the local authority's discretion to decide whether a particular child is in need of services.

Child-minding and Day Care

Local authorities are under a duty to provide such day care for children in need within their area, who are aged five or under and not yet attending schools 'as is appropriate' (s.18), and may provide day care for other children of the same age even if they are not in need. The Nursery and Child Minders Regulation Act 1948 and all its regulations were repealed and replaced by Part 10 of, and Schedule 9 to, the Children Act 1989, with regulations, which through registration provide a unified regulatory mechanism providing local authorities with the necessary powers to take action where adequate standards are not achieved. Local authorities are under a duty to review both their provision of day care and that provided by others required to register under the Act, and by childminders, for children under eight years. In addition to providing day care, local authorities have a duty under the Act, together with the local education authority, to review provision of day care and the availability of childminders for children under the age of eight, on a three-yearly basis.

Accommodation

Under the Children Act 1989, the provision of accommodation with the consent of parents replaced the previous concept of 'voluntary care'. The avoidance of the use of the term 'in care' for any status other than that of a child who is the subject of a care order was deliberate. The term 'care' had come to have negative connotations and therefore to be unduly stigmatizing for a voluntary arrangement. The legislators chose 'accommodation' as a neutral term for the provision by the local authority of a service which provided care in a foster or residential home on a voluntary basis in partnership with parents.

Mirroring previous provisions relating to 'voluntary' care, section 20(1) of the Children Act sets out the circumstances in which local authorities must accommodate children in need.

> Every local authority shall provide accommodation for any child in need within their area who appears to them to require accommodation as a result of:
> (a) there being no person who has parental responsibility for him;
> (b) his being lost or having been abandoned; or
> (c) the person who has been caring for him being prevented (whether or not permanently, and for whatever reason) from providing him with suitable accommodation or care.

The section, as were its predecessors, is drafted in a way that embraces any possible circumstances in which a child might need to be physically cared for in an emergency or as part of a plan.

The provision of accommodation is a voluntary arrangement to which in most circumstances all those with parental responsibility (see pages 51–4) must agree, unless they are willing to take over the care of the child, and the child's wishes and feelings must be ascertained and 'given due consideration'. Anyone with parental responsibility may remove the child from accommodation at any time unless the person who made the arrangement has a residence order in their favour (s.20(7) and (8)). Children in need who have reached the age of 16, whose welfare the authority consider likely to be seriously prejudiced if accommodation is not provided, may also be provided with accommodation regardless of the wishes of anyone with parental responsibility. The position of 'Gillick competent' children under the age of 16 is less clear, particularly if a person with parental responsibility wishes to remove them from accommodation against their wishes (for a detailed account, see Bainham, 1998: 338–9).

Local Authorities' Responsibilities for 'Looked After' Children

Accommodated children may be boarded out in foster homes, placed with relatives, or in residential homes, schools or hostels. Children in accommodation, together with those who are the subject of emergency protection orders or are in care (see Chapter 10), or on remand (see page 143), come within the category of being 'looked after' by the local authority. There are both general duties, set out in section 22 of the Act, and very detailed regulations in regard to all children who are 'looked after' (DoH, 1991a, vols 3 and 4).

The primary general duty of any local authority looking after any child as set out in section 22(3) is:

(a) to safeguard and promote his welfare; and
(b) to make such use of services available for children cared for by their own parents as appears to the authority reasonable in his case.

Where the Children Act provisions differ from their predecessors is in the statutory duty laid on local authorities when reaching their decisions in regard to the child. Section 22(4) provides that

Before making any decision with respect to a child whom they are looking after, or proposing to look after, a local authority shall, so far as is reasonably practicable, ascertain the wishes and feelings of –

(a) the child;
(b) his parents;

(c) any person who is not a parent of his but who has parental responsibility for him; and

(d) any other person whose wishes and feelings the authority consider to be relevant,

regarding the matter to be decided.

When reaching their decisions the local authority are required to give 'due consideration' to 'such wishes and feelings of the child as they have been able to ascertain' having regard to his or her age and understanding, and to those of anyone else they have consulted. They must also take account of the child's 'religious persuasion, racial origin and cultural and linguistic background' (s.22(5)). Where, to protect the public from serious injury, a local authority has to exercise their powers in relation to a child in a way that is not consistent with the general duties outlined they are empowered to do so – for instance, by placing the child in secure accommodation (s.22(6)).

Regulations regarding the placements of all children 'looked after' by the local authority, which includes those in accommodation as well as in care, are detailed and elaborated on in volume 3 of the Department of Health's guidance (DoH, 1991a) and in the Placement of Children (General) Regulations 1991 and the Placement of Children with Parents Etc. Regulations 1991.

Secure Accommodation

The use of 'accommodation provided for the purposes of restricting liberty' by local authorities for children whom they are looking after is subject to restriction, both in terms of the circumstances in which children may be locked up, and the maximum periods for which this may last. Liberty may only be restricted if the following criteria are satisfied (s.25(1)):

(a) that –
    (i)   he has a history of absconding and is likely to abscond from any other description of accommodation; and
    (ii) if he absconds he is likely to suffer significant harm; or
(b) that if he is kept in any other description of accommodation he is likely to injure himself or any other persons.

If the above criteria are satisfied a child may be kept in secure accommodation for up to 72 hours without a court order. Children under the age of 13 may only be placed in secure accommodation with the direct authority of the Secretary of State. If the local authority propose to restrict liberty for more than 72 hours, or an aggregate of 72 hours in a 28-day period, it must obtain a court order. The restrictions on the use of secure accommodation do not apply to children subject to detention under mental health legislation, but they do apply to all children accommodated by health or local education authorities or in residential care, nursing or mental nursing homes. Children in voluntary children's homes and registered children's homes may not be kept in secure accommodation (DoH, 1991a, vols 1 and 7). The fact that the child has been placed in secure accommodation does not restrict the power of anyone with parental responsibility to remove an accommodated child at any time (s.20(8)).

Secure accommodation orders Applications for secure accommodation orders for children in care or in accommodation, apart from those who are remanded into accommodation as a result of committing criminal offences, are made to the family proceedings court (or the county or High Court). If granted, which they must be if the court finds the criteria satisfied (*Re M (A Minor) (Secure Accommodation Order)* [1995]), the order may be for up to three months in the first instance and may be renewed on application to the court for periods of up to six months (Children (Secure Accommodation) Regulations 1991, reg. 11). The order should only be made for the shortest period, up to the maximum, considered necessary. In *Re W (A Minor) (Secure Accommodation Order)* [1993], Booth J identified the draconian nature of a secure accommodation order. She held that magistrates were wrong to make an order for three months when the guardian *ad litem*, supporting the making of the order, had recommended a period of five weeks as being sufficient. Applications with regard to children on remand are made to the youth or other magistrates' court and last for the period of the remand up to a maximum of 28 days.

Where a child is the subject of a secure accommodation order, the local authority must hold a review within a month, and at intervals not exceeding three months to satisfy themselves that the criteria for keeping the child in secure accommodation still apply, and whether any other accommodation would, having regard to the child's welfare, be appropriate (reg. 15).

In all secure accommodation proceedings the child must be legally represented, or have refused such representation, and there are no financial eligibility requirements. In non-criminal proceedings applications to keep children in secure accommodation are proceedings in which a children's guardian must be appointed unless the court is satisfied that an appointment is not necessary in the interests of the child.

Section 1 of the Children Act 1989, which makes the child's welfare the court's paramount consideration on any question respecting his or her upbringing, does not apply to the provisions of Part III of the Act under which applications for secure accommodation are made (*Re M (A Minor) (Secure Accommodation Order)* [1995]). The general duty of the local authority to safeguard and promote the child's welfare applies (s.22(3)). (For a more detailed discussion of the regulation and use of secure accommodation, see Ball, McCormac and Stone, 2001: ch. 9.)

Aftercare

The margin heading for section 24 of the Children Act 'Advice and assistance for certain children' reflects a real difficulty with terminology, in that only children who are the subject of care orders can be referred to as being 'in care'. This is because the duties and powers in section 24 apply to all children who have been looked after by the local authority, including those who have been accommodated in health service or voluntary provision after reaching the age of 16, and who are still under 21. The Act initially provided that all those in the above category, who appear to be in need and ask for help, must be advised and befriended and, where necessary, given assistance in kind or, in exceptional circumstances, in cash.

Research undertaken by Stein and his colleagues at the University of Leeds have systematically identified the plight of children moving into adulthood from the public care system and promulgated best practice in regard to their support (Stein, 1991; Biehal et al., 1995; Frost and Stein, 1995). The Labour government in its first administration recognized the extent of the disadvantage in terms of the poor educational achievement, low employment prospects and homelessness and propensity for criminality suffered by children leaving the public care and introduced legislation intended to impose greater requirements on local authorities to provide services to support such children into independent living.

The Children (Leaving Care) Act 2000, implemented in October 2001, through amendment of section 24, provides additional safeguards for 16- and 17-year-olds who have been 'looked after' after their sixteenth birthday by placing additional duties on local authorities. These include the provision of a 'pathway' plan mapping out a clear route to independence; provision of an personal adviser; and continuing assistance for 18–21-year-olds with education, training and employment. More controversially, social security benefits previously available to care leavers are replaced by a new financial regime administered by local authorities. Although this is intended to provide a comprehensive package more easily accessible than the variety of benefits previously available, commentators raise concerns regarding the adequacy of the ring-fenced budget and the potential for inconsistencies in its administration as between authorities (Howard, 2001).

Services for Families

Schedule 2, Part I to the 1989 Act sets out the range of services which local authorities are under either a duty or have power to provide. The mandatory provisions include: the identification of children in need and the provision of information about available services; the maintenance of a register of disabled children and the provision of services for disabled children which enable them to lead as normal lives as possible; the prevention of abuse and neglect and the committing of crimes by children; provision to reduce the need to bring care or criminal proceedings; the provision of services for children living with their families, including family centres, and enabling children living apart from their families to live with them. There is also a duty when considering day or foster care to consider the different racial groups represented in the area. The services which local authorities are empowered to provide include assistance to enable a suspected abuser to leave the home in order to allow a child to remain.

Co-operation Between Authorities

In an attempt to ensure a co-ordinated approach to the provision of services by, for instance, health, housing and education as well as social services, section 27 of the Children Act authorizes local authorities to request help from other agencies and health authorities in the provision of services under Part III. The agency whose help is sought is under a duty to comply with the request 'if it is compatible with their own statutory or other duties and does not unduly prejudice the discharge of their functions'. The provision provides a useful reminder to other agencies of the expectation of co-operation. However, the decision of the House of Lords in *R* v. *Northavon District Council ex parte Smith* [1994] supports the view that, although section 27 may be helpful in its underscoring of the desirability of interagency co-operation, when tested, the value of the provision is seen to be more symbolic than real. In the *Northavon* case, the Lords, overturning the decision of the Court of Appeal, ruled that the duty under section 27 did not require a housing authority to overturn their finding of intentional homelessness and provide accommodation for a family with children. Reliance was placed on the extent to which the provision of housing to this family would exacerbate the wait of others on the housing list and therefore 'unduly prejudice' the discharge of the housing authority's functions. The court suggested that, if the housing authority would not accede to the request to house the family, the onus was on social services to protect the children of the family by providing financial assistance towards accommodation for the family or exercising other powers available to them under the Children Act 1989.

Chapter 9
Children in Need of Protection

Revised Department of Health guidance on interagency co-operation in child protection work, *Working Together to Safeguard Children* (Department of Health, Home Office and Department for Education and Employment, 1999; Assembly for Wales, 2000) continues to emphasize the difficulty of striking the right balance between avoiding unnecessary intrusion in families whilst protecting children at risk from significant harm. This chapter sets out the main child protection duties and powers of local authorities. Understanding of the impact of these provisions in practice needs to be acquired through familiarity with the overview reports of the outcomes of research programmes into all aspects of the child protection system published by the Department of Health (Department of Health, 1995; Aldgate and Statham, 2001).

Research evidence gives rise to concerns that the philosophy underpinning the Children Act 1989 may not be permeating practice. Child protection conferences and registers, and subsequently Area Child Protection Committees, shortly to get statutory rights, came into being in response to a number of tragic child abuse cases in which children such as Maria Colwell, Jasmine Beckford and Kimberly Carlile died following involved professionals' failure to exchange and act on relevant information regarding the child and the family (DHSS, 1976; Blom-Cooper, 1985; 1987). Although central to the child protection system within each local authority, conferences and registers have no statutory status, relying on policies and procedures determined and implemented locally, through interpretation of local authorities' powers and duties as set out in legislation, and Departmental Guidance (Department of Health, Home Office and Department for Education and Employment, 1999; Assembly for Wales, 2000). An overview of the findings of the studies within a programme of studies covering all aspects of child protection procedures suggest that, contrary to the lessons that were supposed to have been learned from the investigation into child abuse in Cleveland in 1987 (Butler-Sloss, 1988), local authorities were intervening and invoking child protection procedures on the basis of injuries to children without paying proper regard to the child's wider situation (DoH, 1995). The much needed provision of support services under Part III of the Act were observed in a number of the studies to have been ignored, whilst the social workers concentrated on a bureaucratic response to the injuries sustained (Farmer and Owen, 1995).

A recent review of the next tranche of Department of Health funded studies, reflects on the continuing rise in the numbers of children looked after by local authorities on care orders rather than being accommodated on a voluntary basis. This suggests that the practice identified by Farmer and Owen may be persisting (Aldgate and Statham, 2001: 49).

The Duty to Investigate

Local authorities will be put under a duty to make investigations into a child's circumstances either when there is information which gives 'reasonable grounds to suspect that a child who lives, or is found, in their area is suffering or is likely to suffer significant harm' (s.47) or they are informed of the making of an emergency protection order, or the placing of a child in police protection. The duty may also arise as a result of a court direction to investigate (s.37) (DoH, 1991a).

When put under a duty to investigate, local authorities have to take all reasonable steps to ensure that access to the child is obtained, and refusal of access, or of information about the child's whereabouts, constitutes grounds for obtaining an emergency protection order, and a duty to do so unless workers are 'satisfied that his welfare can be satisfactorily safeguarded' in some other way.

It is at this stage that, as part of its investigation, the local authority may convene a child protection conference to enable all professionals with a knowledge of the child to share information and to reach a decision as to whether the child's name should be entered on the child protection register and, if so, the category (or categories) of abuse to be recorded (DoH, 1991b: para. 6.40). Child protection conferences, although currently of immense significance within the child protection system, do not, as we have seen, have any statutory status. Additionally, research evidence suggests that the detailed guidance set, out in the *Working Together to Safeguard Children* document and its predecessors, is capable of such a range of diverse interpretation that there are huge variations in practice concerning both the convening and conduct of case conferences and the placing on and removing of names from the register (Thoburn and Lewis, 1992; Gibbons et al., 1995b).

Court-ordered Investigations

Where a court becomes sufficiently concerned about children who are the subject of any other family proceedings, to consider the need for care or supervision, they may order the local authority to investigate the child's circumstances (s.37), and consider whether to apply for a care or supervision order, provide services or assistance for the child or the family, or take any other action. When a court orders an investigation under section 37, provided there is reasonable cause to believe that the threshold conditions in section 31 are satisfied (s.38), it may at the same time make an interim care or supervision order and appoint a children's guardian for the child. The local authority must report back within eight weeks and inform the court of any action it proposes to take. Action could, where it is believed that the threshold conditions under section 31(2) (see page 89) exist, include applying for a care or supervision order within the existing proceedings, or offering services under Part III. Where the local authority proposes to take no action, it must give the court reasons for that decision.

Compulsory Intervention

The shift towards the use of voluntary arrangements rather than compulsory intervention is at the heart of the Children Act 1989. As already suggested, research indicates that this may not be being followed in practice (DoH, 1995). The Final Report of the Children Act Advisory Committee specifically warned against the use of voluntary arrangement where the threshold conditions for the making of a care or supervision order existed, and a voluntary arrangement might cause delay in addressing fundamental problems (DoH, 1997). There will, also, always be cases in which compulsory measures will be required because co-operation is either not forthcoming or is insufficient for the protection of the child. Immediately after implementation of the Children Act 1989 there was an initial fairly dramatic drop in the number of care orders made, however since 1992 numbers have risen steadily, whereas use of supervision orders rose initially and then declined (Table 9.1). The incidence of the use of emergency protection orders (EPO), which also dropped dramatically when the Children Act came into force, when compared with the use of place of safety orders under the previous legislation, have remained remarkably stable between 1992 and 1998 (Table 9.1), but have since risen.

Table 9.1   Number of care orders and emergency protection orders made annually, 1992–2000

Order	1992	1993	1994	1995	1996	1997	1998	2000
EPO	2423	2546	3144	3054	2565	2393	2473	2232
Care order	2267	3221	4173	4241	4498	4537	4910	6298
Supervision	937	1203	1325	1318	1161	1072	829	1362

Children's Guardians

To help maintain the focus on the child's welfare, in most public law proceedings a CAFCASS children's guardian, previously a guardian *ad litem* (see page 48), will be appointed to safeguard the interests of the child. The role of the children's guardian, is, as far as is possible, to ascertain the child's wishes and feelings, instruct the child's solicitor, participate in directions hearings – including advising the court on parties, the timetable for the proceedings, the making of interim orders – and to prepare a very detailed report for the court. The details of the appointment, powers and duties of children's guardians are set out in the court rules (the Family Proceedings Courts (Children Act) Rules 1991, Rules 10 and 11 as amended by the Family Proceedings Courts (Children Act) (Amendment) Rules 2001). Where the child and the children's guardian disagree over the child's needs, a child of sufficient age and understanding may give his or her own instructions to his solicitor, and the children's guardian will represent his or her own views to the court, with legal representation where necessary.

In the past, the position regarding the independence of guardians *ad litem* was somewhat anomalous in that their role required them to provide an independent scrutiny of the work of local authority social workers and to make their own recommendations to the court, whilst being members of panels of guardians *ad litem* and reporting officers administered by the same authority, which payed their fees. The establishment of CAFCASS (see page 47) has to a large extent remedied that anomaly, however, there is considerable concern that the way in which the agency has been set up may lead to an impoverished and restricted service so far as children in public law proceedings are concerned (Timmis, 2001; White, 2001).

The Protection of Children in an Emergency

The immediate protection of children in any kind of emergency can only be achieved by the provision of wide powers, available without delay, either to ensure that a child is removed from a situation of danger or remains in one of safety when threatened with removal. Preventing abuse of such powers requires that they shall only be exercisable in circumstances in which immediate protection for the child cannot be secured in any other way, last for the minimum necessary time, and be open to challenge at the earliest opportunity. The contrasting dissatisfactions with place of safety orders under the Children and Young Persons Act 1969 informed the provisions in Part V of the Children Act (Blom-Cooper, 1987; Butler-Sloss, 1988; Ball, 1989). The extent to which the former imprecise and broadly framed provisions allowed discrepant, and sometimes abusive, practice explains the detail contained in Part V, which leaves relatively little margin for discretionary interpretation.

Emergency Protection Orders

The emergency protection order is intended for use only in real emergencies: anyone may apply to a court or, with leave of the justices' clerk, to a single justice who is a member of the family proceedings panel, *ex parte* (without anyone who might oppose the application either being present or being served notice) for an order, on the grounds that:

> there is reasonable cause to believe that the child is likely to suffer significant harm
> if ... he is not removed to accommodation provided by or on behalf of the applicant;
> or ... he does not remain in the place in which he is then being accommodated, or
> where enquiries are being made by a local authority, anyone authorised by them, or
> by the NSPCC, and they are denied access to the child. (s.44)

An EPO may be made for up to eight days, and the child or anyone with parental responsibility may apply to a court for discharge of the order after 72 hours, provided they were not served notice and were not present when the order was made.

Under section 44(4) while an emergency protection order is in force, it:

(a) operates as a direction to any person who is in a position to do so to comply
    with any request to produce the child to the applicant:
(b) authorises –
    (i)   the removal of the child at any time to accommodation provided by or
          on behalf of the applicant and his being kept there; or
    (ii) the prevention of the child's removal from any hospital, or other place,
          in which he was being accommodated immediately before the making
          of the order, and
(c) gives the applicant parental responsibility for the child.

If the applicant for the EPO does not have adequate information regarding the child's whereabouts, but believes that another person does, the court or justice making the order may add a direction requiring that any other person disclose, if asked to do so by the applicant, any information regarding the child's whereabouts (s.48(1)).

An EPO may be extended once for up to seven days if the court has reasonable cause to believe that the child will suffer significant harm if it is not extended. During the period that an EPO is in force the local authority will have limited parental responsibility and will therefore be able to make day-to-day decisions in regard to the child, whilst parents retain their parental responsibility subject to the EPO. There is a presumption of reasonable contact between parents and child, however the court may lay down requirements both regarding the contact which shall or shall not take place and concerning more than routine medical treatment or investigation – which a child 'of sufficient understanding to make an informed decision' has a statutory right to refuse (s. 44(7)) (DoH, 1991a, vol. 1; *Gillick* v. *West Norfolk Health Authority* [1986]).

This right is not an absolute one. In circumstances where it decides that the welfare of the child requires it, the High Court may exercise its inherent jurisdiction to override a 'Gillick-competent' child's refusal to accept medical treatment (*South Glamorgan County Council* v. *W and B* [1993]).

Part IV of the Family Law Act 1996 amended section 44 to include the power to include a requirement excluding a person from the place where the child lives, for the duration of the EPO or a lesser time, if there is reasonable cause to believe that if the 'relevant person' is excluded 'the child will not be likely to suffer significant harm, even though the child is not removed' (s.44A(2)(a)(i)). The exclusion requirement can only be made if there is someone else who is able to look after the child in the home who consents to the order being made. A power of arrest may be attached to the exclusion requirement (s.44A(5)), or the court may accept an undertaking (s.44B(1)).

Police Protection

Since Victorian times, the police have had an extra-judicial power, enshrined in successive statutes, to respond to the need to provide emergency protection for children (Masson, Oakley and McGovern, 2001). The current provisions in the Children Act 1989, provide, as with EPOs (above), a considerably more circumscribed power than that available under previous legislation. Under section 46, where a constable has reasonable cause to believe that a child would otherwise be likely to suffer significant harm, the officer may remove the child to, or ensure that he stays in, a place of safety. The section sets out in great detail the steps that must be taken by the constable to ensure that parents, the local authority and the designated police officer responsible for enquiring into the case are informed, and that the child's wishes and feelings are considered. Police protection may only last for up to 72 hours; however, during that time the designated officer may apply for an emergency protection order under section 44 which will run from the start of the period in police protection. A recent study showed no evidence of such applications being made (Masson, Oakley and McGovern, 2001).

In their study of the use of police protection over eight forces, Masson and her colleagues found very wide variations in the use of the power with some evidence of good practice. In general the researchers identify the need for better information on the powers, together with considerable training and improved recording, in many of the forces and in social services departments. It was suspected, although it could not be demonstrated, that informal arrangements amounting to, though not recognized as, use of powers under section 46 may have been quite common.

Police Warrants

Where it is either apparent at the time of the application for an EPO, or subsequently, that anyone attempting to exercise power under the order is being, or is likely to be, denied entry to premises or access to the child, a court or single justice may issue a warrant authorizing a police constable to exercise those powers using force if necessary (s.48(9)).

Entry of Premises to Save Life and Limb

The Police and Criminal Evidence Act 1984 (s.17(1)) restates the common law power of the police to enter and search any premises for the purposes of 'saving life or limb'. Where appropriate, exercise of this power could be followed by reception of a child into police protection.

Recovery Order

Where a child in care or the subject of an emergency protection order or in police protection has been removed or run away from care, or is being kept away from any person who has care of the child as a result of that order, the court may issue a recovery order under section 50. The order operates as a direction to produce the child, and authorizes their removal by any authorized person, and the entry and search of specified premises by a police constable. Taking or keeping a child in these circumstances constitutes a criminal offence (s.49) unless the premises at which the child is being kept is a voluntary home, registered children's home, or foster home issued with a certificate as a refuge under section 51 of the Act (The Refuges (Children's Homes and Foster Placements) Regulations 1991; DoH, 1991a, vol. 4).

Child Assessment Order

When introduced by the Children Act 1989, the child assessment order (CAO) was a new order which had no parallel in previous legislation. Child assessment orders may be applied for only in court, on notice, by a local authority or the National Society for the Prevention of Cruelty to Children (NSPCC) (as 'authorized person') on the grounds that there is reasonable cause to believe that the child is suffering or is likely to suffer, significant harm; that an assessment of the child's health and development are necessary, and that it is unlikely that a satisfactory assessment will be made in the absence of an order (Children Act 1989, s.43). If the court hearing the application believes that the circumstances justify the making of an EPO, it should make one instead of the order applied for. Guidance suggests that CAOs will only be appropriate in cases in which 'a decisive step to obtain an assessment is needed ... and informal arrangements to have such an assessment carried out have failed' (DoH, 1991a, vol. 1: para. 4.8). Early predictions that the order would be rarely sought and made have proved correct in that only 82 child assessment orders were made in 1994 and the incidence is so low that there is no reference to CAOs in the *Judicial Statistics* for 2000 (Lord Chancellor's Department, 2001). It may be that the value of the order lies in its persuasive power rather than actual use.

Chapter 10
Care and Supervision

Care Proceedings

The only means whereby a local authority can assume parental responsibility (other than for the very short term of an EPO in regard to a child under the age of 17, or 16 if married), is by means of a care order made by a court, on the basis that the threshold conditions are satisfied and that the order is likely to contribute positively to the child's welfare (s.1(5)). Under section 31(2):

A court may only make a care order or a supervision order if it is satisfied –
(a) that the child concerned is suffering, or is likely to suffer, significant harm; and
(b) that the harm, or likelihood of harm, is attributable to –
   (i) the care given to the child, or likely to be given to him if the order were not made, not being what it would be reasonable to expect a parent to give him; or
   (ii) the child being beyond parental control.

If a court does not find the threshold conditions satisfied, it may not make a care or supervision order. However, since the proceedings are 'family proceedings' (s.8(4)) the court could, either on application or its own initiative, make any section 8 order (s.10(1)) instead of the order applied for.

Under the Act 'harm' is defined as ill-treatment or the impairment of health or development (further defined in s.31(9) as amended by ACA 2002); and whether harm suffered is significant depends on comparison with 'that which could reasonably be expected of a similar child'.

In *Re M. (Minors: Threshold Conditions)* [1994] the House of Lords upheld the decision reached in *Northamptonshire County Council* v. *S* [1993] and overruled both the Court of Appeal decision to the contrary and that in *Oldham Metropolitan Borough Council* v. *E.* [1994], regarding the appropriate time at which the 'harm or likelihood of significant harm' should be considered by a court. The House of Lords held that the point at which the local authority first intervened was the one at which the court should determine whether the threshold conditions were satisfied – rather than the time of the full hearing – provided that arrangements to protect the child had been continuously in place since the first intervention. The rest of their Lordships speeches in *Re M* were somewhat controversial (Masson, 1994).

Proceedings under section 31 and most other applications for public law orders are commenced in a magistrates' family proceedings court, unless they result from an investigation ordered by a court in private law proceedings under section 37, in which case they are heard by the court ordering the investigation. Cases commenced in the magistrates' court may be transferred up to the local care centre, or laterally to another family proceedings court able to hear the application more quickly.

A justices' clerk's decision regarding allocation of a case to the family proceedings court may be appealed against to a district judge at the care centre, who may either confirm the original allocation or order the transfer of the case to the care centre. Exceptionally, complex cases may be transferred from the care centre to the Family Division of the High Court. The percentages vary slightly from year to year, but in general about 75 per cent of all public law cases are heard in family proceedings courts, 20 per cent in care centres and 5 per cent at first instance in the Family Division.

Interim Orders

Prior to a final hearing, an interim care order or supervision order or any private law orders under section 8 of the Act may be made on the basis that there are reasonable grounds to believe that the threshold conditions exist (s.38). The presumption that delay is harmful, and the provision within the court rules for directions hearings and the establishment of timetables for proceedings, was initially interpreted as meaning that any interim order beyond the first, which may be for up to eight weeks, would have to be well justified. In practice, evidence of serious delays in children's cases, suggest that, in many cases, a succession of interim orders are being made (Aldgate and Statham, 2001).

Procedure, Section 31A Care Plans and Orders

As soon as an application is made and the venue for the trial is settled, whether it is the family proceedings court or the care centre, a children's guardian will be appointed, and a directions hearing will be arranged. This hearing will be before a district judge at the care centre or, most usually, a justices' clerk but, in some areas, a magistrate or magistrates at the family proceedings court. Parties are either present or represented, and the rules provide for the children's guardian to advise the court on issues regarding the child's welfare. The purpose of the hearing is to sort out important preliminary details regarding the parties to the proceedings, the likely length and timetabling of the final hearing, deadlines for the submission of witness statements and the report of the children's guardian, the commissioning of a report(s) from one or more expert witness(es) and so on – all with a view to avoiding unnecessary delay before the matter can come to a final hearing for resolution. When the House of Lords rejected the Court of Appeal's proposal for 'starred care plans', which when approved by the court would only be able to be altered with the approval of the court making the care order (Tolson,

2001), on the grounds that the court was going beyond the judicial and into a law-making role (*S (Minors); W (Minors)* [2002]), they nonetheless supported the Human Rights Act principle behind the Court of Appeal's decision. The Government responded by hastily inserting amendments to sections 26 and 31 of the Children Act 1989 into the ACA 2002. Under s.31(3A):

No care order may be made with respect of a child until the court has considered a section 31A care plan.

When this provision comes into force, a local authority applying for a care order will have to prepare, and keep updated, what will be known as a 'section 31A care plan' (and any care plan on the basis of which an existing care order was made will be treated as a section 31A plan). At any review of the case of a child in care a person approved for the purpose under section 26(2)(k) will under subsection (2A): participate in the review; monitor 'the performance of the authority's functions in respect of the review'; and, where appropriate refer the case to a CAFCASS officer (see page 47). The CAFCASS officer's functions in respect of a referred case will be detailed in regulations.

All reports and witnesses' statements have to be exchanged before the hearing which results in magistrates having to read and assimilate a considerable volume of paperwork in advance. Courts, including the magistrates' family proceedings courts, have to give reasons for their decisions, and all parties have a right of appeal (see Figure 1.1). Although the proceedings are single-stage civil proceedings, courts have to be satisfied that the threshold criteria set out in section 31(2) are met before they can make a care or supervision order. The other orders available, whether or not the threshold conditions are satisfied, are:

1   A care order.
2   A supervision order to the local authority (see below).
3   Any section 8 order.
4   A special guardianship order (CA 1989, s.14A).
5   A family assistance order under section 16.

As in all proceedings under the Act, the court has to be satisfied, before making any order, that making the order 'would be better for the child than making no order at all' (s.1(5)).

Appeals

Appeals from decisions made in the magistrates' family proceedings court are heard in the Family Division of the High Court, and from care centres and the Family Division to the Court of Appeal (Civil Division) (see Figure 1.2).

With leave, there may be a final appeal to the House of Lords on an issue of public importance. The basis on which an appellate court will intervene to overturn a decision of the court which tried the case was authoritatively stated in the House of Lords in a case regarding custody under earlier legislation (*G* v. *G (Minors: Custody Appeal)* [1985]) In that case, Lord Scarman's analysis of the grounds for allowing an appeal in such proceedings was quoted approvingly.

> But at the end of the day the court may not intervene unless it is satisfied either that the judge exercised his discretion upon a wrong principle or that, the judge's decision being so plainly wrong, he must have exercised his discretion wrongly. (*B* v. *W (Wardship: Appeal)* [1979] at 1055F)

In *G* v. *G* their Lordships went further, elaborating that the appellate court should only interfere if it was satisfied that the court of first instance had not only reached a decision with which the appellate court might disagree, but had exceeded 'the generous ambit within which a reasonable disagreement is possible'. In fact it had reached a decision which was 'so plainly wrong' that it must have 'erred in the exercise of its discretion'.

All this means that appellate courts, which only see transcripts of evidence, the judgment, if the case was tried by a judge, or the magistrates' findings of fact and reasons for reaching their decisions, and hear legal argument, are very reluctant to overturn the decision of courts of first instance. Unlike the appellate court, the first court saw the witnesses and heard them give their evidence.

The Effect of a Care Order

The effect of a care order, which lasts until the child is 18 unless discharged, is to give the local authority parental responsibility for the child with the power to override that of the parents, who retain the right to exercise any aspects of their parental responsibility which is not in conflict with local authority decisions in respect of the child's upbringing (Children Act 1989, s.33). Local authorities do not acquire the right to change the child's religion, consent to the child's adoption, or appoint a guardian. It was generally accepted, though with reluctance by the judiciary, that courts could not add requirements to care orders, except in regard to the contact that a child in care may have with parents and others (s.34). This principle was briefly undermined by the Court of Appeal decision that where the court making the care order 'stars' items in a care plan, these should not be altered without reference to the court which makes the order (*Re W & B; Re W (Care Plan)* [2001]). It is now subject to sections 31A and 26(2A) of the 1989 Act (see page 90).

Children in care, together with those in accommodation under the Act or other legislation, come under local authorities' duty to children 'looked after' by them, which are set out in section 22(3) (see Chapter 8).

Contact Between Children in Care, Parents and Certain Other People

When a child is the subject of a care order, parents and others may not apply for a contact order under section 8 of the Children Act. However, under section 34, one of the major reforming provisions of the Children Act 1989, local authorities have a duty to allow reasonable contact between a child who is the subject of a care order and parents, guardians and others with parental responsibility, or who have had care of the child immediately before the order was made (s.34(1)). When a care order is made, the court has to satisfy itself as to the arrangements that will be made for contact and invite parties to the proceedings to comment (s.34(11)). Any subsequent variation of contact which is not agreed by the parents, can be the subject of an application to court. The only way in which a local authority can lawfully refuse to allow contact between children in care and the persons mentioned above, except for up to seven days in an emergency situation, to which special provisions set out in section 34(6) apply, is by means of a successful application to court for permission to terminate contact (s.34(4)).

Prior to implementation of section 34, the amount of parental access (the term used prior to the Children Act) to children who were the subject of care orders was entirely at the discretion of the local authority. The magistrates' juvenile court could only become involved if the local authority served notice that they were terminating all access and the parent responded by seeking an access order from the court under provisions hastily inserted into the 1980 Act in 1983 (Child Care Act 1980, s.12A–F). Prior to that time, the matter of access where the child was the subject of a care order giving the local authority parental rights and duties to the exclusion of the parents, was solely within the discretion of the local authority under powers given to it by Parliament. The courts, following a well-established legal principle, would not intervene (*A* v. *Liverpool City Council* [1982]). Apart from their very limited recourse to the juvenile court if access was terminated, parents had to rely on non-statutory good practice guidance produced by the Department of Health and Social Security (DHSS), which actively encouraged the maintenance and fostering of links between children and care and their families. Sadly the guidance was neither widely adhered to nor enforceable (Millham et al., 1989).

The consequences of local authorities' failure to maintain meaningful contact between children in care and their parents were identified by a major DHSS-funded research programme. The findings highlighted the need for a statutory presumption of reasonable contact between parent and child and a recourse to the courts at an early stage where, for whatever reason, such contact was being denied (Millham et al., 1986; 1989). Following these recommendations, the aim of the section 34 provisions was, as nearly as possible, to equate the position of parents with a child in care with the non-residential parent under private law.

Judicial decisions have confirmed the extent to which section 34 provides the only statutory limitation on a local authority's exercise of discretion (subject to the requirements of regulations made under the Act) in regard to children in care. It is a limitation which prevails over any presumption that courts must not make orders which interfere with a local authority's plans for a child.

> Parliament has given to the court and not to the local authority, the duty to decide on contact between the child and those named in s.34(1). Consequently, the court may have the task of requiring the local authority to justify their long-term plans to the extent only that these plans exclude contact between parents and child. (*Re B (Minors) (Care: Contact: Local Authority Plans)* [1993] per Butler-Sloss LJ; see also *Re E (A Minor) (Care Order: Contact)* [1994]).

Supervision

Supervision orders under the Children Act 1989, s.35 and Schedule 3, Part I, like care orders, may only be made if the threshold conditions in section 31 and the principles in section 1 are satisfied. A supervision order, which does not give the local authority parental responsibility, puts the child under the supervision of a designated local authority for up to one year. The order may be discharged by a court at an earlier date or extended for up to a maximum of three years. The order may contain directions that the child reside in a particular place, or comply with directions given by the supervisor to participate in particular activities for up to a maximum of 90 days. Schedule 3, paras. 4 and 5 give detailed directions regarding the consents that have to be given and the criteria for including requirements as to medical or psychiatric treatment under a supervision order (DoH, 1991a, vol. 1).

There is also a provision in the Act to include requirements for up to 90 days in relation to a responsible person, defined as any person with parental responsibility or any other person with whom the child is living. These requirements include taking reasonable steps to ensure that the child complies with directions given by the supervisor, or ensuring that the child complies with requirements to participate in activities or receive treatment (Schedule 3, para. 3).

If a child is the subject of a supervision order, and the local authority wish to replace that order with a care order, contrary to the position under previous legislation where an application could be made to vary an existing order, a fresh application under section 31 for a care order, re-establishing the existence of the threshold conditions (s.31(2)) must be made (*Re A (Supervision Order: Extension)* [1995]).

Child Safety Order

Under sections 11 and 12 of the Crime and Disorder Act 1998, local authorities can apply to the magistrates' family proceedings courts for child safety orders on children under the age of 10 years. The grounds for making an order are that:

1 the child has committed an act which would amount to an offence if committed by a person over the age of ten, and an order is necessary for the purpose of preventing further such acts; or
2 the child has contravened a ban imposed by a curfew notice; or
3 has acted in a manner which caused or is likely to cause harassment, alarm or distress to a person not in the same household as himself.

The standard of proof is the civil standard of the balance of probabilities, rather than the criminal standard of being satisfied beyond reasonable doubt. The order, which does not require the consent of the parent(s) or child, requires that the child be under the supervision of a local authority social worker or youth offending team member (see Chapter 14) may be made for a maximum of three months or in exceptional circumstances for up to 12 months. Requirements considered desirable in the interests of securing the child proper care and attention, or preventing the kind of behaviour that led to the order being made, may be attached to the order, and a parenting order may at the same time be made against the child's parent or guardian under section 8 of the Act (see page 161).

If the child fails to comply with the order, the court may either vary the order by cancelling or adding provisions or revoke the order and make a care order under section 31 of the Children Act 1989. In contrast to the requirements if the child is subject to a supervision order (see above), in these circumstances the 1998 Act specifically provides that the care order may be made whether or not the threshold conditions set out in section 31(2) are satisfied (s. 12(7)).

Chapter 11

Adoption

Adoption practice has altered almost beyond recognition within the last 25 years (Lowe, 2000), and at last adoption law is being reformed to better meet the needs of children requiring permanent placement outside their birth families. The Adoption and Children Act 2002 (ACA 2002) is likely to be implemented in 2003. After a brief introduction, the first part of this chapter sets out existing adoption law under the Adoption Act 1976 (AA 1976) and the Adoption (Intercountry Aspects) Act 1999 (A(IA)A 1999), and the second outlines the main reforms contained in the ACA 2002.

When adoption was first introduced into English law in 1926 the objective of the legislation was to provide a permanent and secure home for orphans or illegitimate babies with childless couples, thereby creating new nuclear families. At the beginning of the twenty-first century there are very few baby adoptions and many older and often damaged children are in need of the security of a permanent home, some without the total legal severance from their birth family on which current adoption provisions are predicated.

Under the Adoption of Children Act 1926 and all subsequent legislation, an adoption order effects a complete and virtually irrevocable legal transfer of a child from one family to another. While a detailed consideration of adoption law is beyond the scope of this book, and those working in the field will need to make reference to a specialist work (see for instance, Lowe and Douglas, 1998, or Cretney and Masson, 1996, for the pre-2002 Act law), issues concerning adoption feature in many areas of child-care practice. Until the last quarter of the last century, adoption law reform was primarily concerned with better regulation of the process, and with more closely equating the position of adopted children with those of birth children within a family.

The Adoption Process Under the Adoption Act 1976

Local authority social workers may be involved in adoption proceedings specifically because adoption is being considered for children on their caseload, or because they may have to prepare the very detailed report required by the court in all adoption cases under Schedule 2 to the Adoption Rules 1984. There is a sense in which all social workers are adoption workers since the AA 1976 places on all local authorities a statutory duty to:

establish and maintain within their area a service designed to meet the needs in relation to adoption, of:

(a) children who have been or may be adopted,
(b) parents and guardians of such children, and
(c) persons who have adopted or may adopt a child,
and for that purpose to provide the requisite facilities, or secure that they are provided by approved adoption societies. (s.1(1))

The fact that the making of an adoption order effects such a profound change in a child's legal status is mirrored in the strict requirements laid down for all stages of the adoption process. An adoption order can – even if all the parties are in agreement – only be made by an authorized court, that is in the magistrates' family proceedings court, a designated adoption county court (Lord Chancellor's Department, 2001) or, in certain circumstances, the High Court. Currently the statutory provisions and procedural rules are to be found in the AA 1976, Adoption Rules 1984, the Adoption Agency Regulations 1983, the Adoption (Amendment) Rules 1991, and the Adoption (Intercountry Aspects) Rules 2001.

In order to ensure the 'normality' of the new family and that the child's welfare is the first consideration, the law provides strict requirements as to who may adopt or place for adoption, how the process is conducted, the consent or dispensing with the consent of the natural parents and how the interests of the child are both assessed by the agency and put before the court. An independent checking mechanism by the appointment of a CAFCASS reporting officer for the parents or, where necessary, a children's guardian to safeguard the welfare of the child, is built into the system to ensure that all the legal requirements have been met and that the order is in the child's interests.

At the heart of all the statutory provisions, but not overriding any of the procedural rules, is the requirement that:

> the court or adoption agency shall have regard to all the circumstances, the first consideration being given to the need to safeguard and promote the welfare of the child throughout his childhood; and shall so far as is practicable ascertain the wishes and feelings of the child regarding the decision and give due consideration to them, having regard to his age and understanding. (AA 1976, s.6)

Safeguarding the child's welfare may be better achieved by means of other orders which make a less drastic alteration in his legal status than the total legal severance from the birth family effected by adoption. Under the Children Act 1989, in any family proceedings the court may make orders other than those applied for – for instance, a residence order (see page 62) instead of an adoption order.

Residence orders may be made by courts hearing adoption applications whether or not the parents have agreed to adoption. The order gives the person(s) in whose favour the order is made parental responsibility (see page

53) for the duration of the order as well as determining 'with whom the child is to live' (s.8(1)) and may have any conditions the court considers necessary attached. Residence orders differ from adoption in that they only convey limited parental responsibility and generally come to an end when the child is 16, although need not do so if the court considers the case exceptional (s.9(6)). Parental responsibility is limited to the extent that the child's name may only be changed with the consent of all those with parental responsibility, or the court's direction; apart from holidays of up to a month, the child may not be taken out of the United Kingdom without similar consents, and carers with a residence order cannot appoint a guardian for the child in the event of their death, nor can they consent to the child's adoption.

Freeing for Adoption

An adoption order is made, provided all the formalities are in order and the court decides that the making of the order is in the child's interests, following an application by the prospective adopters. The consent of the natural parents will have either have been given or will have been dispensed with by the court on one of the grounds set out in section 16 of the Act.

Under current provisions, in cases in which either the child is already in the care of the agency and the issue of parental consent is in doubt, or where the mother has decided that she wants the child adopted before any specific application is ready, the agency may apply to the court for an order freeing the child for adoption (s.18). The effect of the order, to which the parents must consent, or their consent be dispensed with, is to extinguish existing parental responsibility and vest it in the agency which will hold it until an adoption order is made. Natural parents will be informed if an order has been made or the child placed for adoption after a year, unless they sign a declaration that they do not wish to be further involved. If they have not signed the declaration and the child has not been placed, they may apply for revocation of the freeing order.

Freeing orders have proved problematic in practice. Applications have been subject to long delays, and, once freed, children are effectively in a legal limbo until adopted, or they reach adulthood without a family (Lowe et al., 1993; *Re C (Adoption: Freeing Order)* [1999]). In addition, children may have been placed and be well settled with prospective adopters before the freeing application is heard, to the great disadvantage of birth parents wishing to contest the order.

Adoption Law Reform

The ACA 2002 has had a lengthy gestation. In 1989, once the Children Act 1989 was on the statute book, an interdepartmental group began a review of adoption law. The group commissioned research and published working papers prior to producing its report, *Review of Adoption Law*, as a consultation paper in 1992. The review, which was widely welcomed, though also subject to some criticism, made wide-ranging recommendations aimed at keeping adoption as part of a legal framework which recognized the diverse needs of older children seeking permanent new families. After a somewhat incomplete White Paper (Department of Health, 1993) and two further consultation documents, in 1996 the government published a draft Adoption Bill which also incorporated the Hague Convention on Intercountry Adoption. Key issues in the bill proved contentious and with a small majority the Conservative government decided not to proceed.

Adoption law reform was not high on the political agenda of the incoming Labour government; not, that is, until pressure was put on local authorities to get more 'looked after' children adopted, by making increasing the numbers a performance indicator of good practice. This combined with the personal and high profile interest that the Prime Minister took in adoption in 2000 renewed the momentum for reform of the law.

A White Paper, *Adoption: A New Approach*, which addressed only a few of the areas of reform identified in all earlier proposals and made no reference to the others was published immediately before Christmas 2000 (Department of Health, 2000c). The Adoption and Children Bill, incorporating the *Adoption: A New Approach* proposals and many of those in the 1996 Bill, as well as introducing welcome amendments to the Children Act 1989, had its first reading in March 2001, but fell when Parliament was prorogued for the general election in June. Later in the summer, National Adoption Standards for England and Wales were published by the Department of Health. In October an amended version of the earlier bill was introduced into the House of Commons. The bill was the subject of an unusual Special Standing Committee procedure in the Autumn of 2001, and was eventually enacted a decade after publication of the *Review of Adoption Law* (DoH and Welsh Office, 1992). The length of the process and the level of consultation at various stages allowed much redrafting and the resolution of several but not all contentious issues.

The long awaited incorporation of the Hague Convention on Intercountry Adoption was enacted in the Adoption (Intercountry Aspects) Act 1999. That Act is so far only in force to the extent that bringing a child into the UK for the purposes of adoption without following the procedures set out in the Adoption of Children from Overseas Regulations 2001 is outlawed. This followed a highly publicised case, which demonstrated the worst features of an unregulated trade in children and the urgency of the need to incorporate the Convention into domestic law (Brown, 2001). The ACA 2002 will incorporate some sections of the A(IA)A 1999, but regulations to give effect to the Convention and Central Authorities, and the text of the Convention will come into force in england, Wales and Scotland under the 1999 Act.

The Adoption and Children Act 2002

The Act replaces the AA 1976 and much of the A(IA)A 1999, and introduces important amendments to the Children Act 1989. The government's intention is that the new Act will underpin its programme to increase the use of adoption as a route out of local authority care and improve the performance of the adoption service. The key aspects of the Act are:

- the alignment of adoption law with the principles and concepts of the Children Act 1989;
- an increase in the responsibilities of local authorities for the provision of services and support for all affected by the adoption process;
- placement with consent and placement orders replace freeing for adoption;
- a new single ground for dispensing with parental consent to adoption or the making of a placement order;
- adoption agency responsibility for arranging access to birth records for adopted adults and providing other background information for adopters and adopted people;
- the introduction of a new special guardianship order for children requiring a secure permanent home outside their birth family, for whom adoption is not appropriate (see Chapter 6);
- parental responsibility for step-parents by agreement or court order;
- other amendments to the Children Act 1989, already referred to (Chapters 5 and 6).

Alignment With the Children Act 1989

Section 1 of the 2002 Act requires a court or adoption agency coming to any decision relating to the adoption of a child to make 'the child's welfare throughout his life' its paramount consideration (s.1(2)) and repeats several of the Children Act principles. The checklist (s.1(4)) in part mirrors that in section 1(3) of the Children Act, but is significantly different in content and in its application to adoption agency as well as court decisions.

> The court or adoption agency must have regard to the following matters (amongst others) –
> (a) the child's ascertainable wishes and feelings regarding the decision (considered in the light of the child's age and understanding),
> (b) the child's particular needs,
> (c) the likely effect on the child throughout his life of having ceased to be a member of the original family and become an adopted person,
> (d) the child's sex, background and any of the child's characteristics which the court or agency considers relevant,
> (e) any harm which the child has suffered or is at risk of suffering,

(f)   the relationship which the child has with relatives, and with any other person in relation to whom the court or agency considers the relationship to be relevant, including –

    (i)   the likelihood of any such relationship continuing and the value to the child of its doing so,

    (ii) the ability and willingness of any of the child's relatives, or of any such person, to provide the child with a secure environment in which the child can develop, and otherwise to meet the child's needs,

    (iii) the wishes and feelings of any of the child's relatives, or of any such person, regarding the child.

When placing a child for adoption the agency is required to give due consideration to the child's religious persuasion, racial origin and cultural and linguistic background.

Local Authority Adoption Services

Part II of the Act considerably increases the responsibilities of local authorities to provide

> a service designed to meet the needs, in relation to adoption, of –
> (a) children who may be adopted, their parents and guardians,
> (b) persons wishing to adopt a child, and
> (c) adopted persons, their parents, natural parents and former guardians;
> and for that purpose must provide the requisite facilities (s.3(1))

and an assessment of the person's need for support services under section 4.

The detail of these responsibilities will be set out in regulations, and local authorities may arrange for any of the facilities to be provided by registered adoption agencies or other prescribed persons, provided that it is the responsibility of the local authority to ensure that 'help may be given in a co-ordinated manner without duplication, omission or avoidable delay' (s.3(5)).

There is understandable concern amongst Directors of Social Services Departments and voluntary organizations as to whether these additional responsibilities, and especially post-adoption services, will be adequately resourced.

Independent review of adoption agencies determinations   The government gave a commitment in the White Paper, *Adoption: A New Approach* (2000) to provide people whom the agency has indicated are unlikely to be accepted as prospective adopters with the right to request referral to an independent panel. Regulations will be introduced to deal with such reviews as well as other determinations by agencies such as the release of confidential information and decisions regarding allowances.

Eligibility to Adopt

The eligibility to adopt provisions in the Adoption and Children Bill initially mirrored those in the 1976 Act in providing that only married couples and single people could adopt. Pressure from a wide range of child welfare related organizations, seeking to increase the pool of prospective adopters, persuaded the government to allow a free vote at third reading in the Commons on an amendment extending eligibility to unmarried couples in a secure relationship. At the time of writing it is not clear whether this amendment, passed by an overwhelming majority, will survive attack in the House of Lords.

Placement with Consent and Placement Orders

The current freeing for adoption provisions are generally agreed to be very unsatisfactory. The placement provisions in the Act are the fruit of a lengthy debate and will hopefully achieve the objectives of ensuring that decisions about the child's need for adoption and the parents' consent, or the decision to dispense with that consent is taken much earlier in the adoption process than under the 1976 Act. The provisions are intended to avoid delay for the child, and to provide an opportunity for parents to oppose the local authorities' plans for the adoption of their child before placement.

Placement with parental consent   Where an adoption agency is satisfied that each parent with parental responsibility or guardian of a child has consented to the child being placed for adoption with identified adopters, or with prospective adopters to be chosen by the agency, and has not withdrawn the consent, the agency may place the child. At the same time consent may be given to the making of an adoption order in the future. At the time of writing, these provisions are not finalized.

Placement Orders

> A placement order is an order made by the court authorising the local authority to place a child for adoption with any prospective adopters who may be chosen by the authority. (s.20(1))

A court may not make a placement order unless the child is subject to a care order, or the court is satisfied that the conditions for the making of care and supervision orders under the Children Act 1989, s.31(2) are met, and the parents consent, and have not withdrawn their consent, or their consent should be dispensed with (see below).

Although there was early agreement about the need for placement orders, framing the provisions proved difficult and contentious. Those who had been critical of previous less demanding grounds for the making of placement orders were relieved when the government agreed that they should mirror the care order threshold conditions (Children Act 1989, s.31(2), see Chapter 10).

Where a local authority is satisfied that a child who is looked after either in accommodation or under a care order ought to be placed for adoption, the circumstances in which it must or may apply for a placement order in respect of a child are set out. During that process the child is regarded as being looked after by the local authority.

Any person may apply to have a placement order revoked with the leave of the court. Leave can only be given if a year has passed since the making of the placement order, the child is not placed for adoption, and there has been a change in circumstances.

Parental responsibility   While a child is placed for adoption with the consent of parents, or the authority is authorized to place the child, or there is a placement order in force, the adoption agency concerned has parental responsibility. Prospective adopters with whom the child is placed also acquire parental responsibility. The agency may determine the extent to which that of the parents or guardian or the prospective adopters is to be restricted.

Contact   When an adoption agency is authorized to place a child for adoption any existing contact orders under the Children Act 1989 cease to have effect, and no further applications can be made under that Act. Instead the people detailed in the Act, which include, the child, the agency and any parent or guardian, may apply as of right for contact and anyone else may seek leave to make an application. Where the application is by the child or the agency the court may order any contact it considers appropriate or may refuse to allow contact between the child and any named person mentioned in the subsection. When dealing with other applications, the court may make any order it considers appropriate for contact between the child and the applicant. At the time of making a placement order, the court may on its own initiative 'make any provision it considers appropriate for contact between the child and any person named in the order'. Supplementary provisions regarding variation or revocation of contact orders made under the section, and the temporary suspension of arrangements in an emergency for up to seven days in order to safeguard or promote the child's welfare are set out in detail.

The removal of children who are or may be placed for adoption   Section 29 sets out detailed prohibitions on the removal of children who are placed for adoption or provided with accommodation by an adoption agency prior to placement, or in regard to whom an application for a placement order is pending. Where parents who have consented to placement for adoption withdraw their consent, the requirements in regard to return of the child, and sanctions for non-compliance are set out.

For non-agency cases there are similarly detailed rules.

Dispensing with Parental Consent

The *Review of Adoption Law* (DoH and Welsh Office, 1992) identified the need to replace the existing grounds for dispensing with parental consent and properly recognized that the finality of adoption required that any decision to dispense with parental consent should only be taken if a high threshold was satisfied. The criteria suggested in the review was subsequently endorsed by the Adoption Law Reform Group in its thoughtful critique of the existing law and proposal for its reform (Adoption Law Reform Group, 2000).

The suggested test was that in addition to the parent not being able to be found or being incapable:

> A parent's consent to adoption should be dispensed with only if the court is satisfied that the advantages of adoption would be so significantly greater for the child than any alternative option as to justify overriding the wishes of parents. (DoH and Welsh Office, 1992: para. 12.4)

Instead, the Act, unless further amended sets out a test which many consider does not adequately reflect the gravity of the decision the court is taking.

> (1) The court cannot dispense with the consent of any parent or guardian of a child to the child being placed for adoption or to the making of an adoption order in respect of the child unless the court is satisfied that –
> (a) the parent or guardian cannot be found or is incapable of giving consent, or
> (b) the welfare of the child requires the consent to be dispensed with.

There is a little more protection for birth parents in that courts considering applications to dispense with parental consent will have to apply the checklist in section 1(4). Also, as the decision to dispense with consent is an order of the court, section 1(6) applies:

> The court or adoption agency must always consider the whole range of powers available to it in the child's case (whether under this Act or under the Children Act 1989); and the court must not make any order under this Act unless it considers that making the order would be better for the child than not doing so.

Disclosure of Information About a Child's Adoption

Under previous legislation, adopted adults could only access their original birth certificate through the Registrar General, and had to seek other information from the adoption agency. The ACA 2002, through detailed regulations, will lay duties on adoption agencies regarding the gathering and secure storing of personal information in regard to all adoptions. The Act provides that the agency will be the source of information for all parties to an adoption. It will have responsibilities in regard to the provision to prospective adopters of information about the child, and of some information for birth parents, as well as being the point of access for an adopted adult seeking their original birth certificate and other personal information.

Special Guardianship

The interdepartmental working group responsible for the *Review of Adoption Law* (1992) endorsed the continued need for adoption orders which effect an irrevocable transfer of the child from the birth to the adoptive family. They also recognized that some, particularly older, children need a permanent secure placement outside their birth family, but without the final legal severance of adoption. To meet this need the group proposed a status of *inter vivos* guardianship to provide much more security than a residence order. The new order was designed to reflect the complex needs of children seeking permanent new homes outside their birth families by adding greater flexibility to the system. *Inter vivos* guardianship was omitted from the draft bill in 1996, however, it was picked up during the Prime Minister's consultative process in 2000, renamed 'special guardianship' in the White Paper *Adoption: A New Approach* (Department of Health, 2000c), and enacted through the introduction of very detailed new sections 14A–G into the Children Act 1989. Special guardianship is addressed in detail in Chapter 6.

PART III
VULNERABLE ADULTS

Chapter 12
Community Care

There is no one piece of legislation that governs the provision of community care services for vulnerable adults. Different services, such as home care, residential care and day care are provided under various statutes which date back to the National Assistance Act of 1948. Users of community care services include older people, people with mental health problems, sensory disabilities, physical disabilities and learning disabilities. Services for people with HIV/AIDs and drug and alcohol problems are also provided under community care legislation. Different assessment regimes and specific services apply to people who come within the definition of 'disabled'. This situation has arisen because the National Health Service and Community Care Act 1990 was not a consolidating statute, and refers back to previous pieces of legislation for service delivery. The 1990 Act introduces in section 47 a duty to assess for community care services, but does not describe the services that are to be provided: this is what is meant in legal terms by 'needs led assessment'. Legislation since 1990 has introduced new rights for carers and powers to enable local authorities to make direct payments to service users instead of directly providing services.

Community Care Assessments

The National Health Service and Community Care Act, s.46(1) requires each local authority, after consultation with health and housing authorities, and voluntary organizations, to prepare and publish a plan for the provision of community care services in their area.

The duty to assess an individual's need for community care services is contained in section 47 of the National Health Service and Community Care Act, which states:

(1) ... where it appears to a local authority that any person for whom they may provide or arrange for the provision of community care services may be in needs of any such services the authority –
   (a) shall carry out an assessment of his need for those services; and
   (b) having regard to the results of that assessment, shall decide whether his need call for the provision by them of any such services.

It is the appearance of need that triggers the duty to assess and the threshold for such an assessment has been described as 'very low' (*R* v. *Bristol CC ex parte Penfold* [1998]). The person's financial circumstances and ability to purchase services elsewhere are not relevant to the duty to assess; it is also irrelevant that the local authority may not provide the particular services that the applicant may be assessed as needing. Subsections (1)(a) and (1)(b) of s.47 are distinct, with the duty to assess standing separately from the power to provide services.

The assessment under s.47 has to be at a level appropriate to the complexity of the presenting problem and the risk involved. The *Managers' Guide to the Implementation of the Act* (DoH, 1991d) proposes six levels of assessment ranging from a simple assessment of a need, for instance, of a disabled car badge, which may be carried out by a member of the reception staff, through to a full multidisciplinary assessment where care needs and risk are complex and high.

A comprehensive assessment of need should take into account all the following factors: physical needs, psychological needs, accommodation, finance, education and leisure, carer's needs, risk and transport (Practitioners' Guide, 1991). Need may be prospective, for example where the person is in hospital or in prison. However, even if the assessment identifies a need for community care services, it does not follow that these services must be provided; under section 47(1)(b) the authority must make a separate decision whether all or some of the assessed needs call for the provision of any community care services. To what extent then can the local authority take its own limited resources into account when making this decision? The question was considered by the House of Lords in *R* v. *Gloucestershire County Council, ex parte Barry* [1997]. The majority of the House of Lords in that case decided that resources could be taken into account both when deciding what the local authority would accept as a 'need' and in deciding how to meet that need. The case concerned the withdrawal of home help and laundry services from disabled service users considered not a high risk in the community. However, resources were not the only factor; the person's level of disability and the benefit that they would derive from services were also relevant factors to be taken into account. The local authority would also be acting unlawfully if it fettered its discretion by applying eligibility criteria rigidly so that individual circumstances were not considered. For example, a general policy not to provide a domestic cleaning service would have to be flexible enough to meet the needs of a person with a medical condition that disclosed a need for a clean environment. Although 'needs' can be redefined against tighter eligibility criteria, depending upon the local authority's resources, this must follow a proper reassessment process. In the *Gloucestershire* case, simply sending out a letter to existing service users telling them that their service would be reduced, was not a lawful reassessment of their needs.

Community Care Services

The definition of 'community care services' is contained in section 46(3) of the National Health Service and Community Care Act 1990, as:

Services which a local authority may provide or arrange to be provided under any of the following provisions.
(a) Part III of the National Assistance Act 1948;
(b) Section 45 of the Health Services and Public Health Act 1968;
(c) Section 21 of and Schedule 8 to the National Health Service Act 1977; and
(d) Section 117 of the Mental Health Act 1983.

The services that local authorities have a duty or a power to provide under these statutes are in some cases limited to particular groups of service user. The relevant sections within Part III of the National Assistance Act are section 29 which confers a power to provide services for disabled people, and section 21 which imposes a duty (through Ministerial Directions under the section) to provide residential accommodation 'for persons who by reason of age, illness or disability, or any other circumstances are in need of care and attention which is not otherwise available to them'. The duty is limited, except in cases of 'urgent need' to those who are 'ordinarily resident' within the area of the local authority.

There were a number of cases in which asylum seekers successfully sought to bring themselves within the scope of section 21 of the National Assistance Act as 'persons in need of care and attention not otherwise available to them'. Section 95(3) of the Immigration and Asylum Act 1999 has removed local authority duties towards asylum seekers if the need arises solely because they are destitute (as opposed to being elderly or disabled). Local authority duties towards, older people who could self-fund their own residential accommodation were tested in *R* v. *Sefton Metropolitan Borough Council, ex parte Help the Aged* (1997). The Court of Appeal held that the relevant test of whether accommodation was 'otherwise available' lay in the application by all local authorities of the guidance on income and capital limits contained in the *Charging for Residential Accommodation Guide (CRAG)*, updated twice yearly, and issued under section 22 of the National Assistance Act. Thus local authorities could not impose their own interpretation of the financial limits below which individuals would receive financial assistance with accommodation in contravention of the *CRAG* guidance. Legislative effect was given to this decision by the Community Care (Residential Accommodation) Act 1998.

Section 45 of the Health Services and Public Health Act 1968 contains a power to promote the welfare of older people. Relevant services provided under this section are domiciliary care, meals on wheels, the provision of warden services and family placement schemes. No directions have been given under this section, with the consequence that services vary considerably from one part of the country to another. The power under section

21 and Schedule 8 to, the National Health Service Act 1977 to provide services for people suffering from illness, recovering from illness, and for the prevention of illness is commonly used in respect of mental health services. Directions in LAC (93) 10 require local authorities to provide day-care services; social work 'and related services' and sufficient social workers in their area to act as approved social workers for the purposes of the Mental Health Act 1983. There is also an approval given for services specifically for people who are alcoholic or drug-dependent. The provision of aftercare services under section 117 of the Mental Health Act 1983 for people who have been compulsorily detailed under sections 3, 37, 47 or 48 of that Act, is in itself a community care service. It then follows that residential accommodation provided upon discharge from hospital comes within section 117. There is no power to charge for section 117 services; LAC (2000) 3 in this respect confirms the decision of the Court of Appeal in *R* v. *Richmond London Borough Council, ex parte Watson* [2000].

Disabled Persons

The legal definition of who is a disabled person is contained in section 29 of the National Assistance Act 1948, which enables local authorities to make arrangements for promoting the welfare of persons:

> aged 18 or over who are blind, deaf or dumb or who suffer from mental disorder of any description, and other persons aged 18 or over who are substantially and permanently handicapped by illness, injury or congenital deformity or such other disabilities as may be prescribed by the Minister.

Section 47(2) of the National Health Service and Community Care Act 1990 requires the local authority to identify people whom they are in the process of assessing as 'disabled'. This then means that an additional assessment should be carried out under the provisions of section 4 of the Disabled Persons (Services, Consultation and Representation) Act 1986. The Disabled Persons Act of 1986 provides the assessment regime for the making of arrangements to provide services under the Chronically Sick and Disabled Persons Act 1970. There are advantages in flagging up disability in this way: first, because the range of services listed in section 2 is somewhat wider than the range of services available under other community care legislation and, secondly, because once the need for such services has been established, the local authority is under a duty (not a power) to provide them. The 'service list' in section 2 of the Chronically Sick and Disabled Persons Act covers:

1   the provision of practical assistance in the home;
2   the provision of, or assistance in obtaining wireless, television, library or similar recreational activities;
3   the provision of recreational activities outside the home;

4 the provision of or assistance with travel facilities;
5 the provision of any works of adaptation in the home or any additional facilities designed to secure a person's greater safety, comfort or convenience;
6 facilitating the taking of holidays, whether arranged by the local authority or otherwise;
7 the provision of meals in the home or elsewhere;
8 the provision of, or assistance in obtaining a telephone or any special equipment necessary to enable that person to use a telephone.

Carers

It is good practice to take account of carers' needs in any assessment carried out under section 47 of the National Health Service and Community Care Act. Carers who provide a substantial amount of care on a regular basis are entitled upon request to a statutory assessment in their own right under the Carers (Recognition and Services) Act 1995. This legislation applies also to young carers (C1(95)12), and to those who are 'intending' to provide care, for example upon the discharge of a relative from hospital. It is a prerequisite of a carer's assessment under the 1995 Act that the person for whom they are caring is subject to assessment under the National Health Service and Community Care Act 1990. The assessment is of the carer's ability to provide and to continue to provide care, and the local authority is required to 'take into account' the results of that assessment when putting together a package of care for the person to whom the care is provided. The Carers (Recognition and Services) Act 1995 also applies when the local authority are carrying out an assessment of a disabled child for the purposes of Part III of the Children Act 1989 or section 2 of the Chronically Sick and Disabled Persons Act 1970. Though the Carers (Recognition and Services) Act 1995 has not been repealed, its provisions have been largely superseded by the Carers and Disabled Children Act 2000, which gives carers aged 16 or over a right to free-standing assessment even if the person for whom they are caring refuses either assessment or services provision by the local authority. The 2000 Act enables local authorities to make available 'carers services'; the only definition of such services is that they should 'help the carer care for the person cared for'. Section 2 of the Act acknowledges that it will be necessary to decide whether a service is a carer's service or a community care service, but states that a carer's service cannot include anything of an 'intimate nature'. Section 5 enables direct payments to be made to carers in lieu of services, and there is also a power (s.3) to introduce a voucher system for respite care. Those with parental responsibility for a disabled child are also entitled to a carer's assessment under the Act and may receive vouchers and direct payments in lieu of services under section 17 of the Children Act. There is both policy and practice guidance under the 1995 and 2000 Acts.

Direct Payments

The Community Care (Direct Payments) Act 1996 has enabled local authorities, for the first time, to make available cash payments in lieu of directly provided community care services. With such payments, which have no statutory maximum or minimum, the individual can purchase the services of a personal assistant to meet their assessed community care needs. The original scheme, which was limited to disabled people between the age of 18 and 65, has now been extended by regulation, to older people, and to disabled 16- and 17-year-olds by section 7 of the Carers and Disabled Children Act 2000 (which introduces a new s.17A into the Children Act 1989). The recipient must be both willing to accept a direct payment and be able to manage such a payment, with assistance if necessary. The amount of assistance to be given is not specified, and some creative schemes have developed whereby local groups of disabled people have provided advice and payroll services to facilitate the taking on of employer responsibilities by disabled people. The independence that direct payment schemes can encourage is in itself a contribution to the 'best value' arguments for their effectiveness. Direct payments are not confined to people with physical disabilities; they should be equally available to people with learning disabilities or mental health needs. Excluded are patients subject to guardianship or receiving aftercare under supervision. Regulations (the Community Care (Direct Payments) Regulations 1997) prohibit the use of direct payments to secure services from a spouse or partner or close relative living in the same household. A close relative is defined as a parent or parent-in-law, a son or daughter, son-in-law, daughter-in-law, stepson or stepdaughter, brother or sister, aunt or uncle, grandparent, or the spouse or partner of any of these.

Compulsory Removal from Home

Receipt of community care services or admission to residential care is in all cases dependent upon the consent of the person receiving the service. There is, however, one instance in which compulsory removal from home outside the terms of the Mental Health Act 1983, can be effected and that is by the use of section 47 of the National Assistance Act 1948. The power of removal under section 47(1) applies only to persons who:

1   are suffering from grave chronic disease, or, being aged, infirm or physically incapacitated, are living in insanitary conditions, and
2   are unable to devote to themselves, and are not receiving from other persons, proper care and attention.

The usual circumstances are cases of self-neglect, where there are also public health concerns. Compulsory removal from home is a grave infringement of civil liberties, and the procedure by which it is accomplished is unlikely to meet the due process requirements of Article 6 of the European Convention on Human Rights. Application is made to the magistrates' court for the area in which the premises are situated. The procedure is for the 'proper officer', the Community Physician, to certify in writing to the local authority that an order is necessary. The local authority may then apply to the court for an order which may be for a period of up to three months, extendable for a further three months at a time. The patient must be given seven days' notice of the hearing, but there is no requirement that the person who is the subject of the proceedings is present, nor is legal aid available for their representation.

The patient, or anyone on their behalf may, having given seven days' notice to the local authority, apply for discharge of the order after six weeks. Removal may be to a residential home or hospital or 'other suitable place'. There is an emergency procedure under section 1 of the National Assistance (Amendment) Act 1951 which enables an application without notice to be made. The emergency procedure has in fact become the norm. Under the 1951 Act two medical opinions are required; usually the patient's general practitioner will provide the second opinion but, in contrast to the Mental Health Act 1983 there is no requirement that either doctor should have personal knowledge of the patient. They must certify (s.1(1)) that 'it is necessary in the interests of that person to remove him without delay'. Under this procedure, the initial period of detention is for three weeks.

Protection of Property

When anyone is admitted to hospital under the above provisions, or to accommodation provided under Part III of the 1948 Act, the local authority has a statutory responsibility to take reasonable steps to mitigate loss or damage to that person's property. Under section 48(2) of the National Assistance Act 1948 there is a power of entry to premises in order to carry out this duty. Local authorities have detailed procedures, usually involving the drawing up of inventories to ensure that their responsibilities for protection of property are met.

Chapter 13

Mentally Disordered People

A more detailed knowledge of mental health law is required by those appointed as approved social workers under the Mental Health Act 1983 than can be provided by a general text such as this and several specialist texts are available (Hoggett, 1996; Rashid, Ball and McDonald, 1996; Bartlett and Sandland, 2000). In addition, a historical perspective, such as that provided by Hoggett, is necessary not only to appreciate the considerable changes that have occurred in the twentieth century in the statutory framework which determines the limits of intervention in the lives of mentally disordered people, but also to understand much of the present legislation. All local authority social workers, even if not authorized to exercise them, need to be aware of the statutory powers that exist in relation to the mentally ill and those with learning disabilities, and the legal restraints that should prevent abuse of those powers.

The law relating to the treatment of mentally disordered patients in England and Wales is contained in the Mental Health Act 1983, which consolidated much of the 1959 Mental Health Act with substantial amendments introduced in the Mental Health (Amendment) Act 1982. Although the provisions of the 1983 Act differ substantially in detail from those of the 1959 Act, the principle on which treatment is provided – the innovative cornerstone of the earlier Act – has not altered:

> Nothing in this Act shall be construed as preventing a patient who requires treatment for mental disorder from being admitted to any hospital or nursing home in pursuance of arrangements made in that behalf and without any application, order or direction rendering him liable to be detained under this Act or from remaining in any hospital or mental nursing home in pursuance of such arrangements after he has ceased to be so liable to be detained. (Mental Health Act 1983, s.131(1))

The powers to admit or detain mentally disordered people in hospital compulsorily can only be considered when all attempts to persuade the patient to accept treatment on a voluntary basis have failed, and then only in circumstances which meet the detailed requirements set out in the Act.

The *Memorandum on Parts I to VI, VIII and X Mental Health Act 1983* (Department of Health and Welsh Office, 1998) and the *Code of Practice* (Department of Health and Welsh Office, 1999), give guidance on their implementation of the Act. The 1999 *Code of Practice* places greater emphasis than previous codes on the patient as an individual with rights, and also emphasizes the need for different agencies to co-operate. A particular concern is that black people are overrepresented in all parts of the psychiatric system (Bartlett and Sandland, 2000). There are a number of guiding principles that underlie the Code (Chapter 1); these are that people to whom the Act applies (including those being assessed for possible admission) should:

- receive recognition of their basic human rights under the European Convention on Human Rights;
- be given respect for their qualities, abilities and diverse backgrounds as individuals and be assured that account will be taken of their age, gender, sexual orientation, social, ethnic, cultural and religious background, but that general assumptions will not be made on the basis of any one of these characteristics;
- have their needs taken fully into account, though it is recognized that, within available resources, it may not always be practicable to meet them in full;
- be given any necessary treatment or care in the least controlled and segregated facilities compatible with ensuring their own health or safety or the safety of other people;
- be treated and cared for in such a way as to promote to the greatest practicable degree their self-determination and personal responsibility, consistent with their own needs and wishes;
- be discharged from detention or other powers provided by the Act as soon as it is clear that their application is no longer justified.

The 1999 Code also explicitly states (para. 1.2) that the delivery of all mental health services is framed within the Care Programme Approach (CPA) set out in Circular HC (90) 23/LASSL(90)11. The CPA provides the framework for all patients referred to the specialist psychiatric services, both in hospital and in the community. The key elements of the CPA are stated in the Code to be:

- systematic arrangements for assessing people's health and social care needs;
- the formulation of a care plan which addresses those needs;
- the appointment of a care co-ordinator to keep in close touch with the patient and monitor care;
- regular reviews and if need be, agreed changes to the care plan.

Definitions Under the 1983 Act

The legislation refers 'to the reception, care and treatment of mentally disordered patients'. Under section 1(2), mental disorder means mental illness (which is not defined in the legislation), arrested or incomplete development of mind, psychopathic disorder and any other disorder or disability of mind.

Severe mental impairment means a state of arrested or incomplete development of mind which includes severe impairment of intelligence and social functioning and is associated with abnormally aggressive or seriously irresponsible conduct on the part of the person concerned.

Mental impairment means a state of arrested or incomplete development of mind (not amounting to severe mental impairment) which includes significant impairment of intelligence and social functioning and is associated with abnormally aggressive or seriously irresponsible conduct of the person concerned.

Psychopathic disorder means a persistent disorder or disability of mind, whether or not including significant impairment of intelligence, which results in abnormally aggressive or seriously irresponsible conduct on the part of the person concerned.

It is important to note that severe mental impairment, mental impairment and psychopathic disorder all require evidence of 'abnormally aggressive or seriously irresponsible conduct', and that behaviour due solely to promiscuity or immoral conduct, sexual deviancy, drugs or alcohol dependence is excluded from the definition of mental disorder (s.1(3)).

Approved Social Workers

The role and responsibilities of social workers working with mentally ill people were both enhanced and extended by the 1983 Act. As from October 1984, only approved social workers (ASWs) appointed and approved by their authorities 'as having appropriate competence in dealing with persons suffering from mental disorder' can carry out duties under the Act. The post-qualifying training requirement for ASWs involves a programme arranged by the Central Council for Education and Training in Social Work (CCETSW) of at least 60 days' training (CCETSW, 2000).

The powers and duties of the ASW include interviewing patients in a suitable manner; making applications for admissions to hospital or helping nearest relatives to do so; applying to the county court to replace the nearest relative when that relative is preventing, on grounds the ASW considers unreasonable, the patient's removal to hospital (*W* v. *L* [1974]); conveying patients to hospital; entering and inspecting premises in which a mentally disordered person is living; and, if necessary, applying for a warrant to search for and remove the patient (s.135(1)) (see Hoggett, 1996; Rashid, Ball and McDonald, 1996).

The powers of the ASW are described in paras. 2.11–2.21 of the *Code of Practice*. The ASW has overall responsibility for co-ordinating the process of assessment and has responsibility for informing the care co-ordinator (if the patient is on CPA) and the general practitioner, of any action taken.

Nearest Relatives

Relatives are defined under section 26 of the Mental Health Act 1983 with the 'nearest' higher on the list and the oldest in any category taking precedence regardless of sex:

● husband or wife;
● son or daughter;
● father or mother;
● brother or sister;
● grandparent;
● uncle or aunt; and
● nephew or niece.

However, section 26(4) provides that

> where the patient ordinarily resides with or is cared for by one or more of his relatives (or if he is for the time being an in patient in a hospital, he last resided with or was cared for by one or more of his relatives) his nearest relative shall be determined:
> (a)   by giving preference to that relative or those relatives over the others.

Where there are two or more such relatives the nearest relative is determined according to the above list (s.26(4)(b)).

In practice, there are further extensions: for instance, a cohabitee may be regarded as a spouse after six months, and where there are no other relations, after five years a non-relative fellow lodger or landlady may be considered a relative for the purposes of the Act (Hoggett, 1996).

There is no guarantee that having the legal status of nearest relative will also signify emotional closeness. In fact, the reverse may be the case. The European Court of Human Rights has held that it is a breach of Article 8 of the Convention for a legal system to impose a nearest relative who is not able to act in the best interests of the patient, and who cannot be displaced by the patient's application to a court (*J.T.* v. *U.K.* [2000]).

Compulsory Powers

The minimum conditions required by Article 5 of the European Convention on Human Rights for lawful detention of a person of unsound mind were laid down by the European Court of Human Rights in the case of *Winterwerp* v. *Netherlands* (1979). Detention needs to be:

● in accordance with a procedure prescribed by law;
● based on objective medical assessment;

- for a mental disorder of a kind or degree warranting compulsory confinement; and
- continued confinement must be based on the persistence of mental disorder.

Under the Mental Health Act there are three procedures for applying for compulsory admission to hospital, without judicial proceedings, on the application of the nearest relative or an approved social worker supported by the recommendation of one or two doctors, and one procedure – rarely used – for guardianship in the community. A patient already in hospital may become subject to compulsory detention on the basis of a report by the doctor in charge of his or her case, or in more extreme circumstances by a nurse. In addition, the police have the power to remove to a place of safety any person found in a public place who appears to be suffering from a mental disorder and to be in need of care or control, and an ASW can apply for a warrant to authorize the police to enter premises to search for a mentally disordered person and, if necessary, remove them to a safe place. Controversially, it was accepted in the *Bournewood* case (*R* v. *Bournewood Community and Mental Health NHS Trust, ex p. L* [1998]) that people who were mentally incapacitated could be detained in hospital under common law and without the protection of the Mental Health Act 1983 if it was necessary to do so and in their best interests. This is likely, however, to be challenged under the European Convention on Human Rights.

Admission for Assessment

Section 2 of the 1983 Act authorizes the detention of the patient for up to 28 days on an application by the nearest relative or someone authorized by them or by the county court to act on their behalf, or by an ASW, supported by recommendations from two doctors, one of whom must be an approved specialist in mental disorder and both of whom must have examined the patient either together or within five days of each other. The medical recommendation must be based on the fact that the patient

1 is suffering from mental disorder of a nature or degree which warrants the detention of the patient in a hospital for assessment (or for assessment followed by treatment) for at least a limited period; and
2 he ought to be so detained in the interests of his own safety or with a view to the protection of other persons.

Paragraph 2.7 of the Code makes it clear that a section 2 application is appropriate if there is a strong likelihood that the patient will change his mind about informal admission, prior to actually being admitted to hospital.

The applicant is responsible for getting the patient to hospital, and may seek help from the ambulance service or the police. If patients escape, they may be apprehended and returned, but after 14 days from the date of the second medical recommendation authority to detain or admit the patient lapses. If patients reach the hospital within 14 days, authority to detain them lasts for 28 days unless steps are taken to detain for further treatment.

An order for discharge may be made in respect of a patient detained for assessment by the responsible medical officer (RMO), the managers or the nearest relative. If the patient applies to a mental health review tribunal within 14 days of admission to hospital, the tribunal may discharge the patient.

Admission for Assessment in an Emergency

In an emergency an application for assessment may be made with the support of only one doctor, who need not be a mental health specialist, although he or she should, if possible, have previous acquaintance with, and must have examined, the patient within the 24 hours prior to the patient's removal to hospital (s.4).

An emergency application, which authorizes detention for up to 72 hours, may be made either by the nearest relative or by an ASW. The application must not only state that it is 'of urgent necessity for the patient to be admitted and detained', but be supported by a statement from the recommending doctor indicating the length of the delay that would be caused by obtaining a second medical opinion, why this might result in harm and whether the harm would be caused to the patient or to those caring for the patient or to other people (Mental Health (Hospital Guardianship and Consent to Treatment) Regulations 1983, Form 7). After 72 hours, authority to detain the patient lapses, unless a second medical recommendation made (if the initial one was not) by a doctor 'approved as having special experience in the diagnosis or treatment of mental disorder' converts the emergency admission into a section 2 (28 days) admission.

Emergency procedures as introduced by the provisions of the Mental Health Act 1959 (s.29) were originally intended for exceptional use only. As with other similar provisions where the emergency procedure is either less complicated, or less demanding in terms of evidence, in practice the procedure intended for occasional emergency use became the normal route. This gave rise to considerable concern among those working with mentally ill people (DHSS, 1976).

Under the 1983 Act, use of the procedure has been discouraged, in that the categories of person who make application for an emergency admission are restricted to nearest relatives and ASWs. At the same time, stricter criteria for invoking the procedure were introduced and their observance encouraged by the regulations. It is a matter for continuing criticism, however, that patients can still be admitted under section 4 on a medical recommendation given by a doctor who may have no prior knowledge of the patient, nor any experience or expertise in the diagnosis of mental disorder (Hoggett, 1996). The 1998 Memorandum on the Mental Health Act 1983 emphasizes that section 4 should not be used for administrative convenience and is to be confined to situations where there is an immediate and significant risk of mental or physical harm to the patient or others or to property, or a need for physical restraint (para. 24).

Admission for Treatment (s.3)

An application for admission for treatment under this section may be made by the nearest relative or, if the nearest relative objects, someone appointed by the county court to act as such or, with the agreement of the nearest relative, by an ASW. The applicant must have seen the patient within the previous 14 days, and the application must be supported by recommendations by two doctors, one of them an approved specialist, to the effect that the patient

1 is suffering from mental illness, severe mental impairment, psychopathic disorder or mental impairment and his mental disorder is of a nature or degree which makes it appropriate for him to receive medical treatment in a hospital; and
2 in the case of a psychopathic disorder or mental impairment, such treatment is likely to alleviate or prevent a deterioration of this condition; and
3 it is necessary for the health and safety of the patient or for the protection of other persons that he should receive such treatment and it cannot be provided unless he is detained under this section.

Section 3, rather than section 2 is appropriate where the diagnosis is not different from that made under previous section 2 admissions, though para. 5.2 of the *Code of Practice* says that section 3 may also be appropriate 'where a person has not been in regular contact with the specialist psychiatric services'.

The patient may then be detained, in the first instance, for up to six months, then for a further six months and thereafter for a year at a time on the basis of a report from the RMO to the hospital managers which states that continued detention is necessary, using the same criteria as those justifying the initial admission although, on renewal, all forms of mental disorder are subject to the treatability test (s.3(2)(b)).

Subject to certain safeguards, many forms of treatment except those which are irreversible may be administered to patients admitted or detained under section 3 without their consent, provided that a second medical opinion is sought (see also sections 57 and 58, and Hoggett, 1996).

Consent to treatment is dealt with in paras. 212–30 of the Memorandum and Chapters 15, 16 and 31 of the *Code of Practice*. Paragraph 16.5 of the Code clarifies that Part IV of the Mental Health Act does not apply to the treatment of physical disorders 'unless it can reasonably be said that the physical disorder is a symptom or underlying cause of the mental disorder'. This could, for example, cover the artificial feeding of a patient with anorexia: *B* v. *Croydon Health Authority* [1995]. However, in *St. George's Hospital NHS Trust* v. *S* [1998], it was seen as an abuse of Mental Health Act powers to section a mother refusing a caesarean section; this was not 'treatment for the purposes of the Act'.

An advance refusal of treatment for mental disorder does not prevent the authorization of such treatment by Part IV of the Act (para. 15.11, Code of Practice).

While a patient is detained for treatment under section 3, discharge may be by the RMO, the managers or the nearest relative. If the RMO certifies that 'the patient if discharged would be likely to act in a manner dangerous to other persons or to himself' (s.25(d)), discharge by the nearest relative may be blocked. In those circumstances, the nearest relative can apply to a mental health review tribunal. The patient may also apply to be discharged by a mental health review tribunal within the first six months of detention and once during each subsequent period of renewal.

Patients already in Hospital (s.5)

If it appears to the registered medical practitioner in charge of the medical treatment of a voluntary in-patient that an application ought to be made for the patient's detention in hospital, he or she may provide the managers with a report in writing to that effect and the patient may be detained in hospital for 72 hours from the time the report was furnished. Under section 5(4), a nurse may, if no practitioner is available, furnish a report to the managers to record that fact in writing and the patient may be detained for up to six hours. This six hours is subsumed within the 72-hour period if a further application is made by a doctor under section 5(2).

Detention in a 'Place of Safety' (s.136)

A police officer finding a person who appears to be suffering from mental disorder, and to be in need of care or control, in a public place may remove that person to a place of safety if he or she thinks it necessary in their interests or for the safety of others. The section authorizes detention for up to 72 hours for the purpose of medical and social work assessment, the patient most usually being detained in a police station or hospital. Use and possible abuse of the section have attracted attention from researchers and those concerned with the rights of the mentally ill. Although the powers are not widely used outside London, there was evidence of considerable underrecording (Butler, 1975) and some pressure from MIND during the debate on the 1982 Amendment Act both to tighten the criteria and reduce the detention period to a maximum of 24 hours.

Police Warrant Under s.135(1)

An ASW who has reason to believe that a mentally disordered person is not under proper care may apply to a magistrate for a warrant which will empower a police officer accompanied by an ASW and a doctor to enter premises, by force if necessary, and again, if it is considered necessary, to remove the mentally disordered person to a place of safety without formally 'sectioning' the person for up to 72 hours. There is no power to treat the patient without his or her consent under this procedure. Definitions under this section are difficult and there is some suspicion that its apparent very low rate of use masks considerable flouting of the law by the professionals involved (Hoggett, 1996).

Police powers are discussed in para. 317 of the Memorandum and para. 10 of the Code of Practice. The identification of preferred places of safety is a matter for local agreement, though as a general rule it is preferable for a hospital rather than a police station to be chosen (para. 10).

Guardianship

When the 1959 Act was implemented, it was envisaged that compulsory care within the community would replace hospital orders for most patients. In fact only a minute number of guardianship orders were made. The 1983 Act provisions attempt to make guardianship more workable, though there is as yet little indication that many orders, either civil or criminal, are being made.

The rules as to the applicants and medical recommendations are similar to those for compulsory admission to hospital; the application is addressed to the local authority, and the proposed guardian may be an individual approved by the local authority who consents to act, or any social service authority which accepts responsibility. Under the 1983 Act, the guardian has the power to:

1 require the patient to reside at a place specified;
2 attend at places and times specified for the purpose of medical treatment, occupation, and so on; and
3 require that access to the patient may be given to any doctor, ASW or other similar person.

Under the Act, patients may be transferred from hospital to guardianship and vice versa. The duration and termination of guardianship orders are very similar to those for patients admitted for treatment under section 3 (Bartlett and Sandland, 2000; Rashid, Ball and McDonald, 1996).

A positive use of guardianship in respect of the admission of mentally incapacitated patients to residential care is raised as a practice issue in para. 13.10 of the Code of Practice. Guardianship as a limited essential powers order (Hoggett, 1996) can provide the framework within which decisions about current and future care are planned.

Mental Health Act Commission

The Commission was set up by the 1983 Act as a special health authority under the National Health Service Act 1977. Its members who are mostly medical professionals plus a few lawyers and lay people are appointed, and may be removed by, the Secretary of State. The work includes a visiting and inspection function in respect of detained patients, setting up complaints procedures and monitoring compulsory treatment under the Act. It also advises the Secretary of State on the Code of Practice (Department of Health, 1991), which provides a commentary on the needs, rights and entitlements of detained people, and guidance on good practice with informal patients.

Orders Made in Criminal Proceedings

Remands and interim orders under sections 35, 36 and 38 were introduced into the 1983 Act to provide for those cases in which a remand on bail with a condition of psychiatric assessment is considered impracticable, but the alternative of prison does not provide a suitable environment for such an assessment. This is an important issue for probation officers who may need to write pre-sentence reports on mentally disordered offenders for whom use of these provisions may be appropriate (Stone, 2001a).

Remand to Hospital for a Report (s.35)

Any person awaiting trial for an offence (except murder) punishable with imprisonment may, if the court is satisfied on medical evidence that there is reason to suggest that the accused is suffering from mental illness, psychopathic disorder, severe mental impairment or mental impairment (the four categories), may be remanded to a specified hospital with a bed available within seven days for a 'report on his mental condition'. The remand may be for up to 28 days and is renewable for similar periods up to a total of 12 weeks. Offenders detained under this section cannot be compelled to accept treatment.

When a person suffering from a mental disorder is due to be sentenced, section 82(1) of the Powers of Criminal Courts (Sentencing) Act 2000 requires the court to obtain and consider a medical report before passing a custodial sentence unless the court is of the opinion that it is unnecessary to do so (s.82(2)). Furthermore, the likely effect of a custodial sentence on the offender's mental condition and on any treatment which may be available for it, should be considered before such a sentence is imposed.

Remand of an Accused Person for Treatment (s.36)

Persons accused of offences punishable with imprisonment (excluding murder) who are certified by two registered medical practitioners to be suffering from 'mental illness or severe mental impairment of a nature or degree which makes it appropriate for them to be detained in hospital for treatment' may be remanded to hospital for treatment, which under this section cannot be refused.

Interim Hospital Orders (s.38)

This section provides for a convicted offender to be made the subject of an interim hospital order on the evidence of two registered medical practitioners that the offender is suffering from one of the four categories of mental disorder and that 'there is reason to suppose that the disorder from which the defendant is suffering is such that it may be appropriate for a hospital order to be made in his case'.

This order authorizes admission to hospital within 28 days for an initial period of 12 weeks, which may be increased by periods of up to 28 days to a maximum of six months, provided that the offender's legal representative is heard if extensions are made.

Hospital or Guardianship Order (s.37)

A hospital order, which has the effect of an admission for treatment under section 3, may be made by a court sentencing for an imprisonable offence (except murder) on evidence of two registered medical practitioners of the existence of one of the four categories of mental disorder. If an order is made under section 37, the nearest relative does not have the power to discharge the patient, only to apply to the mental health review tribunal on the patient's behalf after six months; patients may make a similar application on their own behalf. The condition must be likely to respond to treatment or warrant guardianship, and the court must consider the order the most appropriate method of disposing of the case (for greater detail and a commentary, see Hoggett, 1996).

Restriction Order (s.41)

> Where a hospital order is made in respect of an offender by the Crown Court and it appears to the court having regard to the nature of the offence, the antecedents of the offender, and the risk of his committing further offences if set at large, that it is necessary for the protection of the public from serious harm so to do, the court may ... order that the offender be subject to the special restriction set out in this section.

The restriction order can only be made in the Crown Court and has the effect of limiting the power to order discharge to the Secretary of State, who has to receive annual reports on the offender, or a mental health review tribunal. Discharge, when authorized, may be absolute or conditional (Rashid, Ball and McDonald, 1996). Probation officers also need to be aware of the power that exists to allow the transfer of mentally disordered prisoners to hospital under sections 47 and 48 with possible restriction under section 49 (Stone, 2001a).

Section 109 of the Powers of the Criminal Courts (Sentencing) Act 2000 provides for imposition of automatic life sentences on defendants convicted of a second serious offence. In *R* v. *Drew* [2002], a life sentence had been imposed following a second conviction for an offence of wounding with intent (included as a serious offence within s.109(5) of the Act). It was accepted that Mr Drew was suffering from a mental disorder within the meaning of the Mental Health Act 1983. He argued that the imposition of an ordinary sentence of imprisonment was a breach of his rights under Articles 3 and 5 of the European Convention on Human Rights, because suitable alternative orders were available under the Mental Health Act 1983. The Court of Appeal held that notwithstanding the stigma of a life sentence and the fact that the courts had in such cases previously encouraged the use of hospital and restriction orders under the 1983 Act, it had always been open for Parliament to say that in defined cases there should be an assumption that the offender presented such a serious and continuing danger to the public that a hospital order with a restriction order would afford inadequate protection. The assumption was rebuttable, and there was no evidence to show that appropriate medical treatment would not be provided; therefore there was no infringement of Convention rights.

Mental Health Review Tribunals

Mental health review tribunals provide an independent specialist forum before which almost all compulsorily detained patients can have their detention reviewed. There is a tribunal for each area health authority and each panel has legal, medical and lay members 'who have such experience in administration, such knowledge of social services or such other qualifications and experience as the Lord Chancellor considers suitable'. A tribunal is made up of at least one member of each group with a lawyer presiding, and the tribunal members may be specially selected for their suitability to deal with a particular problem. Procedures are kept as informal as is possible whilst still conforming to the requirements of natural justice. Hoggett (1996) considers in detail the various applications that may be made to tribunals and the different procedures that apply. Implementation of the Human Rights Act 1998 has resulted in amendments to the law relating to tribunal hearings (see page 21).

Care in the Community

S.117 Aftercare and Supervised Discharge

Patients receiving specialist psychiatric services are subject to the Care Programme Approach (HC (90)23) which provides for the appointment of a care co-ordinator to bridge care in hospital and in the community. Patients compulsorily detained under sections 3, 47 or 48 of the Mental Health Act are in addition subject to the provisions of section 117 of the Act upon discharge from hospital. Section 117 states:

> It shall be the duty of the (District) Health Authority and of the local social services authority to provide, in co-operation with relevant voluntary agencies, after-care services for any person to whom this section applies until such time as the (District) Health Authority and the local social services authority are satisfied that the person concerned is no longer in need of such services.

Section 117 does not specify what sort of aftercare services should be provided, but the duty to make provision continues until the health and social services authority jointly agree that the need for them no longer exists.

Mental health review tribunals may seek to impose conditions of receiving services in the community when using their powers of discharge under the Mental Health Act. However, the Court of Appeal in *R (on the application of K)* v. *Camden and Islington Health Authority* [2001], held that there was no absolute obligation imposed by the Mental Health Act, s.117 on health authorities or social services departments to comply with such conditions.

Concern that certain individuals presented exceptional risks saw the introduction of supervised discharge under the provisions of the Mental Health (Patients in the Community) Act 1995. Grounds for the granting of supervised discharge are that there is a risk of harm or serious exploitation to the patient, or a risk to other people. In a reversal of the sectioning process, the application is made by the RMO, with supporting recommendations from two other professionals, one of whom is an ASW. Supervised discharge gives no power to treat the patient without his consent; and unlike guardianship with which it has some similarities, there is no power to transfer the patient back to hospital, without further legal intervention. However, it provides through controversial supervision registers a mechanism for monitoring the patient's engagement with mental health services following discharge (Barlett and Sandland, 2000: 334–5).

The Court of Protection

Mentally disordered people, whether they are in hospital or not, may not be able to manage their own affairs and may be vulnerable to exploitation. If a mentally incapable person owns even a small amount of property, it is possible that the powers of the Court of Protection may have to be invoked. This court, which is an office of the Supreme Court, exists solely to deal with the affairs of people who are incapable of managing for themselves.

Proceedings in the Court of Protection are usually started by the patient's nearest relative by means of an originating application, but anyone can apply and social workers may find themselves needing to do so on behalf of a client. Before the court can intervene, it has to have a certificate from a registered medical practitioner that the patient is incapable by reason of medical disorder from conducting his or her own affairs, and either a simple certificate if the patient's income is under £1000 and capital under £5000 or, if larger amounts are involved, a sworn affidavit setting out particulars of property and affairs, details of relatives and the grounds for making the application.

The patient must be served with notice of the application or, if the matter is simple, the proposed summary order unless the court considers that the person is incapable of understanding. After that, the patient has at least seven days or until the date of the hearing, whichever is later, in which to object in writing to the court. There is no provision for a patient to be heard in person.

The court can make any relative or anyone else who seems interested in the application a party to the proceedings, and any relative closer than the applicant should be informed. All this can take a considerable time; however, if there is urgent need for immediate protection, the court can make such interim orders as it considers necessary.

Once a patient is subject to the court's jurisdiction, it has exclusive control over all the person's property and affairs and wide powers to fulfil this function for the maintenance and benefit of the patient and family. Unless the patient's affairs are sufficiently straightforward to be dealt with by a simple order, the court will appoint a receiver, who will be empowered in very precise terms to protect the estate and use it on the patient's behalf and will have to render annual accounts. The receiver may be a relative, professional adviser or any other suitable person who is prepared to act. If there is no such individual, the Official Solicitor may be appointed.

The powers of the Court of Protection are massive and its procedures both cumbersome and expensive, in that not insubstantial fees deducted from the patient's property are charged. However, its powers provide protection from exploitation which cannot be achieved in any other way. The court's functions continue until the patient dies or, exceptionally, the court finds that it can discharge the receiver, because patients have recovered sufficiently to manage their own affairs. Other less intrusive, but correspondingly less effective, measures which may be taken in regard to the affairs of mentally incapable people are usefully discussed in the context of legal rights (Cooper, 2000; McDonald and Taylor, 1995).

Review of the Mental Health Act

The White Paper *Reforming the Mental Health Act* (Department of Health and the Home Office, 2000) was published in December 2000 following a review of the 1983 Act in the light of changes in professional practice, social policy and the implications of the Human Rights Act 1988. Proposals include a single pathway for compulsory admission to hospital with scrutiny by a mental health tribunal before a care and treatment plan is put into place. It is also mooted that the role of the ASW could be carried out by other professional groups. There are also particular proposals for the continued detention of high-risk individuals with psychopathic disorders who cannot at present be detained because they are untreatable (dangerous people with a severe personality disorder – DSPD). A draft bill published in June 2002 to enact these proposals was condemned as 'unethical and unworkable' by the President of the Royal College of Physicians and the Vice-president of the Law Society (Shooter and Kirby, 2002). Legislation is likely in 2004.

PART IV
YOUTH JUSTICE

Chapter 14

The Youth Justice System and Pre-trial Decisions

Youth justice is an umbrella term describing the intervention of the police, welfare agencies and courts seeking to control and reform children (10–13 years) and young persons (14–17) who commit criminal offences. When the Labour government came to power in 1997, reform of the youth justice system was a clear policy priority. In opposition, shadow ministers were convinced of the need for a radical reshaping on the basis of substantial evidence of expense, delay and ineffectiveness throughout the system (Audit Commission, 1996; Straw and Michael, 1996). They were also considerably influenced by a very substantial Home Office self-report study of all aspects of young peoples' involvement in crime (Graham and Bowling, 1995). Once in power, the Home Secretary immediately established a Youth Justice Task Force to advise him on proposals for reform. The ensuing White Paper *No More Excuses* (Home Office, 1997), set out a new aim for the youth justice system and made proposals for its achievement through management of the system, new orders and restorative justice oriented strategies. These were subsequently enacted in the Crime and Disorder Act 1998 (CDA 1998) and the Youth Justice and Criminal Evidence Act 1999 (YJCEA 1999). At the same time new civil orders targeted at children below the age of criminal responsibility were introduced. (For more detail of the background and critiques of various aspects of the reforms, see: Fionda, 1999; Wonnacott, 1999; Gelsthorpe and Morris, 1999; Ball, McCormac and Stone, 2001: ch. 1; Ball, 2000.)

The Youth Justice System

The principal aim of the youth justice system, and the duty of all persons carrying out functions in relation to the system, is 'to prevent offending by children and young persons' (CDA 1998, s.37). The aim and the objectives through which it would be achieved were elaborated in an interdepartmental circular (Home Office, 1998), and are restated in the National Standards for Youth Justice published by the Youth Justice Board in 2000. They are:

the avoidance of delay through the swift administration of justice;
confronting young people with the consequences of their offending for themselves, their victims, their families and the community;

interventions to tackle the particular factors which put the young person at risk of
continuing to offend;
punishment proportionate to the seriousness and persistence of offending;
encouraging reparation to victims;
reinforcing the responsibility of parents for their children's behaviour.

At the same time the statutory requirement that all courts when making
decisions regarding children and young people should have regard to their
welfare (Children and Young Persons Act 1933, s.44) remains in place. It
appears inevitable that in some, possibly many, cases there will be a conflict
between the two.

The Youth Justice Board and Youth Offending Teams

The Board is a national body set up under the CDA 1998 to determine youth
justice policy and keep the work of local youth offending teams under review.

The primary responsibility for the provision of youth justice services rests
with local authorities, working within policy imperatives set by the Youth
Justice Board (YJB). Local authorities, with the police and the probation
service, have to provide the comprehensive range of youth justice services set
out in the CDA 1998, s.38(4). These include the provision of: appropriate
adults to safeguard the interests of young offenders being questioned by the
police; bail support; accommodation on remand; reports for courts; persons to
act as responsible officers in relation to a range of court orders; supervision
under community orders or after release from a custodial order; and, the
management of youth offending panels under the YJCEA 1999.

Every local authority, either on its own or in conjunction with others has
established one or more multidisciplinary youth offending teams (YOTs) to
carry out its responsibilities. The membership of YOTs is prescribed in that it
must include a probation officer, a local authority social worker, a police
officer and persons nominated by a health authority and the local education
authority. The YOT manager is clearly identified in policy terms (Home
Office, 1998a) and in the interim report of the evaluation of pilot teams as
being a key appointment with primary responsibility for strategic planning
for the delivery of youth justice services by the YOT (Home Office, 1999).

National Standards for Youth Justice (Youth Justice Board, 2000)
prescribes the role of YOTs and other agencies within the youth justice
system. These standards cover the supervision of offenders, the court process,
the sharing of information, the needs of victims of crime, including reparation
if the victim is willing; the prioritization of the prevention of offending; the
role of the YOT in the local prevention of youth offending; and, require that
intervention is fairly and consistently achieved in a way that values and
respects cultural and racial diversity.

Youth Courts

The magistrates' youth court is a criminal court. Prior to 1991, the juvenile court had a dual criminal and care jurisdiction. The Children Act 1989 removed care and related civil proceedings from the juvenile court to the family proceedings court, and the Criminal Justice Act 1991 brought 17-year-olds – previously treated as adults – within the jurisdiction of the renamed youth court for trial and sentence, but not for remand purposes (s.68). Sentencing powers for young offenders differentiate between the 10–15-year-old defendants and the 16–17-year-olds, who may be sentenced as 'near adults'. The CDA 1998 introduced a range of new orders (see below) many of which overlap with penalties already in existence.

Throughout the formulation and implementation of the innovative reforms which have established the YJB and YOTs, there has been no fundamental reform of the youth court. The changes that have occurred are managerial and jurisdictional: managerial, in that youth courts are required to comply with National Standards as they affect the courts, and are subject to targets set by the YJB for the completion of each stage of a young offender's progress through the system; jurisdictional, in the range of new orders available, and particularly in the substantial limit placed on youth court panel magistrates' exercise of discretion in sentencing by the introduction of the mandatory referral order for first-time offenders. In his review of the working of the criminal courts, Lord Justice Auld recommended that young offenders charged with grave crimes (see pages 158–62) should no longer be tried in the Crown Court (Auld, 2001). In the White Paper *Justice for All* (Home Depaartment, 2002), the Government proposes strengthening the jurisdiction of the youth court. If the proposals are enacted, young offenders charged with grave crimes will be tried in a youth court, charied by a High Court judge, instead of the Crown Court.

Constitution

Lay justices who sit in the youth court are elected to the youth court panel for a three-year term by all the magistrates in their petty sessional division, or are selected by the Lord Chancellor for the Inner London panel. They should normally be under the age of 50 when first appointed and have experience of dealing with young people and 'a real appreciation of the surroundings and way of life of the children who are likely to come before the courts' (Home Office Circular, 1979). The extent to which these requirements are met varies greatly depending on the policies of the individual bench and on the availability of suitable candidates. Research suggests that scant attention is paid to the age and suitability of panel members, and that their level of understanding of the problems of the children who appear before them and of their sentencing powers may be limited (Ball, 1995; Ball and Connolly, 1999). Youth panel justices are expected to undertake some additional training and to visit community homes run by local authorities and prison service establishments for young offenders. District judges (Magistrates' Courts) also sit alone in the youth court.

Procedure

In order to prevent those appearing in the youth court coming into contact with adult offenders, the Rules provide that youth courts should be held, where possible, in a different building or on a different day from adult courts. At the very least, the youth court may not be held in the same room in which an adult court has sat or will sit within one hour (1933 Act, s.47(2)). Arrangements have to be made for separate waiting areas for those attending youth courts. The physical settings in which they are held and the suitability of the facilities available have been shown to vary as randomly as all other aspects of the juvenile justice system (Hilgendorf, 1981; Parker, Casburn and Turnbull, 1981; Parker, Sumner and Jarvis, 1989; Brown, 1991).

There are strict rules that exclude members of the general public from the youth court. The press are allowed to attend and report, but reports must not contain information, such as names, addresses and school attended, which is likely to lead members of the public to be able to identify anyone involved in the proceedings who is under the age of 18. Where it is considered to be in the public interest, courts may, giving its reasons, order that certain information likely to lead to identification of a young offender may be published (for a detailed account of these rules, see Ball, McCormac and Stone, 2001: ch. 7).

The procedure for trial and sentencing in the youth court is very similar to that for adult defendants, with additional rules regarding time limits and the explanations that have to be given to defendants and their parents.

Time limits   One means of achieving the principal aim of the youth justice system – to prevent offending by children and young people – has been identified as the need to present an offender quickly with the consequences of his or her behaviour by ensuring that there is no unnecessary delay between offence and sentence. The Youth Justice Board has published a template showing the various stages involved in a case involving a young offender from arrest through to sentence, and the government has set time targets for each stage (Youth Justice Board, 1999). In addition, statutory time limits, set under the Prosecution of Offences Act 1985, apply where a defendant is in custody. The 1985 Act was amended by the CDA 1998 to allow special time limits to be set for offences dealt with in the youth court with new regulations specifying the maximum period for specific stages (Prosecution of Offences (Youth Court Time Limits) Regulations 1999; Ball, McCormac and Stone, 2001: paras 7.25–7.31).

Jurisdiction of the Youth Court

There is no criminal responsibility for persons under 10 years of age. Children aged 10–13 were, under the legal principle of *doli incapax*, formerly presumed to be incapable of forming criminal intent unless they can be shown to have known that what they were doing was seriously wrong. This safeguard was removed on implementation of section 34 of the CDA 1998.

Almost all criminal proceedings against 10–17-year-old defendants begin and finish in the youth court. Currently, where a child or young person is charged with homicide trial has to take place in the Crown Court and it may do in relation to a range of other offences where the charge and the nature of the child's involvement in the offence are sufficiently serious to require a very substantial sentence (see pages 157 and 158).

Arrest and the Criminal Process

Juveniles arrested by the police have rights regarding arrest and interrogation under the Police and Criminal Evidence Act 1984 (PACE) and accompanying Codes of Practice (Home Office, 1995 and 1999), in addition to those for adults described in Chapter 19. For the purposes of detention and remand 17-year-olds are treated as adults and not juveniles.

Juveniles may not be arrested or interviewed at school, except in exceptional circumstances (PACE, Code C, para. 11.15). Juveniles may not be subject to voluntary searches by the police (PACE, Code A, notes of guidance 1D).

When a juvenile is brought to a police station under arrest, the custody officer must contact the child's parent or carer or an 'appropriate adult' (see page 140) and ask them to attend the police station; questioning of the juvenile must not begin before the adult arrives unless authorized in cases of grave urgency by a superintendent or officer above (Code C, para. 13.1).

Juveniles, like adults, must be informed of their right to have a solicitor present at the police station; if the appropriate adult considers that legal advice should be taken, interrogation must not start until such advice has been obtained.

Juveniles should not be detained in police cells unless there is nowhere else they can be properly supervised. They may not be placed in a cell with a detained adult (Code C, para. 8.8).

The rules relating to fingerprinting and the collection of other bodily samples are similar to those for adults with added protection of the requirement of the consent of an appropriate person: that is, the person himself or herself if aged 17; the young person (14–16) and their parent or guardian; and for children (10–13) a parent or guardian (for further details regarding the rules relating to identification, see Ball, McCormac and Stone, 2001: paras 3.41–3.48).

Appropriate Adults

The Royal Commission on Criminal Procedure which reported in 1981 regarded it as essential that a juvenile being interviewed by the police should have an adult, other than the police, present.

> Juveniles may not readily understand the significance of questions or of what they themselves say and are likely to be more suggestible than adults. They may need the support of an adult presence; of someone to befriend, advise and assist them to make their decisions. (Para. 4.103)

The requirement that when the police interview an arrested juvenile (or other vulnerable persons), whether at a police station or elsewhere, they may only do so in the presence of a parent or guardian or other appropriate adult was introduced as a result of this recommendation and is set out with great clarity in PACE Code C.

> It is important to bear in mind that, although juveniles or persons who are mentally ill or handicapped are often capable of providing reliable evidence, they may, without knowing or wishing to do so, be particularly prone in certain circumstances to provide information which is unreliable, misleading or incriminating. Special care should therefore always be exercised in questioning such a person and the appropriate adult should be involved if there is any doubt about a person's age, mental state or capacity. Because of the risk of unreliable evidence it is also important to obtain corroboration of any facts admitted whenever possible. (PACE Code A, notes of guidance 11B)

The Audit Commission (1996) identified the cost in social workers time of acting as appropriate adults, also research had produced conflicting evidence as to their effectiveness in the role (Evans, 1993; Bucke and Brown, 1997). The CDA 1998 made the provision of trained appropriate adults for juveniles one of the duties of YOTs, and volunteers are now recruited and trained to fulfil the role according to national standards. National standards (Youth Justice Board, 2000) place responsibilities on appropriate adults which go further than their traditional role at the police station.

> When a young person has been charged, if his or her parents, primary carer or other adult relative were not present at the interview with the police, the appropriate adult must contact them within 24 hours or prior to court, whichever is sooner to inform them and offer information about the court appearance. They must remind them that the young person's failure to attend court would be an offence. (Ibid., para. 2.4)

Diversion: Reprimands and Final Warnings

The Crime and Disorder Act 1998, ss. 65 and 66, replaced the existing non-statutory system of police cautions for minor offences with a formal diversionary system of reprimands followed by warnings (often referred to as 'final warnings') prior to a court appearance (for an elaboration on the reforms, see Ball, McCormac and Stone, 2001: ch. 4).

> The police, who are responsible for issuing reprimands and warnings can only do so if a police constable has evidence that a juvenile
> has committed an offence;
> there is sufficient evidence for a realistic prospect of conviction if he were to be prosecuted;
> the juvenile admits the offence;
> the juvenile has not been previously convicted of an offence; and
> the constable is satisfied that prosecution would not be in the public interest.
> (CDA 1998, s.65)

Guidance (Home Office, 2000a) to the police indicates that first-time offenders should normally receive a reprimand for a less serious offence. Second-time offenders who have been previously reprimanded cannot receive a further reprimand and should be warned or charged. Second-time offenders who have received a warning cannot receive a reprimand and should not receive a further warning, they should be charged unless the current offence is not serious and the previous warning was over two years ago. Third-time offenders who have been previously reprimanded and warned should be charged, unless the exception above applies. Fourth-time offenders who have previously been reprimanded or warned must be charged. They cannot receive a further warning.

Transitional provisions allow for cautions imposed prior to the implementation of section 67 of the CDA 1998 to count on the basis of one as a reprimand and two as a warning.

Reprimands and warnings will only very rarely be regarded as an appropriate response to an indictable offence (see page 201), and diversion from prosecution is never an option for the most serious offences such as murder or rape.

The Administration of Reprimands and Warnings

Reprimands and warnings have to be given orally by a police officer in the presence of an appropriate adult, for an offender under the age of 17, in a police station or other place specified by the Secretary of State.

Reprimand   The police officer giving a reprimand must specify the offence which led to it, make it clear that the reprimand is a serious matter and that any further offending behaviour will, in all but the most exceptional case, lead to a warning or prosecution. The offender must also be told that a record of the reprimand will be kept at least until the offender is 18, may be cited in future criminal proceedings and, if the offence is covered by the Sex Offender Act 1997, the young person is required to register with the police for inclusion on the sex offenders register.

Warnings   Although guidance to the police (Home Office, 2000a) sets out a three-tier structure of warnings, restorative conferences, restorative warnings and standard warnings, there is not yet any evidence of the extent to which the different tiers are being used.

Restorative conferences involve the offender, his or her family and the victim in a meeting at which the warning is administered as part of an attempt to confront the offender directly with the impact of his or her offence on the victim and decide on appropriate reparation. Such conferences can only take place if all parties are willing to participate.

Restorative warnings may be given where the victim, although not present, is willing for his or her views about the impact of the offence to be represented when the warning is administered.

Where the victim does not wish to be involved, or the offence is 'victimless', a standard warning without a restorative element will be administered.

The content of warnings is set out in detail in guidance (Home Office, 2000a: para. 72) and offenders and parents must be given a written copy (ibid.: Annex G). The warning will trigger immediate (within one working day) referral to the local YOT for assessment and participation in a rehabilitation (change) programme. Following a warning, offenders appearing in court for subsequent offences will not generally be able to be dealt with by way of a conditional discharge.

YOTs Responsibilities for Assessment and Rehabilitation (Change) Programmes

An assessment tool, known as ASSET, has been developed for the YJB by the University of Oxford Centre for Criminological Research. ASSET provides a core form with a number of ancillary forms for special purposes such as bail assessment or the assessment of risk of serious harm from the young person. The ASSET forms, which are accompanied by a very detailed set of explanatory notes, are designed to be constantly updated and to accompany a young offender wherever he or she goes in the youth justice system. The *National Standards for Youth Justice* (Youth Justice Board, 2000) specify when ASSET should be used and set a timetable within which assessment should take place (ibid.: para. 5.3). If the assessment indicates the need for a rehabilitative programme, the YOT is required to produce a programme that is consistent with reparation agreed in a restorative conference and address 'the factors that contributed to the offending and opportunities for reparation to victims' (ibid.: para. 5.4). The programme must also take account of the offender's school, work or religious commitments.

YOTs are required to set out how assessment work and rehabilitation (change) programmes are to be delivered, including details of the organizations to be involved in the delivery, as part of their annual youth justice plans.

The report of an early evaluation of the working of the system of reprimands and warnings expresses concern that in many cases the intrusive nature of the assessment appears disproportionate to the seriousness of the offence (Evans and Puech, 2001).

Securing Attendance at Court

The treatment of young offenders in terms of granting bail to secure attendance at court is largely similar to that for adults (pages 199–201, and Ball, McCormac and Stone, 2001: ch. 9). The main differences are in regard to remands, where the option to remand in prison custody only applies to 17-year-olds, and the power to restrict the liberty of young offenders aged 10–16 on remand is subject to strict criteria and depends on age and gender. Youth offending team managers must provide a bail information service at each court to provide factual verified information to assist the Crown Prosecution Service (CPS) to decide whether there is information which would allow them to seek a remand on bail rather than to local authority accommodation or secure facilities.

Remand to Local Authority Accommodation

If bail is refused, the court may remand any defendant aged 10–16 to local authority accommodation, either with or without conditions. Keeping a young offender in accommodation designed to restrict liberty either requires application to court for a secure accommodation order (Children and Young Persons Act, s.23 as most recently amended by the CDA 1998, ss. 97 and 98, and Schedule 7, para. 39, to the Criminal Justice and Courts Services Act 2000) or a court ordered security requirement (see below). When a court is considering a remand to a secure facility it will normally ask the YOT to make an assessment.

Defendants aged 10 or 11 years The local authority can apply either to a youth court, other magistrates' court or to the family proceedings court for a secure accommodation order, provided that the criteria set out in the Children Act 1989, s.25 are satisfied (see Chapter 8). The approval of the Secretary of State is required for the use of secure accommodation for children under the age of 13.

Boys aged 12–14 and girls under 17 years   A court may only make a security requirement when remanding the defendant if the statutory criteria are satisfied and the defendant is legally represented or has refused representation. Before making the requirement the court must consult the designated local authority as defined in section 23 of the Children and Young Persons Act 1969 (C&YPA 1969). On imposing a security requirement, the court must state its opinion that the requirement is necessary to protect the public from serious harm and its reasons for reaching that opinion. The local authority may also apply for a secure accommodation order under the Children Act 1989, s.25, as above.

Boys aged 15 or 16   In addition to the above, courts may remand 15- and 16-year-old boys to prison accommodation. Under national standards, the YOT manager must ensure that a vulnerability assessment of the defendant is undertaken and has responsibility for making the arrangements to place the defendant in the correct establishment. This will normally be a prison or remand centre, but if it is considered that because of his 'physical or emotional immaturity or propensity to harm himself' such a placement would be undesirable, and there is local authority secure accommodation available, he may be remanded to that accommodation instead.

The Criminal Justice and Police Act 2001 section 130, which came into force nationally in September 2002, extends courts' powers to remand 12–16-year-olds to secure accommodation or prison service accommodation on the basis of a recent history of repeatedly committing imprisonable offences while remanded on bail or to local authority accommodation. The court must be of the opinion that having considered all the options, only a secure remand would be adequate to protect the public from harm or to prevent the child or young person from committing further imprisonable offences. The National Association for the Care and Resettlement of Offenders (NACRO) estimate that the low threshold set by the 'imprisonable offences' criteria will result in a significant increase in the demand for secure places (NACRO, 2002).

The Trial Process

Procedure in the youth court is governed by the Magistrates' Courts (Children and Young Persons) Rules 1992. Much of it, including the balance of proof and the actual trial process mirrors that in the adult courts with some variations as to the information that may be before the court.

Following a finding of guilt in the youth court, the offender and his or her parent(s) must be given the opportunity to address the court, whether or not the defendant is legally represented. Brown's observations in the late 1980s led her to be critical of the stereotypical assumptions and limited perceptions revealed by magistrates' impressions of parents gained from such exchanges (Brown, 1991).

Previous reprimands and warnings will be cited in court together with any report of failure to participate in a rehabilitation programme following a warning.

Pre-sentence reports, prepared according to national standards, are reports in writing prepared by a member of a YOT, a local authority social worker or a probation officer 'with a view to assisting the court to determine the most suitable method of dealing with the offender' (Powers of the Criminal Courts (Sentencing) Act 2000 (PCC(S)A), s.162(1)). They are mandatory in cases where a court is considering a custodial sentence, or the more punitive community sentences (PCC(S)A 2000, ss.81 and 36(3)). These requirements run parallel to much older provisions which allow the local authority to determine the matters on which to report, but these also allow the court to demand any or further information, which the authority is then under a duty to provide (C&YPA 1969, s.9).

The issues outlined above and an account of other special considerations applied in regard to youth are addressed in much more detail elsewhere (Ball, McCormac and Stone, 2001: chs 11 and 12).

Chapter 15

Sentencing in the Youth Court

The relatively straightforward sentencing structure – discharges, fines, community sentences and custody – applicable to young offenders as well as adults, set out in the Criminal Justice Act (CJA) 1991, is now somewhat more complicated in regard to juveniles. Reforms introduced by the Crime (Sentences) Act (C(S)A) 1997, the CDA 1998 and the YJCEA 1999 have resulted in many new orders, some of which do not fit conveniently into the existing structure (Ball, McCormac and Stone, 2001: ch. 11). All earlier sentencing powers are now consolidated in the Powers of the Criminal Courts (Sentencing) Act 2000 (PCC(S)A 2000).

Discharges, Fines and Other Financial Penalties

Discharges

The basic details of absolute and conditional discharges are set out on page 203. Prior to recent reforms, conditional discharges were routinely imposed on many youth court defendants. They accounted for more than half of disposals of offenders aged 10–11, and almost a quarter of males aged 15–17 sentenced in 1998 (Home Office, 2000). The government's perception of the ineffectiveness of conditional discharges in achieving the principal aim of preventing offending, will result in use of the sentence being substantially reduced. Offenders who have received warnings may only in exceptional circumstances be conditionally discharged for an offence committed within two years of the warning (CDA 1998, s.66). Those appearing for the first time in the youth court have to be referred to a youth offending panel, unless they are dealt with by way of an absolute discharge or receive a custodial sentence (PCC(S)A 2000, s.16).

Fines

The power to fine on summary conviction for an offence is restricted as to amount in the case of young offenders. If the adult court would have power to impose a fine of more than the usual maximum of £1000, the youth court may not impose more than £1000 on a child or young person. If the offender is aged under 14, if the maximum fine for an adult is more than £250, the youth court may only impose up to a maximum of £250. Youth courts may not impose fines in addition to making a referral order (PCC(S)A 2000, s.19(4)(b)). The means of the defendant have to be taken into account when imposing fines and the youth court must order that the parent(s) or guardian pay the fine unless satisfied that it would be unreasonable to make the order (PCC(S)A 2000, s.137).

Compensation Order

The principles regarding courts' powers to order the payment of compensation are the same for young offenders as for adults (see page 202) and the maximum of £5000 for each offence is the also the same. Unlike fines, compensation orders may be combined with referral orders, action plan orders and reparation orders (see below). For a full account of financial penalties and powers of enforcement, see Ball, McCormac and Stone, 2001: ch. 15.

Non-custodial, Non-community Orders

These 'inelegantly titled' orders – referral orders, reparation orders and orders for petty persistent offenders – are new sentencing measures which 'make active demand upon a young offender but which do not have the status of community orders and thus are not subject to the statutory restrictions that apply to such orders' (Ball, McCormac and Stone, 2001: ch. 16, para. 16.01).

Referral Order

Introduced by the YJCEA 1999 Part I and now governed by the PCC(S)A 2000, ss.16–32, the referral order is the mandatory order for young offenders pleading guilty on their first conviction unless the court considers the offence so petty that it may be dealt with by an absolute discharge or so serious that custody should be imposed. Following conviction, on a not-guilty plea on a first court appearance, the court has the discretion to make a referral order or impose another sentence. The order, which lasts for the time imposed by the court, refers the young offender to a youth offender panel convened by the YOT where the young person will be required to sign a 'youth offender contract' with the panel to participate in an agreed programme of activities aimed at preventing further offending. If the programme is satisfactorily completed, the referral order is discharged at the end of the compliance period. If the offender fails to comply with the terms of the contract, he or she may be referred back to the youth court and may be sentenced differently for the original offence. National standards specify a timetable for the administration of referral orders and requirements on non-compliance (Youth Justice Board, 2000). Pilot referral order schemes were run in several areas and the order, became available throughout England and Wales in April 2002. At the time of writing little is known regarding the outcome of orders.

Despite general support for the principles and attempted practice of restorative justice with its combination of elements of reparation to victims, promoting reintegration into the community, and the taking of personal responsibility for anti-social behaviour, referral orders were the subject of some comment prior to implementation. Criticism focused on the mandatory nature of the order, the power imbalance as between the panels and the young offender, the potential for panels to be so overwhelmed by the volume of cases that they would be unable to devote sufficient time to engage meaningfully with each offender, and, because legal representation is not allowed before the panels, possible breach under the Human Rights Act 1998, of the right to a fair trial (Wonnacott, 1999; Fionda, 1999; Ball, 2000).

Reparation Order

The reparation order was introduced by the CDA 1998 and is now governed by PCC(S)A 2000, ss.73 and 74. The order, which is not a community sentence, and therefore not subject to the offence being 'serious enough' (PCC(S)A 2000, s.35, see page 150) is designed to provide courts with a means of making young offenders aware of the distress their actions have caused to the victim either by making direct reparation to a victim who is willing, or to the community. The order may be imposed on any offender under the age of 18, who is not bound to be sentenced to a referral order, for any offence except one for which the sentence is fixed by law. The order has to be specified in terms of a number of hours up to a maximum of 24, and has to be completed within three months of the making of the order. The requirements of the order must be commensurate with the seriousness of the offence (s.74(2)). The period of three months cannot be extended which appears to give rise to problems in regard to enforcement of the order (Ball, McCormac and Stone, 2001: paras 16.95a and b).

Reparation orders cannot be made alongside custodial orders or the community sentences specified in section 73(4). Before making a reparation order the court must consider a report indicating the type of work that is suitable for the offender; and the attitude of the victim or victims to the requirements proposed to be included in the order. Where a court has the power to make a reparation order, it must give reasons if it does not do so.

Orders for Petty Persistent Offenders

Where a court would otherwise impose a fine on an offender aged 16 or over who has not paid one or more fines imposed in respect of previous offences, and who would not have sufficient means to pay a fine commensurate with the seriousness of the current offence, the court may, subject to procedural requirements, impose either a community punishment order or a curfew order instead of a fine (PCC(S)A 2000, s.59; Ball, McCormac and Stone, 2001: paras 16.95–16.105).

Community Sentences

A 'community sentence' means a sentence which consists of one or more community orders, of which there are now a substantial number available for young offenders of different ages. Community sentences can only be imposed if the criteria set out in the PCC(S)A 2000 are satisfied:

> s.35(1)   A court shall not pass a community sentence on an offender unless it is of the opinion that the offence, or the combination of the offence and one or more offences associated with it, was serious enough to warrant such a sentence.

and,

> s.36(2)   In forming its opinion, a court shall take into account all such information as is available to it about the circumstances of the offence(s), including any aggravating or mitigating features.

The following community sentences are available for all offenders under the age of 18 (attendance centre orders are available in the adult court for offenders under the age of 21, and curfew and exclusion orders for offenders of any age).

Action Plan Order

Home Office guidance (Home Office, 2000b) indicates that this order, originally introduced as one of the tranche of new orders in the CDA 1998 and now regulated by PCC(S)A 2000, ss.69 and 70, is designed to 'provide a short but intensive and individually tailored response to offending behaviour'. The order may be made where the court is satisfied that the offence is sufficiently serious for a community sentence and considers the order to be desirable in the interests of securing the rehabilitation of the offender and the prevention of further offending by him. The order requires the offender for a period of three months to comply, under supervision, with the action plan 'that is to say a series of requirements with respect to his actions and whereabouts during that period' (s.69(1)(a)).

There are detailed provisions regarding the pre-sentence report for the court, requirements that may be included in the order, the compatibility of the action plan order with other orders, and enforcement (Ball, McCormac and Stone, 2001: ch. 18).

Attendance Centre Order

Attendance centre orders, originally introduced by the Criminal Justice Act 1948, are now regulated by PCC(S)A 2000, s.60. The order, which is available where the criteria for a community sentence are satisfied and the offence is one punishable by imprisonment, requires the offender to attend and participate in a range of activities for the number of hours specified which may be up to a maximum of 24 if the offender is under 16, though should only exceed 12 in exceptional circumstances if the offender is under 14. Detailed rules regarding staffing, attendance and discipline are set out in the Attendance Centre Rules 1995, and reinforced by national standards (Home Office, 1995a). Centres, generally run by the police, are normally open on alternate Saturday afternoons for two or three hours. Offenders aged 16 and 17 may be sentenced up to a maximum of 36 hours. The minimum length of an attendance centre order is 12 hours, unless the offender is aged under 14 and 12 hours would be excessive 'having regard to his age or other circumstances' (s.60(3)(b)).

Attendance centre orders may also be imposed in circumstances in which an adult could be imprisoned in default of payment of a monetary penalty, and on breach of a range of community orders and reparation orders (Ball, McCormac and Stone, 2001: paras 19.21–19.23). Enforcement of attendance centre orders is regulated by Schedule 5 to the PCC(S)A 2000.

Supervision Order

Originally introduced as a new form of statutory supervision for juveniles by the CYPA 1969 with the intention that with additional requirements it would replace more punitive orders with a 'constructive, flexible range of local authority provision', the relevant provisions of the 1969 Act 'encumbered by a welter of amendments and repeals' (Ball, McCormac and Stone, 2001: para. 20.01) are now consolidated in sections 63–68 of the PCC(S)A 2000.

The basic order places the young offender under the supervision of a designated local authority or a probation officer or a member of a youth offending team for a period up to a maximum of three years. The requirements that may be included in supervision orders are set out in Schedule 6 to the Act, and include requirements:

- to live with a named individual who agrees to the requirement;
- to comply with the directions of the supervisor, as elaborated in para. 2(1) for up to 90 days;
- as an alternative to the above, and subject to the conditions set out in para. 3(4) to live as directed, to participate in activities, to make reparation, to be subject to a curfew or to refrain from specified activities;
- where the conditions set out in para. 5(2) are satisfied, to live for a specified period in local authority accommodation;
- provided that the criteria set out in para. 6(1) are satisfied, and the offender consents, to receive treatment for a mental condition; and
- if the offender is of school age to comply with such arrangements for his or her education as are made by a parent and approved by the local education authority (para. 7).

The administration and management of supervision orders is regulated by the National Standards for Youth Justice (Youth Justice Board, 2000) as part of a common code which covers reparation, action plan, referral and parenting orders (CDA 1998, s.8) as well. National standards prescribe a timetable within which initial and follow-up meetings between the supervisor and the young offender must take place and within which plans for reparation, where appropriate, must be discussed with the YOT manager, approved by the YOT and implemented. Thereafter team review of plans must occur at three-monthly intervals or more frequently if required, using the ASSET (see page 142) tool to track the offender's progress.

Enforcement of supervision orders is regulated by provisions in Schedule 7 to the PCC(S)A 2000 and practice required by national standards (Youth Justice Board, 2000).

Curfew Order

Originally introduced for offenders over the age of 15 by the Criminal Justice Act 1991, curfew order powers were extended in modified form to offenders of all ages by the Crime (Sentences) Act 1997 and are now governed by the PCC(S)A 2000, s.37.

A curfew order requires the offender to remain for specified periods of between two and 11 hours at a place specified in the order. The court making a curfew order must have received a report about the place to be specified, the attitude of persons likely to be affected by the order and, where the offender is under 16, information about his family circumstances and the likely effect of the order on those circumstances.

A curfew order invariably includes requirements for the electronic monitoring of the offender's whereabouts during the curfew periods. The 'tagging' requirement involves the offender wearing a wrist or ankle bracelet which relays a signal to monitoring equipment located at the place of confinement and linked through the telephone line to the monitoring centre. A 'tagging' requirement can only be included in a curfew order if monitoring arrangements are in place in the area where the specified place is located. Such arrangements are available nationally for offenders over the age of 16.

Researchers at the Home Office evaluated and analysed trials of curfew orders in three areas during 1995–97 (Mair and Mortimer, 1996; Mortimer and May, 1997; and Mortimer, Pereira and Walter, 1999).

Enforcement of curfew orders are dealt with under the common enforcement code in Schedule 3 to the 2000 Act.

Exclusion Order

Exclusion orders, may stand alone or be imposed as an additional requirement to a community rehabilitation order for offenders aged 16 and 17, but not to supervision orders. The orders were introduced by the Criminal

Justice and Court Services Act (CJCSA) 2000 and are now governed by the PCC(S)A 2000, s.40A. Courts may make an order prohibiting the offender from entering a place, including an area, specified in the order for a period of up to a year for offenders aged 16 and over and up to three months if the offender was under 16 when convicted. The order may and invariably will be accompanied by a 'tagging' requirement. When considering making an exclusion order on an offender under the age of 16 the court is required to obtain and consider information about the offender's family circumstances and the likely effect of an order on those circumstances.

When making an exclusion order the court must explain to the offender 'in ordinary language' the effect of the order, the consequences that may follow non-compliance, including the scope for the court to review the order on the application of the offender, the responsible officer, and the 'affected person' as defined by section 40A(13).

Four adult community penalties – community rehabilitation orders (formerly probation orders), community punishment orders (formerly community service orders), community punishment and rehabilitation orders (CPRO) (formerly combination orders) and drug treatment and testing orders (DTTO) – are available in the youth court for 16- and 17-year-old offenders.

Community Rehabilitation Order

PCC(S)A 2000, s.41(1):

> Where a person aged 16 or over is convicted of an offence and the court by or before which he is convicted is of the opinion that his supervision is desirable in the interests of –
> (a) securing his rehabilitation, or
> (b) protecting the public from harm from him or preventing the commission by him of further offences,
> the court may make an order requiring him to be under supervision for a period specified in the order of not less than six months nor more than three years.

It is a standard requirement in all community rehabilitation orders that an offender in respect of whom an order is made 'shall keep in touch with the responsible officer in accordance with such instructions as he may from time to time be given by that officer and shall notify him of any change of address' (s.41(11)). The standard requirement has been interpreted as being somewhat more demanding than the phrase 'keep in touch with' might imply (Stone, 2001b).

Additional requirements, as set out in Schedule 2 to the Act, may be included in community rehabilitation orders provided that the court has obtained and considered a pre-sentence report (PSR) and the requirements are considered desirable in the interests of the objectives set out above. They include: requirements as to residence; participation or non-participation in specified activities set out in para. 2; attendance at a named probation centre;

provided the additional criteria set out in para. 5 are met, treatment for a mental condition; and, a requirement that the offender receive treatment for drug or alcohol dependency. Two further requirements were introduced by the CJCSA 2000, amending PCC(S)A 2000 by introducing new paragraphs 7 and 8 to Schedule 2, to permit the inclusion of curfew and exclusion requirements with electronic monitoring in community rehabilitation orders.

Schedule 3 to the Act makes detailed provision for dealing with failure to comply with certain community orders including community rehabilitation orders.

The management of community rehabilitation orders is largely governed by national standards, most recently revised in 1995 (Home Office, 1995b).

Community Punishment Order

Introduced in 1973, a community punishment order which may be made, provided that the criteria for passing a community sentence are satisfied, for any imprisonable offence, requires an offender to undertake between 40 and 240 hours of unpaid work during his or her spare time (PCC(S)A 2000, ss.46–50). Where the offender is under 18 and the offence is not one triable only on indictment, the court must obtain and consider a PSR, though this may be one prepared for earlier proceedings (PCC(S)A 2000, s.36). The order which is administered through the probation service is subject to national standards, designed to ensure that the work is suitably demanding with some uniformity in the content of work schemes. National Standards for Youth Justice (Youth Justice Board, 2000) specify that 16- and 17-year-olds subject to community punishment orders must be supervised according to the adult standards. Prior to implementation of the Crime and Disorder Act 1998, offenders had to consent to the making of the order. There is some question as to whether making orders requiring unpaid work without consent may be found to be in breach of Article 4 of the ECHR.

Offenders who breach the requirements of a community punishment order may be returned to court and sentenced differently for the original offence. The detailed provisions for enforcement are set out in Schedule 3 to the PCC(S)A 2000, and in national standards (Stone, 1999).

Community Punishment and Rehabilitation Order

The former combination order, introduced by the Criminal Justice Act 1991 to provide a high-tariff non-custodial integrated sentence which combined the punitive and reparation elements of community service with the supervision element of probation was renamed by the CJCSA 2000 'to give the sentence a more transparent identity as well as an unambiguously punitive ethos' (Ball, McCormac and Stone, 2001: para. 24.01). Under the PCC(S)A 2000, s.51, the CPRO may require up to 100 hours of community punishment combined with a minimum of 12 months' and a maximum of three years' supervision by a probation officer which may include any of the additional community rehabilitation order requirements. The court must obtain and consider a PSR before determining the suitability of the offender for a CPRO.

As often happens with new sentences, whatever the intention of legislators, magistrates' sentencing practice is unpredictable. The tariff position of CPROs, contrary to the intention that the order should be high tariff, is now somewhat ambiguous (Ashworth, 2000: 289–90). Use of CPROs by magistrates when relatively minor offenders are perceived to need a combination of punishment and help may ignore the overall restriction on the offender's liberty to the extent that the sentence is no longer commensurate with the seriousness of the offence. Eleven per cent of all 12,800 persons sentenced to combination orders in all courts in 1998 were under the age of 18.

Community punishment and rehabilitation orders are enforced under Schedule 3 to the PCC(S)A 2000. National standards specify that for enforcement purposes unacceptable absences from either the punitive or rehabilitative element will be treated cumulatively. As with community punishment orders, 16- and 17-year-olds must be supervised according to the adult standards (Youth Justice Board, 2000: s.7).

Drug Treatment and Testing Order

The DTTO (PCC(S)A 2000, ss.52–58), which was introduced in the Crime and Disorder Act 1998, is intended to replace the requirement to receive treatment for drug dependency under a community rehabilitation order. The order is targeted at offenders whose offending behaviour is clearly linked to drug dependency and guidance (Home Office, 1998b) suggests that the volume of offending may be a more important consideration than the seriousness of individual offences, although offenders under the age of 18 who are otherwise suitable should not be ruled out just because they 'do not yet have a long criminal record' (ibid.: para. 11).

A DTTO may be made where a court, which has obtained and considered a PSR, is satisfied that

- the offender is 'dependent on or has a propensity to misuse drugs', and that
- the dependency or propensity 'is such as requires and may be susceptible to treatment', and that
- arrangements can or have been made for the treatment intended to be specified in the order, and
- the offender consents to the order.

The obligations of a DTTO are complex but basically require the offender to submit to residential or non-residential treatment for the duration (minimum, six months and maximum, three years) of the order, and to provide samples for testing at times and and in such circumstances as are specified (Ball, McCormac and Stone, 2001: ch. 25).

Custodial Sentences

The Labour government came to power in 1997 determined to replace the 'chaotic and dysfunctional range of custodial facilities for young offenders' (Straw and Michael, 1996: 15). To a certain extent they have succeeded, in that there is now only a single custodial sentence that can be imposed by a youth court, the detention and training order. The Crown Court may also impose detention and training orders in addition to the two sentences available to it when sentencing young offenders convicted of murder and other grave crimes under sections 90 and 91 of the PCC(S)A 2000 (formerly Children and Young Persons Act, s.53).

Courts sentencing juveniles are under the same restrictions as to the use of custody as the adult courts.

PCC(S)A 2000, s.79:

> (2) Subject to subsection (3) below, the court shall not pass a custodial sentence on the offender unless it is of the opinion –
>> (a) that the offence, or the combination of one or more offences associated with it, was so serious that only such a sentence can be justified for the offence; or
>> (b) where the offence is a violent or sexual offence, that only such a sentence would be adequate to protect the public from serious harm from him.

Subsection (3) permits a court to pass a custodial sentence on an offender who refuses consent to a community sentence requiring that consent.

Much has been written about the interpretation of the 'so serious' criteria when cases are on or near the threshold (Ashworth, 2000). The most recent judicial guidance can be found in the judgment of Lord Bingham CJ in *R* v. *Howells* (1999) (Ball, McCormac and Stone, 2001: paras 27.04–27.07).

Detention and Training Orders

The detention and training order introduced by the Crime and Disorder Act 1998 and now governed by the PCC(S)A 2000, ss.100–107 is the only custodial sentence available to the youth court.

Under the PCC(S)A 2000, s.100(1) where a child or young person is

> (a) convicted of an offence which is punishable with imprisonment (in the case of a person aged 21 or over), and
> (b) the court is of the opinion that either or both of the threshold criteria specified by the PCC(S)A 2000, s79(2) apply, or the defendant falls within the provisions of s79(3) (failure to consent to certain community sentencing

proposals) the sentence the court shall pass is a detention and training order.

The order requires that the offender is subject for the duration of the order to a period of detention followed by an equal period of supervision in the community. The order is unique as a custodial sentence in that it may only be imposed, whether in the youth court or Crown Court, for specified periods of four, six, eight, 12, 18 or 24 months. Various complications raising the possibility of challenges under the Human Rights Act 1998 as regards the right to a fair trial, possible discrimination as between juveniles and young adults, and the extent to which time spent in custody on remand is taken into account by sentencing courts (PCC(S)A 2000, s.101) have been created by this feature of the sentence (Ball, McCormac and Stone, 2001: paras 28.12–28.27).

As well as satisfying the statutory criteria for the making of a custodial sentence, there are additional criteria which have to be satisfied if the defendant is under 15.

PCC(S)A 2001, s.100(2):

A court shall not make a detention or training order –
(a) in the case of an offender under the age of 15 at the time of the conviction, unless it is of the opinion that he is a persistent offender;
(b) in the case of an offender under the age of 12 at that time unless –
  (i)   it is of the opinion that only a custodial sentence would be adequate to protect the public from further offending by him; and
  (ii) the offence was committed on or after such date as the Secretary of State may by order appoint.

In contrast to earlier legislation, there is no definition of persistence although Home Office guidance reminds courts of that used in regard to fast-tracking procedures: conviction for a recordable offence on three or more occasions and committing another offence within three years, whilst also saying that they are not bound by it (Home Office, 2000c). The Court of Appeal appears to have rejected the fast-tracking criteria in favour of decisions made on the facts of individual cases (*R* v. *Smith* [2000]; *R* v. *Charlton* [2000]).

Section 100(2)(b)(ii) above has not been brought into force and at the present time there is no date set to make 10- and 11-year-olds eligible for detention and training orders.

The custodial period of the order is spent in 'secure accommodation' which includes secure training centres, young offender institutions (YOI), local authority secure accommodation, youth treatment centres and other prison service accommodation. Recent reports by Her Majesty's Chief Inspector of Prisons has been highly critical of the regimes for young offenders in YOIs (Ball, McCormac and Stone, 2001: paras 11.51–11.59).

The supervision period begins at the halfway point of the sentence, that is to say after two months in a four-month sentence and lasts for the rest of the period. Supervision will generally be undertaken by a YOT member but may be by a probation officer or local authority social worker and the offender will be notified as to the supervisor and the prescribed requirements before release from custody. Very detailed requirements as to contact and review of progress are set out in *National Standards for Youth Justice* and Home Office guidance. Failure to comply with supervision requirements may result in breach proceedings before a youth court which may order further detention for the shorter of a period of three months or the remainder of the original sentence. An offender committing a further offence during the supervision period of the order may be ordered to serve the rest of the original period of the sentence in secure accommodation in addition to any penalty for the subsequent offence. The complexity of the provisions where an offender is on the cusp of adulthood has already exercised the courts (Ball, McCormac and Stone, 2001: paras 28.50–28.57).

Young Offenders Charged With Grave Crimes

The power of the Crown Court to sentence for any of the offences specified in the Act, previously exercised under the Children and Young Persons Act 1933, s.53(3), are now governed by section 91 of the PCC(S)A 2000. The offences for which all persons under the age of 18 may be sentenced under section 91(1) are:

1   an offence punishable in the case of a person aged 21 or over with imprisonment for 14 years or more, not being an offence the sentence for which is fixed by law; or
2   an offence under section 14 of the Sexual Offences Act 1956 (indecent assault on a woman); or
3   an offence under section 15 of that Act (indecent assault on a man) committed after 30 September 1997.

In addition offenders aged 14–17 may also be sentenced on conviction of an offence under section 91(2) under

1   section 1 of the Road Traffic Act 1988 (causing death by dangerous driving); or
2   section 3A of that Act (causing death by carelss driving while under the influence of drink or drugs).

Where young offenders fall into the above categories

if the court is of the opinion that none of the other methods in which the case may be dealt with is suitable, the court may sentence the offender to be detained for such period, not exceeding the maximum term of imprisonment with which the offence is punishable in the case of a person aged 21 or over, as may be specified in the sentence (PCC(S)A 2000, s.91(3)).

Detention under section 91 may only be imposed following trial in the Crown Court (see page 137 for proposals for reform of this jurisdiction). It is up to the youth court on the advice of the clerk and the prosecution to identify eligible cases which appear to merit a greater penalty than 24 months detention and training and to commit to the Crown Court for trial (*R* v. *Learmouth* [1988]. It is at least possible that there may be an advantage in some eligible cases, where 24 months detention and training might be a long enough sentence, in the case being dealt with by a similar length sentence under section 91 in order possibly to ensure the use of appropriate secure accommodation or to avoid the circumstances in which 18 months is perceived to be too short, but 24 too long (Ball, 1998). Where the grave offender is ineligible for a detention and training order either because he is under 12, or not a persistent offender, section 91 detention is the only custodial sentence available.

A discretionary sentence of detention for life may be imposed on a young offender in the most exceptional circumstances (Ball, McCormac and Stone, 2001: paras 29.20–29.29) and young offenders may be liable to an extended sentence under PCC(S)A 2000, s.85(2) for sexual or violent offences as defined by section 161(2).

Time Spent on Remand

Any time spent on remand in custody or the equivalent of custody in local authority secure accommodation counts towards the time to be spent under a section 91 sentence.

Place of Detention

The responsibility for placement of section 91 detainees is shared between the YJB, when alerted by YOTs to a likely sentence, and the Prison Service 'Section 91 Unit'. The YJB's published *Juvenile Secure Estate Placement Strategy* (Youth Justice Board, 2000: para. 13) sets out the placements to be used for offenders according to age and sex with some absolute and some aspirational requirements. For instance, under 12-year-olds must be placed in local authority secure accommodation whilst girls aged 15–16 'should normally be given priority' for places in a local authority unit or secure training centre, but those aged 10–14 (and 15–16-year-olds girls on remand) take precedence.

Young Offenders Charged With Murder

A person under the age of 18 convicted of murder has to be sentenced to be detained during Her Majesty's Pleasure (HMP). The sentence is only passed on a very few young people each year (Ball, McCormac and Stone, 2001: para. 29.75, quote a maximum of 26 in 1997 and a minimum of 10 in 1998 during the five years 1994–98). The mode of trial for very young defendants and the involvement of the executive in the form of the Home Secretary in the sentencing process have been challenged in the domestic courts and the ECtHR (ibid.: para. 29.76). Following the decision of the ECtHR in *T.* v. *United Kingdom* and *V* v. *United Kingdom* [2000], the Lord Chief Justice issued a Practice Direction setting out the procedures to be followed to avoid distress and enable the young person to understand and participate in the proceedings. These apply whether young defendants are tried in the Crown Court or a youth court (*Practice Direction* [2000]).

As a result of a further finding in the same case that even the modified involvement of the Home Secretary operative since the House of Lords decision in *R.* v. *Secretary of State for the Home Department ex p. Venables and Thompson* [1998] was in breach of the defendants' right to a fair trial under Article 6(1) of the Convention, the Home Secretary is no longer involved in either setting the tariff or determining an early release date. The Home Secretary will set the tariff recommended by the Lord Chief Justice who will determine the tariff in accordance with the approach set out in *Practice Statement (Juveniles: Murder Tariffs)* [2000]. In effect new HMP cases are now equated with adult life imprisonment, with age being treated as one mitigating factor in tariff setting. The new process may be open to further challenge under the Human Rights Act 1998 since it precludes consideration of tariff changes for progress (Arnott and Creighton, 2000).

There is abundant research evidence of the extent to which young offenders detained under the equivalent provisions under earlier legislation (Children and Young Persons Act 1933, s.53) have suffered multiple disadvantage in their lives. In a long-term study Bullock, Little and Millham (1998) determined that regardless of early experiences in terms of the blunt measurement of reconviction within two years of departure, the outcomes were best from specialist centres, next best from less intensive local authority settings and worst from prison custody.

Orders Against Parents

There are two orders which seek to make parents more responsible for their children's offending behaviour.

Binding Over to Exercise Proper Control

Courts sentencing offenders under the age of 16, except when making a referral order (see page 148 above), have a duty to exercise the power, with the consent of the parent or guardian, to order the parent or guardian to 'take proper care of him and exercise proper control over him' and enter into a recognizance of up to £1000. The purpose of the bind over is to prevent further offending. If the court does not exercise the power, it must state in open court its reasons for not doing so. This bind over was originally introduced by the Criminal Justice Act 1991 and is restated in the PCC(S)A 2000, s.150(1). Where offenders are aged 16–17, the court may bind over the parents but are not under a duty to do so. In fact courts routinely decide against use of the bind over (see Ball, McCormac and Stone, 2001: para. 14.04).

Parenting Orders

In an attempt to provide parents with support rather than simply the threat of financial penalty through forfeiture of a recognizance, a controversial new order against parents was introduced in the CDA 1998, s.8. The order, which may be made in civil as well as criminal proceedings, is available where a child has been convicted of an offence, or made the subject of an anti-social behaviour order, or a sex offender order. In addition parenting orders may be made where a person is convicted of failing to comply with a school attendance order, or of failure to secure a child's regular attendance at school (see Chapter 17). The order is controversial because it attempts to remedy through coercion and within a very short timescale, family difficulties which are likely to be deeply entrenched. Several commentators have expressed concern that stigmatizing parents in this way may result in more teenagers being rejected and made homeless (see, for instance, Ball, McCormac and Stone, 2001: paras 11.38–11.43).

As with the bind over, where a defendant in criminal proceedings is aged under 16, the court has a duty to make a parenting order if it is satisfied that:

> the parenting order would be desirable in the interests of preventing the commission of any further offence by the child or young person.

If it is not so satisfied the court must state in open court that it is not and give its reasons.

There is no requirement for a court making a parenting order to consider a PSR, although Home Office guidance (Home Office, 2000d) suggests that courts will need some information about family circumstances before doing so.

A parenting order requires the parent for a period of not exceeding 12 months to comply with requirements specified in the order, and to attend 'such counselling or guidance sessions as may be specified in directions given by the responsible officer' (CDA 1998, s.8(4)(b)), not more than once a week for up to three months. The sessions to be timed where possible so as not to interfere with the parents' religious beliefs, and any work or educational commitments.

The court has discretion as to whether to include, and the nature of, further requirements. These might require the parent to ensure that the child attends school regularly, avoids certain areas, or attends a programme to address specific problems such as substance abuse or anger management. These requirements may last up to 12 months, but guidance suggests that where the child is subject to a shorter order, for instance a three-month action plan order, the parenting order requirements should be tailored to the same length (Home Office, 2000d).

Parenting orders are the subject of *National Standards for Youth Justice* (Part 7) which set out a timetable and details of expected contact. In pilot trials of the order, take up, except in one area, was very low. It was also apparent that efforts to involve parents of offenders in parenting sessions on a voluntary basis were unlikely to be successful (Holdaway, Davidson, Dignan, Hammersley, Hine and Marsh, 2001).

Where parents fail without reasonable excuse to comply with a parenting order they are guilty of a non-arrestable and non-imprisonable summary offence with a maximum fine not exceeding level 3 on the standard scale. If prosecuted, the case will be heard in the adult and not the youth court.

PART V
LEGAL ISSUES
FOR CLIENTS

Chapter 16

Housing

Modern housing law is about the right of an occupier not to be unreasonably deprived of his/her home and only to pay a fair rent for it, the efforts of landlords to let out their property at the greatest profit and yet retain the greatest freedom of disposal of it, and the rules of law which determine the rights and wrongs of a particular situation and interprets the application of statute law to particular arrangements.

It is often confusing to a layperson that, technically, the law is still concerned with the land on which buildings stand rather than the houses, flats, garages or factories which are the subject of the vendor or purchaser's interest.

Housing law is a vast and complex subject about which few social workers have or need detailed knowledge, but there are three topics about which social workers need sufficient knowledge to advise their clients or help them to get appropriate advice. These are:

1 eviction;
2 unlawful eviction and harassment; and
3 homelessness (Housing Act 1996, Part VII).

Following a brief introduction to the different relationships that may exist between individuals and the 'land' (including any building on that land) that they occupy to set them in context, these topics will be looked at in more detail.

An individual may:

1 *own* the land – as a freehold owner; or
2 have *exclusive* use of the land for a slice of time in return for payment or services, as tenant; or
3 have *permission* to be on the land as a licensee without having a tenancy (as are guests in hotels, students in college, residents in homes, patients in hospital and so on); or
4 be on the land *without permission* as a trespasser.

The occupier's rights and duties are determined by his/her relationship to the land. In particular, the distinction between a *tenant* and a *licensee* is important because tenants have statutory protection from eviction and rent increases under the Rent and Housing Acts and licensees have very little, although they may be entitled to protection from immediate eviction. Where two people share accommodation on a permanent basis, there is, therefore, in terms of security of tenure, a considerable advantage in a joint tenancy. This is because, if one party dies or leaves, the other will only have a right to remain (and a duty to pay the rent and so on) if they are already a tenant. If the remaining party is only a licensee, they will have no right to assume the tenancy. Trespassers have no protection, except for recourse to the courts, if undue force is used against them.

It is an overriding principle that it is the law, and not the parties, which determines the form of the relationship. A landlord may not, for instance, evade the consequences of what is effectively a tenancy by describing the tenant as a 'licensee'.

Eviction

If a landlord wishes to regain possession of his or her property, he or she can only do so, whether or not the tenancy is at an end, if the tenant agrees, without unlawful pressure, to leave. If the tenant does not agree to leave, and

1　the tenant breaks a term of the lease or tenancy agreement;
2　the tenant is paying on a weekly or monthly basis and is protected by the Rent Acts; or
3　the tenant is paying on a weekly or monthly basis but is not protected by the Rent Acts

then the landlord must give valid notice to quit and get an eviction order from the county court. Only then will he or she be entitled to evict the tenant, with the help of the bailiff if necessary.

It is important for social workers to advise their clients that they should not leave on threat of a court order, and that, unless they are agreeable to leaving, any tenant served with a county court summons for possession should seek immediate legal advice (available under the Community Legal Service funding 'legal help' scheme, see page 10 above) as to their rights and how to contest the landlord's application. Although the client may not be ultimately successful in retaining the accommodation, they may well be able to get an extension of time before the eviction order can be executed. If no application is made to the court on behalf of the tenant, the landlord may, provided the formalities are satisfied, be granted an immediate eviction order, which is then difficult to challenge.

Unlawful Eviction and Harassment

Although different types of lettings of property made at different times have different types of protection in regard to repossession of the property by the landlord, most lettings come within the protection set out in the Protection from Eviction Act 1977, s.1(2):

> If any person unlawfully deprives a residential occupier of any premises of his occupation of the premises or any part thereof, or attempts to do so, he shall be guilty of an offence unless he proves that he believed, and had reasonable cause to believe, that the residential occupier had ceased to reside in the premises.

People are unlawfully evicted if they are physically evicted from the premises they are entitled (see above) to occupy without an eviction order being in force (unless the very limited exception introduced by the Housing Act 1988 applies). Being denied entry through, for instance, the locks being changed, amounts to eviction. Harassment involves making life so unpleasant that the tenant leaves, or stays but fails to complain to the rent officer or public health inspector of the treatment – such as tipped refuse, water or power turned off, abuse and so on – to which he or she is subjected. Both unlawful eviction and harassment are actionable as criminal proceedings under the Protection from Eviction Act 1977 as amended by the Housing Act 1988 or in civil proceedings.

All in all, landlords are well advised always to seek a court order before evicting an occupier, and social workers should act at once to seek legal advice on behalf of a client threatened with eviction. The 'residential occupier' definitions in section 1 of the 1977 Act protect almost anyone living on premises except certain trespassers or licensees whose licence has ended.

Criminal proceedings are only rarely pursued, usually by the Tenancy Relations or Harassment Officer of the local authority. Where they are brought, the delay is often too great to benefit the evicted person, except, possibly, in terms of compensation. Civil proceedings in the county court are more likely to be of benefit to the injured party. In civil proceedings he or she may seek damages and/or an order of the court, called an injunction, which identifies the person bound by it and makes him or her liable for contempt of court, punishable by a fine or imprisonment, for failure to comply. A full injunction is normally made at the end of what may be lengthy proceedings, but in an emergency an occupier who can be shown to have acted without delay may apply with an affidavit to a court or a judge in chambers for an *ex parte* injunction which will last for a few days until a court hearing *inter partes* (see Glossary).

At full hearing, damages may be awarded. These may be special to cover actual loss; general, for shock and injury; or aggravated, when the treatment has been particularly brutal or offensive, to teach the landlord a lesson, as the case described in the Court of Appeal as 'a cautionary tale for landlords who are minded unlawfully to evict their tenants by harassment or other means' illustrates (Lord Donaldson in *Tagrov* v. *Cafane and Another* [1991]).

In order to help a client obtain relief, speed and specialist legal advice from a law centre or private practitioner is essential. It is important to make a note of any incidents which may amount to harassment and, where there are witnesses, to obtain their names and addresses and, if possible, a written statement from them.

Housing Allocations

All housing authorities are now required to keep a register of those who apply to them for housing; this register is then used to allocate either secure or introductory tenancies and to make nomination to registered social landlords, such as housing associations, for new tenancies. Only 'qualifying persons' can be on the housing register; this excludes asylum seekers and applicants who are intentionally homeless. Local authorities may also exclude people with a history of anti-social behaviour or rent arrears, though section 164 of the 1996 Act gives a right of review in respect of non-inclusion or removal from the register. Section 167(1) requires local authorities to have allocation schemes, though they can decide whether these are to be organized by points or date order or be quota based. However, priority categories to whom 'reasonable preference' should be given are specified. These are:

- people occupying insanitary or overcrowded housing housing;
- people occupying accommodation that is temporary or occupied on insecure terms;
- families with dependent children;
- households consisting of or including someone who is expecting a child;
- households consisting of or including someone with a particular need for settled accommodation on medical or welfare grounds;
- households where social or economic circumstances are such that they have difficulty in securing settled accommodation;
- people who are homeless.

Anti-social Behaviour

There is a wide range of activities that may be considered to constitute anti-social behaviour, including 'vandalism, noise, verbal and physical abuse, threats of violence, racial harassment, damage to property, trespass, nuisance from dogs, car repairs on the street, joyriding, domestic violence, drugs and other criminal activities such as burglary' (Department of the Environment, 1995). There is also a range of legal remedies, both at common law and in statute. The tort of nuisance applies to conduct which causes unreasonable interference with the quiet enjoyment of property. The Environmental Protection Act 1990, as amended by the Noise and Statutory Nuisance Act 1993, creates a new category of statutory nuisance (s.79).

The Noise Act 1996 enables local authorities to investigate complaints and serve warning notices in respect of excessive noise from a dwelling at night. Section 10 provides a power of entry by warrant to search for, seize and dispose of equipment such as audio and stereo equipment.

The Crime and Disorder Act 1998, s.1 enables a local authority to apply to a magistrates' court for an anti-social behaviour order (ASBO) in respect of any person over the age of 10, who has acted in 'a manner that caused or was likely to cause harassment, alarm or distress to one or more persons not of the same household as himself'. Though the order is made in civil proceedings, breach of the order is a criminal offence. The criminal justice approach to problems of anti-social behaviour is reflected in Home Office guidance (Home Office, 2000d). The guidance urges local authorities, housing associations and the police to work together with the Probation Service and community organizations in developing local strategies to deter and respond to anti-social behaviour. The Social Services Department should be consulted and the individual's needs assessed before deciding whether an ASBO should be made.

Housing law also contains provisions to deal with anti-social behaviour. The Housing Act 1996 extended the grounds for repossession of secure tenancies in both the public and private sectors to include anti-social conduct by tenants and their families where nuisance or annoyance is caused to a person residing, visiting or otherwise going about a lawful activity in the locality. There is also a power (s.152) to apply for an injunction to exclude from local authority properties persons who have used or threatened violence to tenants. Part V of the Housing Act 1996 also enables local authorities and housing action trusts to grant 'introductory tenancies' for a period of up to one year, during which time there is no security of tenure. This enables the landlord to test out the tenant's ability to adhere to the usual conditions of a tenancy. The landlord can obtain possession at the end of the year by application to the court without any need to prove grounds such as anti-social behaviour or non-payment of rent. Following possession, the local authority will owe only the same duty to the former tenant as it would to any other homeless applicant.

Homeless Persons

Local authorities have had statutory duties towards homeless families since the Housing (Homeless Persons) Act of 1977, but the extent of that duty has been modified by the current legislation which is the Housing Act 1996 Part VII. Nevertheless, the basic concepts of homelessness, priority need, not intentionally homeless, and local connection, remain. A substantial body of case law has grown up around the statutory provisions. The 1996 Act will itself be amended when the Homelessness Act 2002 is brought into force.

Homelessness

Section 175 of the Housing Act 1996 defines a person as being 'homeless' if he or she has no accommodation available for occupation in the United Kingdom or elsewhere by himself or herself and any member of his or her family living with him or her and any other person who normally lives with him or her 'in circumstances which the housing authority considers it reasonable for that person to do so'. Accommodation is 'available' if there is some place which the claimant is entitled to occupy as owner or tenant, or he or she has a court order entitling him or her to occupy. In the same way, an occupier who has a contractual or bare licence or entitlement to occupy because the landlord has not obtained a possession order, cannot qualify as homeless under the Act. On the other hand, lack of a place to park a mobile home or moor a houseboat counts as 'homelessness'. People living in accommodation which is 'unsuitable' because it is unfit, or incapable of adaptation to meet their disability needs are also homeless under the Act; homelessness in these situations does not equate with rooflessness. Under section 117 of the Act it is not reasonable for a person to continue to occupy accommodation if it is probable that this would lead to domestic violence against him or her. A person is 'threatened with homelessness' (s.175(4)) if it is likely that he or she will become homeless within 28 days.

Priority Need

The original legislation was designed to protect vulnerable people and to ensure that the lack of a home would not result in families being split up. Prior to the 1977 Act, homeless families were often in a catch-22 situation where the children were in care because of lack of accommodation and the parents were not entitled to accommodation because the children were in care. Under section 189 of the 1996 Act, the following have priority need of accommodation:

1   a pregnant woman or a person with whom she resides or might reasonably be expected to reside;
2   a person with whom dependent children reside or might reasonably be expected to reside;
3   persons who are vulnerable as a result of old age, mental illness, handicap or physical disability or other special reason; and
4   a person who is homeless or threatened with homelessness as a result of an emergency such as flood, fire or other disaster.

Intentional Homelessness

The onus of proof is on the local authority to show that a person has become homeless intentionally. Section 191 of the 1996 Act says that:

A person becomes homeless intentionally if he deliberately does or fails to do anything in consequence of which he ceases to occupy accommodation which is available for his occupation and which it would have been reasonable for him to continue to occupy.

A person is also treated as having become homeless intentionally if he enters into an arrangement under which he is required to cease to occupy accommodation which it would have been reasonable for him to continue to occupy, and the purpose of the arrangement is to enable him to become entitled to assistance under the Act (s.191(3)).

However, if the loss of accommodation arises from a genuine ignorance of a legal right to continue occupation, the person should not be treated as being intentionally homeless. This might occur where a tenant, given notice to quit, left premises because he or she was unaware of the right to remain in occupation until the expiry of a court order. A person who was mentally incapable of managing their affairs would also not be intentionally homeless because of failure to keep up financial commitments.

A Local Connection

Applicants must be accepted by the authority to which they apply 'unless he and anyone who might reasonably be expected to live with him has no connection with that authority and does have a connection with another' (Housing Act 1996, s.198). A person may have a local connection because he or she either lives, or once lived, in an area, or because he or she is employed there, or because of any special circumstances. Anyone who is homeless as a result of domestic violence does not have to establish a local connection in the area to which application is made.

Local Authority Duties

The Housing Act 1996 imposes different duties upon housing authorities according to the needs of the area and to the eligibility of those who apply as homeless. Under s.179, local authorities have a duty to ensure that advice and information on homelessness is available to all people in their area (not just those who make an application). Section 1 of the Homelessness Act 2002 places a duty upon housing authorities to formulate a homelessness strategy, with assistance from the Social Services Department. Applicants who are accepted as homeless, but who are not in priority need are entitled to advice and assistance from the local authority in accessing suitable accommodation that is available locally. A person in priority need who has become homeless intentionally, is entitled to temporary accommodation as well as advice and assistance. A person whose only local connection is with another local authority will be referred on to that authority. The full 'housing duty' is only owed to those who are homeless, in priority need, not intentionally homeless, and with no local connection elsewhere. Under the Housing Act 1996 the full housing duty was limited to two years. Section 6 of the Housing Act 2002 abolishes this maximum period. However, section 7(3) of that Act provides that the duty comes to an end if the applicant, having been informed of the possible consequences of refusal and of his or her right of a review of the suitability of the accommodation, refuses a final offer of accommodation.

The Code of Guidance on Parts VI and VII of the Housing Act 1996 (Department of the Environment, 1996) advises local authorities on the interpretation of their statutory duties, and reference should be made to the Code when challenging definitions under the Act. Section 8 of the Homelessness Act 2002 also requires local authorities to institute a review system under which challenges based on the suitability of accommodation offered can be challenged. Appeal is to the county court. Where a person is ineligible for assistance, and there are children under the age of 18 in the household, section 213A of the Housing Act 1996 requires the housing authority, subject to the applicant's consent, to refer on to the social services authority.

Children Leaving Care

The Children (Leaving Care) Act 2000, which came into force in October 2001, gives local authorities additional responsibilities towards 16- and 17-year-olds leaving care (see Chapter 8). Specifically in relation to accommodation, the responsible authority has to ensure that accommodation is suitable in regard to the child's health and other needs. Guidance (Department of Health, 2001) states that bed and breakfast should be used only as an emergency.

Chapter 17

Education

Local authorities have considerable statutory obligations under the Education Act 1944, as amended by subsequent Education Acts, to provide and maintain an efficient education service and to ensure that parents, guardians and others caring for children meet their obligations in respect of the children's education; the legislation in this field is both detailed and, because of its vulnerability to political whim, prone to frequent change. It is an area in which children themselves have few rights (Monks, 2002). In terms of their practice, it is suggested that there are three areas of education law with which social workers need to be familiar: the legal consequences following from parental failure to ensure a child's attendance at school; the exclusion of children from school; and, the statutory provisions regarding children with special educational needs.

School Attendance

The legal duty to ensure attendance rests with parents or guardians or, in practice, anyone else caring for a child *in loco parentis*. Every child must receive full-time education, from, at the latest, the term after their fifth birthday until, at the earliest, the end of the Easter term following their sixteenth birthday, if this is before the end of January or on the Friday before the last Monday in May if the birthday falls after the end of January and before 1 September. Under the Education Act 1996, s.411, parents may express a preference as to the school they wish their child to attend. The local education authority's (LEA's) duty to provide efficient full-time education is an absolute legal duty and is not dependent upon the availability of resources (*R* v. *East Sussex County Council, ex parte Tandy* [1998]).

Every LEA has a team of education welfare officers (EWOs) part of whose responsibility is to follow up irregular attendance and to seek to improve it. The nature of the role and the status of EWOs varies markedly in different authorities; in some their role has not developed greatly from that of the school attendance officer, whilst in others they are recognized as social workers within the educational system.

Where there is concern about a child's school attendance, and informal efforts to improve it have failed, the provisions of the Education Act 1996, Part VI, Chapter II, apply:

> If it appears to a local education authority that a child of compulsory school age in their area is not receiving suitable education, either by regular attendance at school or otherwise, they shall service a notice in writing on the parent requiring him to satisfy them within the period specified in the notice that the child is received such education. (s.437)

The parent has 15 days within which to satisfy the LEA that the child is receiving suitable education after which the authority may issue a school attendance order requiring the child to become a registered pupil at a school named in the order. Different provisions apply with respect to children with special educational needs, and parents may be able to negotiate regarding the school at which the child is to become a registered pupil. Once the school attendance order is issued the child's failure to attend the named school renders the parents liable to prosecution by the local authority in the magistrates' court. The usual penalty is a fine, but may be imprisonment.

If parents choose to educate their children at home or to send them to a 'free' school (an independent school not registered as such by the Department for Education) the LEA must satisfy itself that the provision is 'appropriate' and the onus of proof is on the parent. If the authority is not satisfied, it may issue a school attendance order. Even if a child is excluded from school, the LEA is still under a duty under section 19 of the Education Act 1996 to provide 'suitable' education for that child.

Children over the age of 10 years who commit offences and are not attending school may be made the subject of orders in criminal proceedings in the youth court which aim to improve their school attendance (see Chapter 15).

Education Supervision Orders

Under the Children Act 1989, whether or not the parents are proceeded against for failing to ensure their children's attendance at school, the local education authority, having consulted with the local authority social services committee, may apply to the court for an education supervision order (ESO). This order puts a child of compulsory school age who is not being properly educated under the supervision of the local authority (Children Act 1989, s.36 and Schedule 3, Part III). The order requires the supervising officer to 'advise, assist and befriend and give directions to' the child and his parents, with the aim of ensuring that the child receives efficient full-time education suitable to his age, ability and aptitude and any special educational needs he may have. An education supervision order cannot be made in respect of a child in local authority care (s.36(6)). The supervising officer will be an EWO employed by the education authority.

Education supervision order proceedings are family proceedings under section 1 of the Children Act which means that when the court is considering an application the child's welfare must be the paramount consideration, and the court is required only to make an order if it is satisfied that doing so would be better for the child than making no order. Guidance suggests that all possible efforts should have been made to resolve problems of poor school attendance before proceedings are begun. Courts will require detailed reports, the suggested contents of which are also contained in the *Guidance* (DoH, 1991a, vol. 7).

An education supervision order will cease to have effect after one year or when the child reaches school-leaving age, but may be extended on application to the court for up to three years. Persistent failure by a parent to comply with reasonable directions given under an education supervision order constitutes an offence (Sched. 3, para. 18) and the supervising officer is under a duty to draw the attention of the court to the matter. Where a parent or child persistently fails to comply with a direction given under the order, the supervising officer is also under a duty to inform the social services department who must investigate the child's circumstances and consider whether they should take any action, such as care proceedings under section 31 of the Children Act 1989, to secure the welfare of the child.

It is apparent from the fact that the number of ESOs made nationally are not published in judicial statistics with the annual breakdown of other Children Act 1989 orders, that the order is rarely sought.

Exclusion

Exclusions from school, which have risen considerably during recent years, can have immensely damaging consequences for the child involved. School exclusions are regulated under the School Standards and Framework Act 1998. Section 64 provides that the power to exclude pupils from school may only be exercised on disciplinary grounds, by the head teacher, and either permanently or for a fixed period or periods not exceeding 45 school days in any school year. No other form of exclusion is lawful. When a pupil is excluded the headteacher must take reasonable steps to tell a parent if the pupil is under 18, or the pupil himself if 18 or over, of the period of the exclusion, the reasons for it, the right to make representations to the governing body and how to do this. The governing body may direct the headteacher to reinstate the pupil. Under section 67, there is a right of appeal to the LEA against any decision of a governing body not to reinstate a pupil who has been permanently excluded. The procedure on appeal is set out in Schedule 18 to the 1998 Act.

Department for Education and Employment Circular 10/99 entitled *Social Inclusion: Pupil Support*, addresses issues relating to pupil behaviour and discipline, school attendance, exclusion from school and the reintegration of excluded pupils. It places an emphasis on early intervention and prevention through interagency working and partnership with parents.

Special Educational Needs

The *Report of the Committee of Inquiry into the Education of Handicapped Children and Young People*, chaired by Baroness Warnock (HMSO, 1978) led to the enactment of the Education Act 1981, which introduced the concept of special educational provision and special educational needs. The governing statutes are now the Education Act 1996, Part I and the Special Educational Needs and Disability Act 2001. Section 312 of the 1996 Act provides:

> For the purposes of this Act, a child has 'special educational needs' if he has a learning difficulty which calls for special educational provision to be made for him.

> A child has a 'learning difficulty' if:

> (a) he has a significantly greater difficulty in learning than the majority of children of his age; or
> (b) he has a disability which either prevents or hinders him from making use of educational facilities of a kind generally provided for children of his age in schools within the area of the local authority, or
> (c) he is under the age of five years and is, or would be if special educational provisions were not made for him, likely to fall within para. (a) or (b) when over that age.

A child is not to be regarded as having a learning difficulty solely because the language or form of language in which he or she is, or will be taught, is different from the language which has at any time been spoken in his or her home. The 1996 Act preserves the underpinning principle of the Warnock Committee's report, that a child with special educational needs should be educated in an ordinary school rather than a special school provided this does not conflict with the parents' wishes.

Special educational provision is defined as any educational provision for a child under two years of age, and that which is additional to, or different from, educational provision in schools maintained by the LEA for children over two years.

A detailed *Code of Practice on the Identification and Assessment of Special Educational Needs* (Department for Education and Skills, 2002) has been published. This describes an age-related process, varying from additional support from the class teacher to a statement of special educational needs. A local authority which fails to identify a child's special educational needs may be liable in the tort of negligence (*Phelps* v. *Hillingdon London Borough Council* [2000]).

When an LEA decides that a child needs assessment as to whether he or she has special educational needs, a notice must be served on the parents or guardian of that decision and the procedure that will be followed. Parents can also initiate this process. If, following the assessment, the LEA decides that no special provision is required, the parents may appeal to a special educational needs tribunal (SENT) against the decision (Education Act 1996, s.325). The tribunal may dismiss the appeal, order the LEA to make and maintain a statement, or remit the case to the LEA for reconsideration in the light of the tribunal's observations. If the authority decides that special provision is required, it has to make a 'statement' of the child's educational needs and is under a duty 'to arrange that special education provision specified in the statement is made for him unless his parents make suitable arrangements' (s.324(5)). There is a right of appeal from the SENT to the Council of Appeal (Harris, 2002).

Under section 326, the parents may appeal against the content of a statement either when the statement is first made or if it is amended, or if there has been a further assessment and the statement is not amended. The tribunal's powers on hearing the appeal are set out in section 326(3) – inserted by Special Educational Needs and Disability Act 2001, s.5. The LEA are under a duty to ensure that all of the support services specified in the statement are provided, this includes services such as speech therapy in cases where the local health authority is not able to make the necessary provision (*R* v. *Lancashire County Council ex parte M* [1989]).

A statement of special educational needs must be reviewed annually. Sections 5 and 6 of the Disabled Persons (Services, Consultation and Representation) Act 1986 require educational authorities to establish whether a child over the age of 14 who has been statemented is 'disabled' within the meaning of the Act and likely to require support from the social services department when he or she leaves school. Other relevant agencies may also be invited to participate in the drawing up of a 'transition plan'. The Special Educational Needs and Disability Act 2001 extends this requirement of multi-disciplinary co-operation to all reviews of the statement of special educational needs, not just those at 14 plus.

The Special Educational Needs and Disability Act 2001 brings aspects of the Disability Discrimination Act 1996 into the field of education. Section 1 of the Act strengthens the duty upon the LEA to educate statemented children in mainstream schools unless that is incompatible with the wishes of his parent or the provision of efficient education for other children; resources are not a relevant consideration. A new section 332A is inserted into the Education Act 1996 to require the LEA to arrange for the parent of any child with special educational needs to be provided with advice and information about matters relating to those needs. The LEA must also make arrangements for the appointment of independent persons to resolve disputes about the special education provision made for the child or the exercise by the authority of its powers.

A new section 28A inserted into the Disability Discrimination Act 1995 by section 11 of the Special Educational Needs and Disability Act 2001 states that it is 'unlawful for the body responsible for a school to discriminate against a disabled person (a) in the arrangements it makes for determining admission to the school as a pupil, (b) on the terms on which it offers to admit him to the school as a pupil; or (c) by refusing or deliberately omitting to accept an application for his admission to the school as a pupil'. Section 28A (2) also makes it unlawful for the body responsible for a school to discriminate against a disabled pupil in the education or associated services provided for, or offered to, pupils at the school. 'Discrimination' here is less favourable treatment that cannot be shown to be justified (s.28B). There is a further duty (s.28C) to take reasonable steps to ensure that in terms of admission arrangements, and in the education and associated services provided by a school, disabled pupils are not placed at a 'substantial disadvantage'. The LEA must also prepare, in relation to schools for which they are the responsible body, accessibility strategies and plans (s.28D). The Special Educational Needs Tribunal is renamed the Special Educational Needs and Disability Tribunal and can hear claims of discrimination under the 2001 Act.

The LEA's duty under section 19 of the Education Act 1996 to provide 'suitable' education is absolute and not dependent on resources (*R* v. *East Sussex County Council, ex parte Tandy* [1998]). It means efficient education in terms of the child's age, ability and aptitude and any special educational needs he may have (for further reading see Callman, 2001). The Code of Practice 2002 (Department for Education and Skills, 2001) moreover recommends that parent partnership services, for access to information advice and guidance, should be available to the parents of all children with special educational needs, not just those with statements.

Chapter 18
Welfare Benefits

The term 'welfare benefits' is used to encompass benefits payable by the state either on the basis of contributions paid or a particular status – childhood, old age or disability – or entitlement for a variety of reasons to income support. In any consideration of welfare benefits basic distinctions need to be drawn between means-tested and non-means-tested and between contributory and non-contributory benefits. The non-means-tested social security benefits include all those towards which National Insurance contributions are paid, together with those such as child benefit and disability living allowance which are paid on qualification, as of right without contribution or means test. Non-contributory welfare benefits are all income related and therefore means tested. The two categories are considered separately. Benefits for adults of working age are administered by the section of the Department for Work and Pensions (DWP) now known as Jobcentre Plus.

Most claims are dealt with at local offices, to which application should be made, although all claims for certain benefits are processed centrally. Entitlement to most benefits depends on a claim being submitted on the appropriate form, which is usually supplied as part of the booklet describing the benefit. Although a limited amount of backdating may be allowed, those who may be entitled to benefit should be encouraged and helped to claim without delay, as there are strict time limits which can only be extended 'for good cause'. Most initial decisions on claims are taken by the adjudications officer (AO). As part of the government's Citizens' Charter initiative, the former Benefits Agency produced a 'customers' charter' setting out standards of service in regard to such matters as prompt and accurate payment of benefits. The charter sets targets for dealing with claims which vary according to complexity. Child benefit claims should, for instance, be decided within 10 working days.

Some understanding of the legal framework of benefit, most recently codified in the Social Security and Benefits Act 1992, is necessary to comprehend the welfare rights system. A detailed knowledge of application of the provisions, although valuable to social work clients, is, however, beyond the scope of this book. Practitioners faced with practical problems and students seeking more detailed information will find excellent, up-to-date guidance on entitlement and submitting claims in the annually published Child Poverty Action Group *National Welfare Benefits Handbook*. In addition, Disability Alliance and other organizations publish more specialist guides and *Community Care* annually produces a useful welfare benefits wallchart.

Non-means-tested Social Security Benefits

National Insurance Contributions

There are five different classes of contributions paid on the basis of an 'earnings factor' by different categories of people between school-leaving and retirement age which give rise to varying entitlement to benefit (Table 18.1). A fixed percentage of all contributions goes towards funding the National Health Service and the rest towards National Insurance benefits.

Table 18.1   Classes of National Insurance contribution

Class	Paid by:	Entitlement
1	Jointly by employed earners and their employers	All contributory benefits
1A	Employers of employed persons	No benefits
2	Self-employed	All except unemployment
3	Voluntary contributions	Widows' benefit and retirement pension
4	Self-employed with profits above prescribed level	No additional entitlement

The principal benefits, excluding retirement and industrial injuries benefit, are:

1 *Jobseekers allowance.* Jobseekers allowance has replaced unemployment benefit and income support for those required to sign on as available for work. Applicants must 'be capable of work' and 'available for work', both of which are terms with specific meanings within the regulations. 'Capable of work' means not being physically or mentally 'incapable of work' (as defined in terms of incapacity benefit, see below), and legally, in that the applicant must not have an immigration status which prohibits employment, or requires prior acquisition of a work permit.

   Jobseekers allowance is of two types: contribution-based (payable for a period of 26 weeks) and income-based (for those without the necessary national insurance contributions). From March 2001, couples with no dependent children are required to make a joint claim for income-based jobseekers allowance. All claimants must sign a Jobseekers Agreement specifying the conditions upon which they are available for work, and there are penalties for failing to attend training courses or employment interviews. From April 2002, a new agency, called 'Jobcentre Plus' provides a work-focused personal adviser system to anyone claiming a 'working age' benefit, not just jobseekers allowance.

The requirement that applicants must be 'available for work' means that after an initial period, of up to 13 weeks, when, if they previously had employment in what could be regarded as their 'usual occupation', they may concentrate on seeking, and only have to accept work in that occupation, they must be available to accept any suitable job offer at once. People with disabilities can restrict their availability for work provided the restrictions are reasonable, given their physical or mental condition. Carers of 'close relatives' or members of the same household can limit their availability up to a minimum of 16 hours per week.

2   *Incapacity benefit.* In 1995 major changes came into effect in regard to benefits paid to those too ill or disabled to work. Incapacity benefit (ICB) replaced short-term statutory sick pay and long-term invalidity benefit, and introduced a new medical test of incapacity for work. Under the new rules most people who are away from work due to sickness will continue to receive statutory sick pay from their employer for the first 28 weeks as before. After that, all those who have paid or been credited with sufficient contributions will receive ICB from the Benefits Agency. There are two tests for 'incapable for work'. If the claimant has a regular occupation, the 'own occupation' test applies for the first 28 weeks of a claim, after which the 'personal capacity assessment' test is applied. This is a test of the extent to which the applicant's disability impairs performance of certain mental and physical functions. The rules for the test are very complicated, and initially claimants have to fill in detailed and confusing questionnaires. Continued payment of ICB depends on decisions regarding the 'personal capacity assessment' test. Any social worker needing to give assistance or advice in this area would be well advised to consult the CPAG *National Welfare Benefits Handbook.*

3   *Maternity benefit.* Statutory maternity pay (SMP), now the main source of income for pregnant women, is the minimum maternity pay a woman who has worked continuously for the same employer for at least six months, and who satisfies the earnings conditions, is entitled to from her employer. Maternity allowance is payable to pregnant women who satisfy the employment requirements but are not entitled to statutory maternity pay.

4   *Bereavement benefits.* Bereavement benefits have replaced widows benefits, and, in accordance with European Community law, are available to both men and women. Entitlement depends upon the spouses' contributions record and age when widowed. There is a lump sum bereavement allowance, and a widowed parents allowance.

5   *Retirement pensions.* Persons of the current retirement age of 65 for men and 60 for women may qualify for one of the three main categories of retirement pension:

- Category A: payable on the retired person's contribution record;
- Category B: retirement pension payable on a spouse's contribution record;
- Category D: a non-contributory pension paid to people over 80 entitled to no other retirement pension or to a pension of less than the current category D rate.

There is a category C but, as category C pensions are only paid to women who are at least 106 or widows whose husbands had they lived would have been at least 111, there are few claimants.

The government has announced that in order to introduce equality between men and women, the pensionable age for women will be increased gradually to 65 between 2010 and 2020. This change will affect women born after 5 April 1950.

Non-contributory Benefits Relating to Status or Disability

Benefits for children   Child benefit is payable for all children under school-leaving age, or aged 16–19 and in full-time education. Child benefit is also payable in respect of children under 18, living at home, who are registered as available for work or youth training, are not in remunerative employment for 24 hours or more a week, are receiving income support and are not on a youth training scheme. The higher rate of child benefit for lone parents is not available to new applicants.

If a child is looked after by the local authority, either under a care order or in accommodation, child benefit is not payable after the first eight weeks of the child's absence from home. If the child returns home for periods of time it may be payable. Payment is made to a parent or other who is 'responsible' for the child, either because he/she lives as a child of the family or the parent pays at least the current rate of benefit for maintenance of the child.

Benefits for severely disabled people   Severely disabled people may be entitled to a disability living allowance (DLA), which has both mobility and care components, or an attendance allowance for those over the age of 65.

- *Disability living allowance – mobility component.* To qualify, a claimant must be aged three or over and under 65 when they first claim. The allowance may be paid at a higher or lower rate depending on the level of disability. The higher rate is most commonly paid to claimants who are unable, or virtually unable, to walk. The lower rate is paid to those who whilst not so severely disabled are unable to walk out of doors without guidance or supervision most of the time.

  Motability, a charity incorporated by Royal Charter, runs a scheme to help people receiving the higher rate of the DLA mobility component to lease or buy a car.

- *Disability living allowance – care component.* The DLA care component is paid to persons so severely disabled mentally or physically that they require attention or supervision from another person most of the time. The rate at which the care component is paid depends on the extent of the disability as measured against the nature of the attendance or supervision required. The lowest rate is paid to those over 16 years who satisfy the hypothetical 'cooking test' – that is, if they were provided with the ingredients, the claimant is so disabled physically or mentally that they could not prepare themselves a main meal. The higher levels of DLA care component are paid when there are additional needs in connection with attention and bodily functions.
- *Attendance allowance.* The rules for claiming this allowance, which is for people over the age of 65, are similar to those for the higher and middle rates of the DLA care component. There is no equivalent to the lowest rate. The lower rate is payable for those needing attention or supervision during the day or the night and the higher rate for those who require assistance throughout 24 hours or who are terminally ill.
- *Invalid care allowance.* This allowance is payable to persons who give regular and substantial care to a person who is receiving the higher or middle rates of the care component of DLA, attendance allowance or constant attendance allowance in respect of industrial or war disablement. To qualify for the allowance the carer must be at least 16 and not over 65, and not be earning more than £72 per week or in full-time education.

Industrial injury benefit   Benefits under the industrial injuries scheme are paid to people who are disabled as a result of an accident at work or a disease caused by their job.

For greater detail consult the Disability Alliance's annually published *Disability Rights Handbook.*

Means-tested Benefits

Entitlement to means-tested benefit is dependent on the applicant satisfying basic conditions as to need, and very low income/capital resources. The main means-tested benefits are:

1   Income support (IS). The main income maintenance benefit for people not in full-time employment.
2   Housing benefit (HB). Benefit paid by local authorities to help people with a low income to pay rent.
3   Council tax benefit (CTB). Benefit paid by local authorities to help people on a low income to meet their council tax liability.
4   Social fund (SF). Payment out of a government fund of discretionary grants to meet various needs, and specific grants payable as of right on eligibility.

Other means-tested benefits include: help with National Health Service charges; free milk and vitamins; free milk and school dinners; housing renovation and other local authority grants and services; and discretionary grants for people with disabilities.

Family credit and disability work allowance have been replaced by new tax credits to encourage people to take up employment. The minimum period of employment is 16 hours per week, and capital limits apply.

Income Support

Income support is the main income maintenance 'safety net' benefit. It is a non-contributory benefit for people who are exempt from signing on for work (for example, lone parents with children under the age of 16), or those who work for less than 16 hours per week. Those 'regularly and substantially engaged' in caring for a disabled person may also qualify. Income support can also be claimed to 'top up' other benefits, such as retirement pensions to the level of the minimum income guarantee. The capital limit for claimants in the community is £8,000 (£16,000 in residential care). Entitlement is calculated on the extent to which the income of the claimant, and any partner living with them, falls below their 'applicable amount'. The applicable amount is based on personal allowances for each member of the family, and premiums for any special needs. Any income from other welfare benefits is deducted from the applicable amount. Housing benefit and council tax benefit have to be claimed separately. Income-based jobseekers allowance is paid at the same rates as income support.

Example

Jane Edwards is a single parent aged 27 with a son aged nine.

Applicable amount (2001/02)		
Personal allowance	£53.05	
Allowance for dependent child under 16 years	£31.45	
Family Premium – lone parent rate	£15.90	
Total		£100.40
Income		
Child benefit – first child, lone parent with protected rights	£17.77	
Total income		£17.55
Income supplement (applicable amount, less income)		£82.85

Sixteen- and 17-year-olds   In addition to satisfying all the other basic rules 16- and 17-year-olds can only be paid income support in their own right if they satisfy particular criteria. These cover a wide range of circumstances and no 16- or 17-year -old should be turned away by the Benefits Agency without careful consideration of their case, including evidence of estrangement from parents. The criteria are set out in great detail in the CPAG *National Welfare Benefits Handbook*.

Sixteen- and 17-year-olds leaving local authority care after 1 October 2001 are however no longer entitled to income support, income-based jobseekers allowance or housing benefit. Responsibility for their maintenance remains with the local authority under the Children (Leaving Care) Act 2000 (see page 78).

Housing Benefit and Council Tax Benefit

Housing benefit is paid by local authorities, although it is a national scheme subject to DSS regulations. Housing benefit is paid to people on low income and who pay rent, regardless of whether they are in work. It may be paid in addition to other social security benefits, or by itself. Council tenants have their housing benefit paid into their rent account as rent rebate; private tenants receive it as a rent allowance paid to the claimant or to the landlord.

Housing benefit can be claimed by persons liable to pay the rent or by their partner. Where there is a joint occupancy by single people, they may all make a claim for their share of the rent. Where a local authority considers a rent too high, or the accommodation unreasonably expensive, they may restrict a rent figure. Housing benefit is calculated on the 'applicable amount' (see above, page 184), the 'eligible rent' – which includes a variety of rent equivalents, but not charges for fuel, water rates, mortgage repayments, meals and so on – any deductions for non-dependants, and the claimant's income.

The very complex law and regulations with an expert commentary on housing benefit and council tax benefit can be found in the CPAG's *Housing and Council Tax Benefits Legislation* and very helpful, though less detailed, guidance in their *National Welfare Benefits Handbook*.

Supporting People (Department of the Environment, 2001) addresses the complexities caused by the growth in housing with care schemes whereby a tenancy is created, usually by a housing association, but personal care is provided by the local authority or voluntary organization. The intention is to shift the costs of care away from housing benefit to the care provider. The scheme should be fully operational by 2003. In the interim, 'transitional housing benefit' is payable to individuals who have received a community care assessment; this includes both a housing element and a contribution to the cost of their care which is then passed on to the care provider.

The Social Fund

The regulated social fund   There are two types of payment available from the social fund. The regulated social fund pays grants as of right to people on very low incomes who satisfy the eligibility criteria laid down in regulations in respect of maternity expenses, funeral expenses and periods of cold weather.

The discretionary social fund   In addition to grants available as of right, the SF provides discretionary grants and loans to meet a range of other needs. The discretionary social fund is different in character to all other social security provision in that:

● payments are discretionary;
● the fund is strictly budget-limited; each district office of the DWP is given an annual budget which it must not exceed;
● most payments are in the form of loans which have to be repaid, usually by deduction from weekly benefit; and
● there is no right of appeal from the social fund officer's decision to an independent tribunal; instead there is a two-stage review system, involving a reconsideration by the office which made the decision and a possible further review of a social fund inspector who reconsiders the case independently.

There are three types of discretionary payment available from the social fund.

● *Community care grants (CCGs)*. These grants are intended to promote community care by helping people to move out of, or stay out of, institutional or residential care, and to assist families under exceptional pressure. Community care grants are only available to people in receipt of IS or who will receive IS when they leave residential or institutional care, and who have very little capital. The purposes for which CCGs are available are set out in regulations and there is a list of priority groups, though this is not exhaustive (CPAG, *National Welfare Benefits Handbook*).
● *Budgeting loans*. Budgeting loans are available to help people who have been in receipt of IS for at least 26 weeks to meet one-off expenses, such as removal expenses, essential items of furniture and so on. Binding directions set out the rules which have to be satisfied. If the applicant qualifies, the decision as to whether or not a loan is granted is a discretionary one made by the social fund officer (SFO) in accordance with guidance as to high, medium and low priority, and the applicant's capacity to repay the loan.
● *Crisis loans*. These are intended to cover expenses in an emergency as the only means of avoiding serious risk of damage to the health or safety of

claimants who satisfy the eligibility rules. There is no requirement that claimants are already in receipt of IS. Social fund officers must consider each application on its merits.

There is no right of appeal to an independent tribunal against decisions regarding the discretionary social fund.

There is a capital limit of £500 for eligibility to apply to the Social Fund (£1,000 if aged 60 or over).

Asylum Seekers and Refugees

The position with regard to entitlement to social security benefits and local authority housing for asylum seekers in the UK is complex. Up-to-date information can be obtained from the Refugee Council website at www.refugeecouncil.org.uk. There are currently different systems in operation according to how and when a person applied for asylum. Since the coming into force of the Asylum and Immigration Act 1996, in-country asylum seekers have not been entitled to income support, or similar income replacement benefits and no asylum seekers have been entitled to child benefit. Responsibility for the support and accommodation of asylum seekers has therefore fallen upon either local authorities, initially through the National Assistance Act 1948, or, more recently, upon the Home Office.

This was the situation until the Immigration and Asylum Act 1999 shifted responsibility for the future support of asylum seekers away from mainstream welfare services to a new national body known as the National Asylum Support Service (NASS). The National Asylum Support Service began operating in April 2002 to provide economic support to asylum seekers through a system of vouchers, and accommodation through a dispersal system away from London and the South East to 'cluster areas' which are nevertheless still supposed to be appropriate to the asylum seeker's language and community. Asylum seekers can apply to NASS for accommodation and support, but only if they are destitute (that is, have no other means of support), or are likely to become so within 14 days. Section 95(3) of the Immigration and Asylum Act 1999 defines a person as destitute if:

(a) he does not have adequate accommodation or any other means of obtaining it (whether or not his other essential living needs are met); or
(b) he has adequate accommodation or the means of obtaining it, but cannot meet his other essential living needs.

Accommodation is provided by contract either with local authorities or private landlords; any liability for council tax rests with the landlord. It has been announced that the much-criticized voucher system whereby recipients were restricted to buying goods at designated shops will be abolished by autumn 2002. The value of the vouchers is set at 70 per cent of income-support levels, and there is no entitlement to 'passport' benefits such as free milk and vitamins. Only £10 worth of the value of the vouchers is available in cash. For pregnant women, there is a one-off maternity payment of £300. The NASS helpline for enquiries is 020 8633 0869: NASS also produces Policy Bulletins on many aspects of asylum and immigration law and these can be viewed at www.ind.homeoffice.gov.uk/. The situation is complex and susceptible to change, but at the time of writing the following categories of support are available for asylum seekers and others

- Support and accommodation from NASS.

  All applicants after 29 August 2000.

- Urgent case payments (90 per cent IS levels) + housing benefit, council tax benefit.

  Port applicants before 3 April 2000. 'Disbenefited asylum seekers' whose claim is refused after September 2000 will receive support from NASS, pending appeal.

- Support and accommodation from local authorities under the Asylum Support (Interim Provisions) Regulations 1999.

  Interim arrangements for in country asylum seekers who made an application before August 2000 will continue pending final appeal.

- Full social security benefits and qualification for the housing allocation.

  Persons with exceptional leave to remain, persons recognized as a refugee in the UK and British citizens habitually resident in the common travel area.
  NB spouses and children who join them and seek asylum will not be entitled to benefits.

- Hard cases support grant (full-board accommodation).

  Available for those have no further appeal rights and who are unable to leave the UK due to physical impediment or exceptional circumstances. From 21 November 2001 includes those who have an application for judicial review pending.

What effect will the Human Rights Act 1998 have on the position of asylum seekers? The European Convention on Human Rights is largely concerned with civil and political rights, rather than economic and social rights. So, in the *East African Asians* case (1973), the European Commission considered that discriminatory immigration legislation could amount to 'degrading treatment' under Article 3 of the Convention. However, there appears to be no entitlement to non-contributory financial benefits because these are not 'possessions' in the sense referred to in Article 1 of Protocol 1 (*X* v. *Netherlands* (1971)).

In English law, section 17 of the Children Act 1989 may impose a duty to provide services (including financial support) to families where there are children in need, irrespective of their immigration status. The local authority's duty under section 21 of the National Assistance Act (NAA) 1948 as interpreted by the Court of Appeal in *R* v *Hammersmith LBC ex parte M* [1997], to accommodate asylum seekers who are destitute no longer applies (NAA, s.21(1A) inserted by the Immigration and Asylum Act 1999, s.116). However, asylum seekers who are 'in need of accommodation' for some other statutory reason such as disability or old age still come within section 21.

Chapter 19

The Criminal Process

The Police and Their Powers

The Police and Criminal Evidence Act 1984 (PACE), as subsequently amended, provides a statutory framework within which the police must operate when investigating crime. Based on the Report of the Royal Commission on Criminal Procedure (HMSO, 1981), the PACE replaced the series of administrative directions known as the 'Judges' Rules', which had previously, somewhat haphazardly, regulated police investigations and the evidence obtained from interrogation. The PACE provisions were based on an approach which sought to give the police more powers to conduct their investigations effectively, and to provide safeguards for suspects through the provision of checks and controls on the exercise of those powers. As Sanders and Young (2000) identify, many PACE rules brought the law into line with police practice or aspirations, whilst others 'have a freedom-enhancing due process character' (page 74). The 1993 Royal Commission on Criminal Justice reviewed many of the PACE provisions, and made recommendations for reform, some of which have been enacted in subsequent legislation. Although the majority of members of the Commission favoured retaining the 'right to silence' of a suspect, over which there has been a long-running debate polarised between police and civil liberties interests, it was subsequently effectively abolished (see page 198).

The PACE is supported by five Codes of Practice which provide an elaborate system of rules for dealing with suspects at all stages of an investigation. The Codes are not statutory in nature and a breach of the rules they contain cannot itself be made the subject of criminal proceedings or the foundation of a civil action for damages. However, the rules are important in regulatory terms because any breach is an automatic breach of police discipline and may be the subject of disciplinary proceedings. In a trial the defence will be able to refer to a breach of the Code, but evidence obtained in breach will not automatically be excluded, although its admission may be grounds for appeal if a 'guilty' verdict was rendered unsafe (*R* v. *Delaney* (1989)). The Codes of Practice have been revised several times, most recently in 1999. They deal with:

(a) stop and search;
(b) search of premises and seizure;
(c) detention, treatment and questioning;

(d) identification of suspects;

(e) tape recording.

For a more detailed account and critique of policing under the Codes than is appropriate here, see Sanders and Young (2000, chs. 2–5).

'Stop and Search'

Under section 1 of the Act, police officers are given the power to search any 'person or vehicle' and 'anything which is in or on a vehicle, for stolen or prohibited articles' and to detain a person or vehicle for the purpose of such a search, provided that there are 'reasonable grounds' for suspecting that stolen or prohibited articles will be found. These include offensive weapons or articles made or adapted for use in burglary, theft, taking a motor vehicle or obtaining property by deception. Less restrictive rules apply under the Knives Act 1997 and various Prevention of Terrorism Acts (Code A, paras. 1.8 to 1.16).

Except where the exemptions apply the Code defines both 'suspicion' and 'reasonable grounds' relatively restrictively:

> Whether a reasonable ground for suspicion exists will depend on the circumstances of each case, but there must be some objective basis for it. An officer will need to consider the nature of the article suspected of being carried in the context of other factors such as the time and place and the behaviour of the person concerned or those with him. Reasonable suspicion may exist, for example, where information has been received such as a description of an article being carried or of a suspected offender; a person is seen acting covertly or warily or attempting to hide something; or a person is carrying a certain type of article at an unusual time or in a place where a number of burglaries or thefts are known to have taken place recently. But the decision to stop and search must be based on all the facts which bear on the likelihood that an article of a certain kind will be found. (Code A, para. 1.6)

The notes of guidance accompanying the revised Code A emphasize the fact that misuse of police powers is likely to lead to mistrust of the police by the community. However, drawing a clear line on reasonableness is problematic. As Sanders and Young (2000: 86) point out, after a review of judicial decisions finding for and against the police: 'it would be difficult to slip a Rizla paper between the material facts of these reasonable suspicion cases which nonetheless reach different conclusions'.

The power to stop and search can be exercised in any place to which the public, or a section of the public, have access but not when people or their cars are on their own private land, or on private land on which they have specific permission to be. Searches on those premises require a search warrant.

The Act (s.2) lays down procedural safeguards to prevent abuse of the power to stop and search. These involve the police having to identify themselves and provide the owner of a vehicle with a written record of the search. The person searched must be detained for no longer than the search takes (Code A, para. 3.3).

Stop and search in anticipation of violence   Additional powers of stop and search were introduced by the Criminal Justice and Public Order Act 1994, s.60 as amended by the Crime and Disorder Act 1998, s.25. Under these provisions, where a senior police officer 'reasonably believes that incidents involving serious violence may take place in any locality in his area' and that invoking the power might help to prevent their occurrence, he may authorize any constable in uniform to stop and search any vehicle for 'offensive weapons or dangerous instruments', and may require anyone to remove a face covering where it is believed that wearing the face covering is wholly or mainly for the purposes of concealing identity. The power, which lasts for up to 24 hours and may be extended for a further six, covers the whole locality for which the officer is responsible. Contrary to the 'stop and search' provisions under PACE, officers operating these powers do not need to have grounds for suspicion of an individual before stopping and searching him or her. They may also seize face coverings in these circumstances.

Powers of Entry, Search and Seizure

Warrants to enter and search premises for evidence of serious arrestable offences are issued on application to a justice of the peace. The application must give reasonable grounds for believing that the offence has been committed, and there is material on the premises likely to be of value and relevant to the investigation, which is not 'excluded', or 'special procedure' material, and that access to the premises is impracticable without a warrant. Warrants to search for records held on confidential files, medical samples and some journalistic material can only be granted by circuit judges (Police and Criminal Evidence Act 1984, s.9).

The police also have limited rights to enter and search premises without a warrant in the circumstances set out in section 17(1) of PACE.

Arrest

The laws relating arrest involve a further example of partial regulation of the exercise of police discretion. There are several lawful purposes of arrest, some traditional: prevent crime, maintain public order, or to facilitate prosecution, by holding in custody prior to charge or to secure appearance in court after breach of an order, and others less so such as the power to return truants to school under the Crime and Disorder Act 1998. Less traditional uses include the developing practice of arrest for the purposes of gathering evidence. It is apparent that laws designed to protect suspects by prohibiting questioning away from a police station, have led to an enormous increase in arrests, in many cases with little likelihood of prosecution (Sanders and Young, 2000: ch. 3).

Arrest by the police without a warrant   Where a constable has reasonable grounds for suspecting that an arrestable offence has been committed, he may arrest without warrant:

1   anyone whom he has reasonable grounds for suspecting to be guilty of an offence;
2   anyone who is about to commit; or
3   anyone whom he has reasonable grounds to suspect to be about to commit an arrestable offence (s.24);
4   anyone who has within the previous month been convicted of a recordable offence, for which he was not held in police custody, for the purpose of taking his fingerprints if he has failed to comply within seven days to a request to attend a police station for this purpose (s.27).

The power of arrest for arrestable offences applies:

1   to offences for which the penalty is fixed by law (for example, murder);
2   to offences carrying a penalty of five or more years' imprisonment;
3   to offences in subsection 2 – some fairly serious offences which were not previously arrestable.

General arrest conditions (s.25)   All other offences carry a limited power of arrest if a constable has reasonable grounds for suspecting that any offence has been committed or attempted, or is being committed or attempted, and it appears to him that service of a summons is impracticable or inappropriate because any of the 'general arrest conditions' are satisfied. These are as follows:

(a) The officer does not know and cannot readily obtain the name and address of the suspect, or he reasonably believes them to be false, or he doubts whether the suspect has given an adequate address for the service of a summons.
(b) There are reasonable grounds for believing that the arrest is necessary to prevent the suspect causing:
   ● physical harm to himself or to someone else;
   ● loss of or damage to property;
   ● an unlawful obstruction of the highway;
   ● an offence against public decency where the public cannot easily avoid the person to be arrested;
   ● to protect the child 'or other vulnerable person from the person to be arrested'.

An arrested person must be told at once, or as soon as is practicable, that he is under arrest and the grounds – even if these may be obvious.

Arrest under warrant An arrest warrant may be issued by a justice of the peace for a serious offence where the offender is unlikely to, or has failed to answer, a summons.

Citizen's arrest Any person has a right to arrest without warrant anyone who is committing, or is reasonably suspected of having committed, an offence. This right has not been affected by the Act.

Detention Where a person attends voluntarily at a police station to assist with an investigation 'he shall be entitled to leave at will unless he is placed under arrest' (s.29), and where a person is arrested anywhere other than in a police station, the Act provides that he should be taken to a police station 'as soon as is practicable'. If there is a delay, the reasons for this must be recorded. Detention in a police station must be in conformity with the provisions of the Act and the custody officer, who will usually be of the rank of sergeant or above and should not be involved in the investigation, must order the release of anyone whose continued detention by the police cannot be justified under the Act.

At the Police Station

Rights of an arrested person to information As soon as practicable after arrival at the police station or after his arrest there, an arrested person must be told of:

1   the grounds of his detention;
2   the right to have someone informed;
3   the right to consult a copy of the Codes;
4   the right to legal advice.

Duties of the custody officer The Act lays down that it is the duty of the custody officer to ensure that a person brought to a police station is charged if there is enough evidence to charge him, or released if there is not, unless there are reasonable grounds for believing that his detention is needed to preserve or obtain evidence of the offence for which he was arrested (s.37). The custody officer must also tell an arrested suspect of his right to have someone informed of his arrest; to receive confidential legal advice free of charge; and to consult the codes of practice.

As soon as is practicable, the custody officer must make a written record of the grounds of detention, preferably in the presence of the suspect who must be told of the grounds. The need for further detention must be reviewed by a review officer, of at least the rank of inspector, who has not been involved in the investigation, after six hours and thereafter at nine-hourly intervals. If the police wish to hold the suspect without making charges after 24 hours, authorization must be given by a superintendent, or officer above, after hearing representations from the suspect or his solicitor, and after 36 hours approval must be obtained from a magistrates' court. The court can approve a further 36 hours (twice) up to an absolute maximum of 96 hours. There is limited provision in the Act for flexible interpretation of the time limits.

Questioning and treatment of persons by the police   The custody officer must take charge of searches of detained persons and make an inventory of the suspect's property. There may only be a search if the officer considers it necessary to make a complete list of his property, and a suspect may only be searched by a constable of the same sex. If a strip search is considered necessary, the reason must be recorded.

Intimate searches are allowed only if authorized by a superintendent or above, on the grounds of reasonable belief that the arrested person might have concealed anything that could be used to cause injury to himself or others, and that he might so use it, and that it could only be discovered by such a search. Detailed rules regarding fingerprinting and the taking of body samples are set out in sections 62 and 63 of PACE as amended by the Criminal Justice and Public Order Act 1994, ss.54–59, and the Crime and Disorder Act 1998, Sched. 8, paras 61 and 62.

When a person is under arrest in a police station, he is entitled, if he so requests, 'to have one friend or relative or other person who is known to him and likely to take an interest in his welfare' told as soon as is practicable that he is under arrest and his whereabouts (s.56). Delay in allowing exercise of this right is theoretically only permissible if strict conditions are met.

Legal advice   An arrested person who is held in custody at a police station or other premises has the right to consult a solicitor of their choice privately at any time (Police and Criminal Evidence Act 1984, s.58). Also under the ECHR the Article 6 'right to a fair trial' requires that everyone charged with a criminal offence has the right to legal assistance, provided free 'when the interests of justice so require' (Art. 6(3)). An interview should not begin without legal advice except in exceptional circumstances set out in the section. The 24-hour duty solicitor scheme should ensure that free legal advice is readily available; however, only solicitors in firms with a Legal Services Commission criminal contract can provide the service and in some areas there are too few contracted solicitors available. Sanders and Young (2000: ch. 4) provide a review of research and an informed critique of interpretations of the rules relating to detention and interrogation at police stations.

Vulnerable Suspects

There are statutory safeguards designed to protect vulnerable suspects, such as juveniles and mentally disordered people or those with learning disabilities, in interview situations and to minimize the risk of interviews producing unreliable evidence. The rules relating to children (10–13) and young persons (14–16) are considered in Chapter 14. People unable to participate properly in interviews because of specific disabilities such as deafness or an inability to understand English must be provided with interpreters. The need for a range of additional safeguards for people vulnerable through age, mental illness or learning disability, is set out with great clarity in Notes of Guidance 11B of Code C.

There is evidence that the police and also police surgeons often fail to recognize mental disorder or disability with the result that many vulnerable suspects are interviewed without an appropriate adult being present (Hodgson, 1997; Williams, 2000).

The 'appropriate adult' in the case of a person who is mentally disordered or mentally disabled is defined under Code C, para. 1.7(b) as

(i)   a relative or guardian or other person responsible for his care or custody;
(ii)   someone who has experience of dealing with mentally disordered or mentally handicapped people but who is not a police officer or employed by the police (such as an approved social worker as defined by the Mental Health Act 1983 or a specialist social worker); or
        as a parent or guardian, or, if in care, the care authority or voluntary organization worker, or a social worker, or
(iii)   failing either of the above, some other responsible adult aged 18 or over who is not a police officer or employed by the police.

No interview with a vulnerable person should take place without an appropriate adult being present unless the interview is extremely urgent in which case the reasons must be recorded in writing and the interview only cover the matters of urgency (Code C, Annex C). Code C para. 11.16 provides that the appropriate adult should be informed that he or she is not expected to act merely as an observer, but has an active role to play: advising the person being questioned; observing whether or not the interview is being conducted fairly; and facilitating communications. Research evidence suggests that this explanation is often cursory or absent (Bucke and Brown, 1997; Hodgson, 1997), and that both parents and social workers very often fail, for a variety of reasons, to provide effective support. Social workers have in the past received little training for the role and may feel threatened by the police culture which they perceive as hostile. There is some indication that the recruitment and training of volunteers under the Crime and Disorder Act 1998 reforms has improved the quality of service provided by appropriate adults acting for young offenders. Williams (2000) indicates the clear need for a similar service for vulnerable adults.

Caution and Charge

The right of silence Code C on Detention, Treatment and Questioning provides that a person whom there are grounds for suspecting of an offence must be cautioned before any questions, or further questions, are put to him for the purpose of obtaining evidence which may be given to a court in a prosecution.

As Sanders and Young suggest, it is in relation to the right of silence and the privilege against self-incrimination that

> [D]ue process and crime control principles clash most fundamentally. For the due process adherent, it is up to the prosecution to find its own evidence, and anything else negates the presumption of innocence. For the adherent to crime control, only the guilty have something to hide. Innocent people have nothing to fear by assisting the prosecution, and have much to gain. (2000: 252)

The common law, and at one time the Judges' Rules which preceded PACE 1984, took a clear due process position. This was, however, first eroded by legislation in regard to specific offences, and subsequently, as a consequence of the government's decision not to follow the recommendation of the majority of the Royal Commission on Criminal Justice (1993) who favoured retaining the 'right of silence', reversed. In 1995, the form of the caution was substantially – and very possibly for some defendants, confusingly – altered on implementation of the Criminal Justice and Public Order Act 1994. The caution reflecting the inferences which may be drawn from an accused's silence has to be given in the following terms:

> You do not have to say anything. But it may harm your defence if you do not mention when questioned something which you later rely on in court. Anything you do say may be given in evidence. (PACE, Code C, 10.4)

Under sections 34–37 of the 1994 Act, courts may draw inferences when defendants rely on facts which they did not mention to the police when they had a reasonable opportunity to do so; fail to testify in their own defence; fail to provide explanations for incriminating objects; and, fail to provide explanations for their presence near the scenes of crimes. Although the ECtHR has ruled that the right of silence lies at the heart of the right to a fair trial under Article 6 of the ECHR, it has also ruled that the right is not absolute (*Condron* v. *UK* [2000]). (For further discussion on the implications of the erosion of the right of silence, see Sanders and Young, 2000: 251–68.)

Recording of interviews Under Annex D of Code C there are detailed requirements relating to written records of interviews (*R* v. *Delaney* (1989)).

Code of Practice, E, sets out the procedures to be followed when interviews at a police station are recorded on tape. The Code is accompanied by detailed notes of guidance to police officers.

When a detained person has been charged, or a person has been informed that he may be prosecuted for an offence, he should be cautioned again. A charged person should be given written details of the offence, the police officer's name and the police station. After the charge is made, questions relating to the offence may not be put, with the exception of those necessary to minimize harm to others, or to clear up an ambiguity. Before any such questions the caution should be administered again.

Fingerprints should only be taken with consent, but may be taken without consent if a superintendent, or officer above, authorizes it on the grounds of reasonable suspicion of the involvement of that person in an offence and that his fingerprints will tend to confirm or disprove his involvement.

Crown Prosecution Service (CPS)

Once the police make the decision to prosecute, the responsibility for the case passes from the police to the CPS who have to decide initially, and continually review, whether to prosecute or continue prosecution. The key criteria applied by the CPS working, within guidance set out in successive codes of practice, is whether the evidence available indicates that there is a realistic prospect of a conviction. For a review and critique of the extensive body of research on the CPS see Sanders and Young (2000: ch. 6).

Securing Attendance at Court

The majority of persons proceeded against in magistrates' courts are summonsed to attend; a substantial minority are bailed by the police and a small minority are remanded in custody by the police pending their first appearance. In 1998 the distribution was:

Summonsed	55%
Police bail	38%
Remanded in custody	7%

Police Bail

A person is bailed when he is released from custody or from police detention to attend court or a police station at a specific time. Failure to attend constitutes a further offence (Bail Act 1976, s.6(1)).

Under section 38 of the PACE, as considerably amended by section 8 of the Criminal Justice and Public Order Act 1994, if the police charge an arrested person they must release him on bail unless:

- his name or address cannot be ascertained; or
- if the offence is imprisonable, the custody officer has reasonable grounds to believe that detention is necessary to prevent him from committing further offences; or
- if the offence is not imprisonable, the custody officer has reasonable grounds for believing that detention is necessary to prevent his causing harm or physical injury to another person or causing loss of or damage to property; or
- there are reasonable grounds for believing that detention is necessary to prevent him from interfering with the administration of justice or with the investigation of offences or a particular offence; or
- the custody officer has reasonable grounds for believing that the detention of the person is necessary for his own protection.

If not released, these defendants may be detained in custody to appear in court within 36 hours. The courts and, since implementation of section 27 of the Criminal Justice and Public Order Act 1994, the police, can attach conditions, such as regular reporting to the police station or keeping away from witnesses, to bail. Where a person, who has been released on police bail with a condition of attending at a police station, fails to report he may be arrested as if for the offence for which he was granted bail.

Court Bail

When a defendant appears in court following arrest, or when a serious case is unfinished, the court has to decide whether to remand the defendant in custody or release him on bail.

Under the Bail Act 1976 there is a presumption that bail will be granted unless there are substantial grounds, which must be entered on the court record, for believing that the defendant, if released, would fail to surrender, commit further offences, interfere with witnesses or otherwise obstruct the course of justice. Bail may be granted unconditionally or subject to conditions, such as that of residence in a bail hostel, imposed to ensure that any of the grounds which might justify remand in custody are avoided. In general, the Bail Act, and in particular magistrates' decisions regarding bail, have been widely criticized both for failing to avoid unnecessary remands and for allowing the release of defendants who have subsequently committed serious offences. Magistrates' decision-making under the Bail Act 1976 has also been criticized for the enormous disparities in rates at which different courts refuse bail, which cannot be accounted for by differences between the cases. Hucklesby (1997) suggests that since magistrates rarely question remand proposals supported by the CPS and the defence, this variation is more likely to reflect disparate decision making by the police and defence lawyers rather than the magistrates.

Variation of bail conditions Where bail has been granted either by a court or by the police, an application may subsequently be made to a court to vary or impose conditions of bail, or to withhold bail (Bail Act 1976, s.5B).

Bail information schemes In many courts the probation service operates bail information schemes under which probation officers provide verified information on offenders to the CPS. Where this happens there is some evidence that prosecutors and magistrates are more likely to grant bail, without there being any corresponding rise in absconding or further offences committed on bail (Mair and Lloyd, 1996; Morgan and Henderson, 1998).

Appeals against bail decisions Under the Criminal Justice Act 1982, appeals against the refusal of bail may be made to the Crown Court or to a High Court judge in chambers. Prior to the implementation of the Bail (Amendment) Act 1993, the prosecution had no right to appeal where they had opposed bail and the defendant was released. Under the 1993 Act where the defendant is charged with an offence carrying a maximum penalty of at least five years, and bail was granted despite being opposed, an appeal lies to a judge in chambers.

Oral notice of appeal must be given without delay, prior to the release of the defendant, and followed up in writing. The defendant is then remanded in custody pending the outcome of the appeal which must be determined within 48 hours.

Statutory limitations on courts' discretion to grant bail Successive governments have responded to media induced panics regarding bail decisions. Under the last Conservative administration restrictions on the granting of bail were introduced by sections 25 and 26 of the Criminal Justice and Public Order Act 1994. Section 25 banned bail for anyone charged with rape or homicide offences – or attempts – who had previous convictions for such an offence. The first Labour administration, in order to comply with the ECHR in advance of implementation of the Human Rights Act 1998, amended section 25 (Crime and Disorder Act 1998, s.56) to a rebuttable presumption against bail in such cases. Under section 26 of the 1994 Act, persons charged with an indictable offence committed whilst on bail 'need not be granted bail' (s.26).

Trial Venue

Most criminal proceedings begin in the magistrates' court and over 90 per cent are concluded there. Magistrates have sole jurisdiction over all summary offences. The most serious offences are triable only on indictment in the Crown Court. A substantial range of cases can be tried 'either way' (Criminal Law Act 1977, s.19) – that is, either by magistrates or in the Crown Court. If the case is triable on an indictment, or is triable either way and the defendant pleads not guilty and elects jury trial, or the magistrates decide that their maximum allowable fine and/or six months' imprisonment would not be an adequate penalty, the defendant will be committed for trial or sentence either on bail or remanded in custody.

Successive governments have sought to reduce cost and delay by reducing the volume of trials in the Crown Court. This has been achieved through systematically recategorizing offences as summary, so that they can only be tried in the magistrates' court; encouraging magistrates to accept jurisdiction in a higher proportion of suitable cases; or, where the evidence supports alternative charges, encouraging the charging of summary offences rather than those triable either way. A more drastic strategy designed to keep a greater proportion of cases in the magistrates' court was recommended by the Runciman Commission (Royal Commission on Criminal Justice, 1993). This would allow the venue for trial to be decided by magistrates alone, removing the defendant's right to chose trial by jury. The government tried to introduce legislation to this effect in 1999 and 2000 but was defeated in the House of Lords. It is committed to trying again in due course. Proposals by Lord Justice Auld (2001) to remove the right of trial by jury for a large range of less serious offences, by introducing a new District tier of criminal courts presided over by a judge and magistrates, were rejected (Home Department, 2002).

Criminal Trials and Appeals

An account of the procedure and evidential requirements of criminal trials and the law relating to appeals is beyond the scope of this book. For those who wish to pursue this aspect of the criminal process, the critical account of both given by Sanders and Young (2000: chs. 9 and 10) is strongly recommended.

Courts' Sentencing Powers

The Powers of the Criminal Courts (Sentencing) Act 2000 (PCC(S)A 2000) consolidated existing sentencing powers, previously found in several major statutes dating back to 1933. Courts in England and Wales have a much wider range of sentences available to them than in many other jurisdictions. Sentencing principles introduced in the Criminal Justice Act 1991, and consolidated into the 2000 Act, suggest a pyramid built up of different bands, with minor sentences at the base and custody at the apex. All courts when sentencing may order the payment of compensation by the offender to the victim or give reasons for not doing so. The compensation may be in addition to a sentence, or as a sentence in its own right (PCC(S)A 2000, s.130). Sentences available for adults and young adults (18–20) will be briefly described below. Youth courts' sentencing powers for young offenders

(10–17), and those of the Crown Court in relation to the trial and sentencing of children and young persons charged with homicide or certain other grave crimes are addressed in Chapter 15. For the leading account and analysis of sentencing principles, policy and practice, see Ashworth (2000).

Sentencing Discounts

The avoidance of a trial results in a massive saving in time and expense and considerable pressure is put on defendants to admit guilt, either by the CPS agreeing to prefer a lesser charge, or through discount for a guilty plea. This was made statutory in the Criminal Justice and Public Order Act 1994 (now PCC(S)A 2000, s.152), which introduced the requirement that courts consider giving a discount for a guilty plea at a level determined by the stage in the proceedings at which the guilty plea was entered.

Discharges

Absolute discharges   Where the court is satisfied that punishment is not appropriate, generally in relation to minor offences, or those where guilt is technical but without any moral blame, it may grant an absolute discharge (PCC(S)A 2000, s.12). The result is that the conviction does not count for most future purposes. Absolute discharges are granted in fewer than 1 per cent of cases.

Conditional discharges   Where the discharge is conditional, the condition is that the offender is not convicted of another offence within a specified period up to a maximum of three years. If convicted within the period, the offender is liable to be sentenced for the original as well as the current offence(s). Conditional discharges are quite widely used, especially for first offenders where the encouragement to avoid further offending may be seen to be more likely to prove effective.

Fines

The fine is the most commonly used sentence. Almost all summary offences and about a third of indictable offences are routinely disposed of by way of a fine. The Crown Court has unlimited powers to fine. In the magistrates' courts maximum fines are banded in five levels. Levels of fine within the maxima for magistrates' courts and in all cases in the Crown Court should be determined having regard to the principle that the fine should reflect the seriousness of the offence and the offender's means. The payment of fines is enforceable through the courts, the ultimate sanction being imprisonment.

Community Sentences

Under the principle of 'commensurability' introduced by the Criminal Justice Act 1991, courts may only impose a community sentence if satisfied that the offence is 'serious enough' to warrant such a sentence. The court then has to decide, with the aid of a pre-sentence report, which community sentence is most suitable for the offender whilst also considering whether the restrictions on liberty the order will impose are commensurate with the seriousness of the offence (PCC(S)A 2000, s.35). The Criminal Justice and Courts Services Act 2000 amends the PCCSA, introducing new orders and renaming others. There are currently seven community orders available for adult offenders.

Community Rehabilitation Orders (CRO) – formerly Probation Orders   See pages 153–154.

Community Punishment Order (CPO) – formerly Community Service Order See page 154.

Community Punishment and Rehabilitation Order (CPRO) – formerly Combination Order   See page 154.

Curfew Order   This order (PCC(S)A 2000, ss.37–40) was originally introduced for juveniles and extended to adults by the Criminal Justice Act 1991. The order requires the offender to remain at home or at some other specified place during specified hours, and the offender may be subject to electronic monitoring to ensure compliance.

Drug Treatment and Testing Orders (DTTO)   See page 155.

Attendance Centre Order   Adult offenders under the age of 21 and fine defaulters aged 21–24 may be sentenced for imprisonable offences or instead of being imprisoned for fine default, to attend an attendance centre provided one is available for 12 hours or up to 36 hours if in all the circumstances 12 hours 'would be inadequate' (PCC(S)A 2000, s.60). Attendance centres are generally run by the police on Saturday afternoons, providing a mixture of physical and other supervised activities.

Custodial Sentences

Principles   Under the PCC(S)A 2000, s.79, courts may only sentence offenders to imprisonment (unless the sentence for the offence is fixed by law) if one of two grounds are satisfied. Either the court has to be of the opinion that the offence was 'so serious' that only a custodial sentence 'can be justified' (s.79)(a)), or 'where the offence is a violent or sexual offence, that only such a sentence would be adequate to protect the public from serious harm from him' (s.79(2)(b)). The only exception to this approach arises where a court indicates that it intends passing a sentence such as a DTTO or a requirement in a CRO which requires the offender's consent, and that consent is refused. In those circumstances a court may pass a custodial sentence instead of the community sentence.

The length of the term to be served in custody (apart from the statutory mandatory sentence of life imprisonment for murder), up to the statutory maximum for the offence, has to be determined by the court applying the general principles set out in section 80 of the PCC(S)A 2000, sentencing case law and guidance from the Court of Appeal. For a detailed critical analysis of policy, the law and practice in relation to custodial sentencing, see Ashworth 2002; Cavadino and Dignan, 2001.

Suspended sentences on imprisonment   Courts may suspend any sentence of imprisonment for two years or less for between one and two years, provided that the offender is aged 21 or over (PCC(S)A 2000, ss.118–121). If during the period of suspension, the offender commits and is convicted of any further offences the court has to activate the suspended sentence, unless of the opinion that it would be unjust to do so. The sentence has had a chequered history. In order to discourage improper use, the Court of Appeal has set out the decision-making sequence to be followed by courts:

(i)   decide whether the case is serious enough for immediate imprisonment;
(ii) if it is, determine the appropriate length of the sentence;
(iii) if the sentence is two years or less, consider whether it might be suspended. (Ashworth, 2000: 293).

Custodial sentences for young adult offenders (18–20)   Offenders aged 18–20 although tried in adult courts, and sentenced under the powers set out above, may not be sentenced to imprisonment. The custodial sentence for young adults is that of detention in a young offender institution and is usually served in an institution designated for that purpose (PCC(S)A 2000, ss.89–99). Also persons of this age may be detained for default or contempt if the court is of the opinion that 'no other method of dealing with him is appropriate' (PCC(S)A 2000, s.108). A person under the age of 21 convicted of murder will be sentenced to custody for life rather than imprisonment for life. Custodial sentences for young adults may not be suspended.

Early release   The discretionary release of prisoners before the expiry of the full sentence has a lengthy history and raises many interesting policy issues (see Ashworth, 2000: 254–61). Release before the end of the sentence imposed has long been used to reduce the prison population, and encourage good behaviour amongst prisoners before and after release. The current scheme was introduced in the Criminal Justice Act 1991. The reform of this system, which would have been introduced had Part II of the Crime

(Sentences) Act 1997 been implemented, was abandoned by the Labour government.

Early release works differently according to sentence length.

- Prisoners sentenced to less than 12 months are released conditionally after serving one half, and are liable to recall for any unexpired portion of their sentence if they commit another offence before the sentence expires.
- Prisoners serving sentences of one year and less than four years are released conditionally after half the sentence is served and are subject to supervision on licence by the probation service until the three-quarters point of their sentence. If the supervision conditions are breached the offender may be fined or recalled to prison. Between the three-quarter point and the end of the sentence, the same provisions on conditional release apply as for sentences of up to one year. Supervision on licence may be ordered by the court to continue until the end of the sentence for sex offenders (PCC(S)A 2000, s.85).
- There is no automatic entitlement to release at the half-way point for prisoners serving four years or more. The normal time for release becomes two-thirds, but the Parole Board may grant a parole licence, which lasts until the three-quarters point to such offenders at any point between the halfway and two-thirds point of the sentence. At the three-quarters point conditional release provisions apply until the end of the sentence.

Prisoners who are being considered for discretionary conditional release have access to their full dossier. They are entitled to discuss the dossier at their interview with a Parole Board member. They also have access to and may comment on the report of that interview. Prisoners are given reasons for the decision reached by the Parole Board.

In order to meet public concerns about periods spent in custody being considerably shorter than the sentences announced in court, the Lord Chief Justice issued directions to judges in 1998. This requires Crown Court judges when passing a custodial sentence to give an explanation of the length of time an offender will spend in custody and the conditions on which he will be released (*Practice Direction* [1998]).

Home Detention Curfew   Prisoners who are serving sentences of between three months and four years and are assessed as presenting a low risk to the public may be released during the last two months before they would be due to be released on licence under a curfew monitored by electronic tagging.

Life imprisonment   Life imprisonment is a discretionary sentence for some very serious offences. Mandatory life sentences have to be passed for murder and under the Crime (Sentences) Act 1997 for a second violent or serious sexual offence. Ashworth (2000: ch. 6) provides a detailed discussion and critique of the complex criminological, human rights, and penal policy issues to which both discretionary and mandatory life sentences give rise.

Previous Convictions

With the aim of allowing people who had not re-offended to put their convictions behind them, mainly for employment purposes, the Rehabilitation of Offenders Act 1974 introduced a system under which, depending on the gravity of the offence as reflected in the sentence imposed, convictions may become 'spent' after a period of time. 'Spent' convictions do not have to be admitted to by those seeking employment, unless the form of employment comes within the wide range set out in Schedule 1 to the Act. It is also a criminal offence for anyone to publicise the spent convictions of another person. The Act has been reviewed and a report has been published for consultation (Home Office, 2002).

PART VI
SCOTLAND

Chapter 20

Social Work Law in Scotland

Janice McGhee

The Scottish Legal Context

Scotland has a separate legal system from the rest of the United Kingdom, with its own courts, system of prosecution and legal profession reflecting the fact that Scotland was a separate nation state until the union of the Scottish and English parliaments in 1707. The Union allowed for the continuance of the distinctive Scottish educational, church and legal systems although legislative power was vested in the United Kingdom Parliament at Westminster. There was a form of administrative devolution from 1885 through the Scottish Office, a department of government, however political pressure for constitutional reform continued to grow in Scotland (Himsworth and Munro, 1999: ix). Following a referendum on 11 September 1997, which expressed very substantial support for the creation of a Scottish Parliament, the government introduced the Scotland Bill into the Westminster Parliament. The bill set out the framework for devolving legislative power to a Scottish Parliament and the Scotland Act 1998 received Royal Assent on 19 November 1998. Elections to the Scottish Parliament by a form of proportional representation were held on 6 May 1999, and it was invested with its statutory powers on 1 July 1999. There are 129 Members of the Scottish Parliament (MSPs).

Part I of the Scotland Act 1998 includes provisions setting out the legislative competence of the Parliament (sections 28–30, Schedules 4, 5) which is in effect restricted to Scots law; it is a 'subordinate legislature' (Himsworth and Munro, 1999: 5). Power is devolved to legislate in a range of areas including social work, health, education, training, housing, law and order. Certain matters are reserved to the UK Parliament and these include for example social security, energy, defence and foreign policy (Schedule 5). The UK Parliament retains the power to make legislation for Scotland in the devolved areas (section 28(7) 1998 Act) however there is a convention that the consent of the Scottish Parliament should be sought before doing so. The Parliament has a tax varying power (Part IV 1998 Act) although there appear to be no immediate proposals to implement this aspect of the Act.

There are also various provisions in place to ensure that Acts of the Scottish Parliament and acts and decisions of the Scottish Executive are competent in terms of the devolution framework set out in the 1998 Act. There is provision to scrutinize these 'devolution issues' raised in the courts (Schedule 6 1998 Act). The Judicial Committee of the Privy Council is the court of last resort in determining devolution issues; and it can also have a role in determining whether a bill is within the competence of the Parliament (pre-Assent scrutiny, section 33) (Paterson et al., 1999: 85).

Part II of the Act sets out the provisions to establish a Scottish Administration and related ministerial functions. There is a Scottish Executive headed by the First Minister, a team of nine ministers, the Scottish law officers, the Lord Advocate who heads the Crown Prosecution Service and the Solicitor General. The remaining parts and schedules of the Act deal with financial provision, the tax-varying power and various other matters.

The Scottish Parliament has introduced 38 Acts to date, many addressing issues where there had previously been a lack of time in the UK Parliament. Acts of the Scottish Parliament (ASPs) apply only in Scotland, as did some Acts of the UK Parliament in recognition of the differing legal and organizational structures in Scotland. The Social Work (Scotland) Act 1968 for example underpinned the creation of local authority social work departments in Scotland. Other UK statutes of course continue to apply equally in both Scotland and other parts of the United Kingdom, for instance, the majority of laws relating to social security and taxation, areas where the UK Parliament has reserved powers.

Despite differing legislation many legal principles are similar in the Scottish and English jurisdictions, such as the paramountcy of the welfare of the child; or address similar issues but adapted to the specific legal context. The Care Standards Act 2000 and the Regulation of Care (Scotland) Act 2001 both address the creation of regulatory bodies for social service provision and social work and social care staff in the separate jurisdictions.

Following major local government reorganization in 1996 (Local Government etc. (Scotland) Act 1994) 32 unitary, single-tier authorities were created with a requirement for a chief social work officer to be responsible for social work services. The 1994 Act removed the need for local councils to have a social work committee and a Director of Social Work. The wide variation in geographical size and population between these authorities, combined with their unitary status, has influenced the pattern and delivery of social work services. Some local authorities have moved towards joint departments of housing and social work, others have reorganized around service provision for specific groups such as children and families, bringing together education and social work services.

Social work services have always been structured differently in Scotland compared to the rest of the UK. There is no separate probation service; duties associated with the probation service in England are carried out by local authority social work departments/divisions in Scotland. These duties are integrated into their remit alongside responsibility for child care, community care and other social service provision. However, since 1990, direct central funding for many criminal justice social work services has been allocated to local authorities from central government (Law Reform (Miscellaneous Provisions) (Scotland) Act 1990). This initiative, along with the publication of National Objectives and Standards for criminal justice social work (SWSG, 1991), has served to further the development of specialist criminal justice teams and services across Scotland. More recently, local authorities have been required by the Scottish Executive to form consortia to allow for the delivery of a greater range of criminal justice social work services in their areas and by April 2002 it is expected there will be 11 mainland groups plus the Islands Councils.

The Regulation of Care (Scotland) Act 2001 provides for the establishment of a Scottish Commission for the Regulation of Care to register and inspect a wide range of 'care services' (defined in section 2) against national standards. Residential and community based services including adoption and fostering agencies are included but not field social work services. Part 3 of the 2001 Act allows for the creation of the Scottish Social Services Council (section 43) with the responsibility to maintain a register of social workers and social care staff (section 44). The Council will have the power to grant or refuse registration, and to remove or suspend someone from the register. Establishing codes of practice outlining standards and conduct of practice for social service staff and employers are also the responsibility of the Council. Both agencies will be operational by 1 April 2002. The role of promoting the education and training of social work and social service staff and approving courses now lies with the new Council. At the time of writing the Scottish Executive had not yet set out its proposals regarding future arrangements for social work education, more specifically the Diploma in Social Work. However, a degree in social work is the most likely basis for the new professional qualification.

The Scottish Legal System

As in England, common law, statute law and European Community law are the main sources of law in Scotland. There is a further important minor source of law, which is relevant, particularly in the context of criminal law. These are the writings of learned jurists from the mid-seventeenth century to the nineteenth century, known as the Institutional Writers. They set down a number of legal principles which may still apply today, often in the absence of a relevant statute or case example (Paterson, Bates and Poustie, 1999: 462–6).

The working of judicial precedent (whereby a decision in a higher court can bind a lower court on the same point of law) operates, but the system of courts is different (see Figures 20.1 and 20.2 for simplified versions). The House of Lords can hear appeals from Scottish courts in relation to civil law matters; criminal appeals are only heard by a High Court of Justiciary Appeal Court based in Edinburgh. There are, of course, separate series of Scottish law reports.

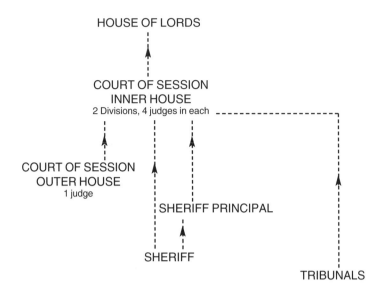

Figure 20.1   The civil courts in Scotland

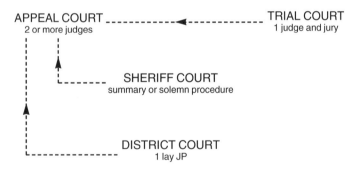

Figure 20.2   The criminal courts in Scotland

Civil Courts

The sheriff court is a local court with both civil and criminal jurisdiction. There are six sheriffdoms in Scotland, which are further divided into sheriff court districts (apart from Glasgow and Strathkelvin). Each sheriffdom has a sheriff principal who has the duty to ensure that the courts' business is carried out in an efficient manner. The sheriff is a professional judge who sits alone, dealing with cases coming to court for the first time (at first instance). The sheriff court's civil jurisdiction is wide: many types of actions can be raised, for example, debt, divorce, disputes relating to children, contract and personal injury. In most cases decisions can be appealed to the sheriff principal of the sheriffdom or to the Inner House of the Court of Session. It is often less costly to raise an action in the sheriff court, although some matters, for instance, judicial review of decisions of administrative bodies, can only be undertaken in the Court of Session.

The Court of Session is the supreme civil court based in Scotland, and sits only in Edinburgh. It is divided into the Outer House and Inner House. The Outer House comprises Lords Ordinary (a courtesy title); judges who sit alone and generally hear civil cases coming to the court for the first time. The Inner House is the main court of appeal for civil cases in relation to decisions taken in the Outer House, where appeal is of right. The Inner House is divided into two divisions of equal standing; one presided over by the Lord President and the other by the Lord Justice-Clerk, the most senior and second most senior judges respectively in Scotland.

Recently the number of senior judges in each of the two divisions of the Inner House was increased from three to four making a total of ten, when the most senior judges are included (Number of Inner House Judges (Variation) Order 2001). Appeals from the sheriff court depend on the procedure used and are possible to the sheriff principal and/or direct to the Inner House. The Inner House also hears the decisions of some administrative tribunals and specialized courts.

The House of Lords (the Appellate Committee) is the final court of appeal in civil matters in Scotland. In cases beginning in the sheriff court appeal is limited to points of law. In civil cases the person bringing the action is called the pursuer (plaintiff in English law) and the other party is known as the defender (defendant in English law).

Criminal Courts

The lowest level of criminal court in Scotland (where minor offences are prosecuted) is the district court, which is located within and administered by the local authorities. There are 56 district courts in Scotland sited in the main towns and cities (Mays, Smith and Strachan, 1999: 28). The procedure is always summary and the court is presided over by a lay magistrate (known as a Justice of the Peace) with legal advice available from an assessor or clerk of the court. Sentencing powers are limited; for example, the maximum period of imprisonment which can be imposed, is 60 days (section 7(6), Criminal Procedure (Scotland) Act 1995). In Glasgow there are also stipendiary magistrates, who are lawyers and have the same sentencing power as the sheriff summary court.

The sheriff court has wide criminal jurisdiction but it is excluded from the most serious crimes, such as murder or rape. Procedure may be solemn (a sheriff sitting with a jury of 15) or in less serious cases, summary (a sheriff sitting alone). However, the court's sentencing powers are limited according to the procedure adopted, for example, the maximum sentence of imprisonment a sheriff sitting with a jury can impose is three years (section 3(3), Criminal Procedure (Scotland) Act 1995). If the sheriff considers that a longer sentence is merited the case can be remitted to the High Court for sentence (section 195, Criminal Procedure (Scotland) Act 1995).

The High Court of Justiciary functions both as a trial court and as the Scottish Court of Criminal Appeal. There is no further appeal to the House of Lords in criminal cases as in England. In practice most serious crimes are prosecuted in the High Court and some offences, such as murder, rape and treason must be tried there. The High Court, as a trial court, sits in Edinburgh and goes out on circuit throughout Scotland to hear cases in various towns and cities. There are four circuits, Home, North, South and West. The High Court is in almost permanent session in the Home and West circuit, which contain the major cities of Edinburgh and Glasgow respectively. Procedure is always solemn. The sentencing powers of the court are unlimited for common law offences, life imprisonment being the maximum penalty.

The Justiciary Appeal Court sits only in Edinburgh. Appeals are possible under both solemn and summary procedure and against conviction, sentence or both. Appeals against conviction are heard by at least three judges and against sentence by no less than two judges. The court hears appeals from the sheriff court, the district court and from the High Court acting as a trial court. Under certain circumstances the Lord Advocate and the prosecutor can appeal if they consider a sentence is 'unduly lenient' (sections 108, 175(4)(4A), Criminal Procedure (Scotland) Act 1995).

The Scottish Criminal Cases Review Commission has the power to refer cases, which have exhausted the appeal process, back to the Appeal Court, where it is thought there may be a miscarriage of justice. The Commission is an independent body and came into operation on 1 April 1999 taking over this power which had previously been exercised by the Secretary of State for Scotland.

Legal Personnel

Lawyers

There are two branches of the legal profession in Scotland: advocates (similar to barristers) and solicitors. As in England clients have direct access to solicitors whilst advocates are always instructed by solicitors; the client cannot directly approach an advocate. The solicitors' professional body is the Law Society of Scotland, which regulates solicitors' conduct and deals with disciplinary matters.

Advocates are members of, and regulated by, the Faculty of Advocates and are lawyers who specialize in court appearance who may also be consulted for opinion in complex legal matters. Only advocates and solicitor-advocates (very experienced solicitors with further training) may appear in the higher courts (the High Court, the Court of Session and the House of Lords).

Judges

Judges in the High Court and the Court of Session are drawn from senior members of the legal profession often from current sheriffs. There are 32 judges in Scotland and three are women. Sheriffs are legally qualified, being principally drawn from advocates and very experienced solicitors. Justices of the Peace are lay magistrates who are advised in relation to the law by a legal assessor or clerk to the court. They also carry out other tasks, for example, they may grant authorization to allow for the emergency protection of a child where it is not practicable for the application to be made to the sheriff for a child protection order (section 61, Children (Scotland) Act 1995).

A Judicial Appointments Board has been established in Scotland to allow for a more open system of judicial appointments where vacancies are advertised. It includes lay and legal members and recommends preferred candidates (and a short-list of approved candidates in order of preference) to the First Minister who will consult with the Lord President of the Court of Session and then recommend a candidate(s) to the Queen. The system was established initially on an administrative basis, but is expected to be placed on a statutory basis when parliamentary time becomes available.

Prosecutors

Prosecution against crime in Scotland is through a public prosecution system (private prosecutions are possible but extremely rare) organized through the Crown Office under the direction of the Lord Advocate who has ultimate control of all prosecutions in Scotland. There is a procurator fiscal service in each sheriffdom, which is delegated control of the prosecution process by the Crown Office although their decisions are subject to consultation and guidance. Procurators fiscal decide whether to prosecute, the charges to be laid, the type of procedure to be used and the level of court in which an accused is to be tried. In more serious cases these decisions are referred to the Crown Office.

There is no provision for an accused to claim a right to a jury trial in Scotland where juries comprise 15 members (12 in England) and may reach a verdict by a simple majority of eight to seven. There are three possible verdicts available to Scottish criminal courts, guilty, not guilty or the charge is not proven, which has the same effect as an acquittal.

Prosecutions in the sheriff and district courts are undertaken by the procurator fiscal and in the High Court by the advocate depute (advocates appointed on a temporary part-time basis to act as Crown Counsel). Criminal law in Scotland has largely been developed by the courts and is a common law system. If an authoritative statement of the law is required the High Court may convene a bench of five or more judges (see *Drury* v. *HMA* 2001, considering the definition of murder and the plea of provocation in the context of such a charge in Scots law).

In contrast the majority of the law regulating criminal proceedings in Scotland is statute based. The Criminal Procedure (Scotland) Act 1995 as amended, supplemented by various Acts of Adjournal of the High Court (Rules of court) contain the key provisions. Case law does assist in the interpretation of these procedural provisions. The intention of these rules is to ensure fairness to the accused and to the public interest.

A distinctive feature of the Scottish criminal justice system is the 110-day rule (section 65(4)(b), Criminal Procedure (Scotland) Act 1995). If an accused has been committed for trial on indictment and remains in custody his or her trial must commence within 110 days of the full committal. If the accused is not committed in custody the period is 12 months from the first appearance on petition for the alleged offence (section 65(1), 1995 Act). If the case does not begin within the time limit the accused must be released and no further action can be taken. On application to the court it is possible to have these limits extended but, in the case of the 110-day rule, this will not be granted if the fault for delay lies with the Crown (Shiels and Bradley and others, 2001: 109).

Evidence

As in the rest of the UK rules of evidence are a highly technical area of law. The standard of proof in civil and criminal cases pertains, as in England, 'on the balance of probabilities' and 'beyond reasonable doubt' respectively. Corroboration of the material facts of a criminal case is required in Scotland, that is, evidence must be submitted from two independent sources. Generally therefore, a confession alone would not be sufficient to convict an accused person. As a general principle hearsay remains inadmissible in criminal proceedings. However, there are a wide range of exceptions to this rule including statutory exceptions (incorporated into sections 259, 260, Criminal Procedure (Scotland) Act 1995). In civil cases corroboration is not required and hearsay is admissible (Civil Evidence (Scotland) Act 1988, sections 1, 2 respectively).

There is no lower age limit on children giving evidence in court but before admitting a child's evidence the judge or sheriff has to ensure that the child understands the difference between truth and falsehood and the requirement to tell the truth (referred to as competency). The child must be admonished to tell the truth, children aged 12 years or over are required to swear or affirm with the expectation those over 14 years will be sworn (*Rees* v. *Lowe*, 1990; *Kelly* v. *Docherty*, 1991).

In civil cases, there is no need for a child witness to be tested for 'competence' before evidence of their prior statements can be introduced to the court (*T* v. *T*, [2000]). Thus statements given by children to police officers or social workers will be admissible, although if a young child is to give evidence directly they will then have to be tested in court for competence. This is most relevant to those situations where evidence regarding grounds of referral to a children's hearing are tested in court, as these are a civil matter. In criminal proceedings prior statements of this kind can only be admitted if the child is in court and is unable or refuses to testify (*MacDonald* v. *HMA* [1999]).

Special provisions for child witnesses in criminal cases were introduced by the Law Reform (Miscellaneous Provisions) (Scotland) Act 1990 and the Prisoners and Criminal Proceedings (Scotland) Act 1993. These included the use of a live television link (see Murray, 1995, for an exploration of the impact of this provision). The provisions were consolidated (brought together) in section 271 of the Criminal Procedure (Scotland) Act 1995 and have now been extended to include vulnerable adult witnesses, being those with a mental disorder or significant impairment of intelligence and social functioning. The Lord Justice-General issued a Memorandum on Child Witnesses suggesting a number of measures that judges/sheriffs can make to reduce the anxiety of children giving evidence including removing wigs, gowns and permitting the child to be accompanied by a friend or relative.

Legal Aid

Legal aid is available for both advice and assistance and criminal and civil proceedings in court. The Legal Aid (Scotland) Act 1986 is the relevant statute and the Scottish Legal Aid Board (SLAB) administers legal aid.

Human Rights

The Human Rights Act 1998 came into force in Scotland on the 2 October 2000, however, the Scotland Act 1998 brought some effects of the European Convention on Human Rights into Scots law at an earlier stage. Section 29 of the Scotland Act 1998 provides that the Scottish Parliament cannot make provisions in an Act, which would be incompatible with Convention rights; and section 57(2) indicates that a member of the Scottish Executive has no power to do any act that would be incompatible with the Convention rights.

An early case was that of *Starrs* v. *Ruxton* [2000], a criminal prosecution. As the Lord Advocate is a member of the Scottish Executive his decisions were subject to the Convention rights from 20 May 1999. The High Court found that the lack of tenure of temporary sheriffs was incompatible with Article 6(1) of the ECHR where 'everyone is entitled to ... an independent and impartial tribunal' when a criminal charge is being determined.

Temporary sheriffs had their contract renewed annually at the discretion of the Lord Advocate, therefore their independence potentially could be seen as compromised. The Bail, Judicial Appointments, etc. (Scotland) Act 2000 formally abolished the role of temporary sheriff (section 6) and a new office of part-time sheriff was created (section 7). In more recent criminal cases the most common human rights issues raised have been related to delay in coming to trial as a potential breach of Article 6 of the ECHR (the right to trial in a reasonable time), for example, *Gibson* v. *HMA* [2001].

It is expected the Human Rights Act 1998 will generate a substantial amount of case law in many areas of social work law. A recent human rights challenge to the hearings system is discussed below.

Children and Families

Child-care legislation is probably an area where the differences between Scotland and other jurisdictions in the UK are most profound. The Children Act 1989 does not apply in Scotland (apart from some very minor aspects), the Children (Scotland) Act 1995 along with the Adoption (Scotland) Act 1978 provides the majority of the legislation in relation to children and families of direct relevance to social workers.

There is no youth court in Scotland, children and young people in need of care and protection, including those who may also have committed offences, are dealt with in a system of lay panels or tribunals known as children's hearings. The children's hearings are serviced on a voluntary basis by lay people, drawn from the child's community, with knowledge of children and family life. Each local authority has a Children's Panel made up of the volunteer members of the public who have been appointed to this role and a Children's Panel Advisory Committee, which has responsibility for recruiting and training lay panel members and ensuring that members carry out their duties satisfactorily.

Children's Hearings

The children's hearings tribunal system in Scotland was originally established under the Social Work (Scotland) Act 1968 and came into operation on 15 April 1971. Part II of the Children (Scotland) Act 1995 and the Children's Hearings (Scotland) Rules 1996, SI 1996/3261 now provide the main legislative basis for the operation of the system. The hearings system was a direct result of the deliberations of the Kilbrandon Committee (1964) which sought to find solutions to the rise in the rate of juvenile delinquency in post-war Scotland. The committee found the legal distinction between juvenile offenders and children in need of care and protection was not meaningful when the underlying circumstances and needs of the children were examined. The central philosophy of the children's hearings system has a clear welfare orientation focusing on the 'needs' rather than the 'deeds' of the child as the basis for decision-making and intervention. The hearing can place the protection of the public from 'serious harm' above the welfare of the child (section 16(5), 1995 Act).

The system operates on the fundamental principle of separating the needs of the child from the establishment of the facts of a case. The courts are only involved where the facts of a case are disputed, in appeals and in cases where more serious offences have allegedly been committed. Children under 16 years of age can only be prosecuted in the criminal courts on the instruction of the Lord Advocate (section 42, Criminal Procedure (Scotland) Act 1995). The age of criminal responsibility in Scotland is currently eight years; however, the Scottish Law Commission have recommended that this age rule be abolished but that there should be a bar on the prosecution of children under 12 years (SLC, 2002).

There is provision for adult courts to remit offenders to the hearings system for advice or disposal including those aged 16 up to 17½ years dealt with in summary courts (section 49, Criminal Procedure (Scotland) Act 1995). This rarely occurs although there has been growing concern about the number of young people aged 16 and 17 years receiving very short prison sentences. The Scottish Executive (2000) responding to the Report of the Advisory Group on Youth Crime (Scottish Executive, 2000b) indicated that the feasibility of a bridging pilot whereby certain young people aged 16 and 17 years would be routinely dealt with in the hearings system would be examined. It is likely a pilot project will be introduced in 2002/03.

The Scottish Children's Reporter Administration (SCRA) was established from 1 April 1996 in response to local government reorganization. Previously each local authority had a reporter's department with responsibility for the children's hearings service. The SCRA is a national non-governmental public body headed by a chief officer, the Principal Reporter and has the responsibility for the management and deployment of reporters throughout Scotland. The term 'Principal Reporter' includes the appointed principal reporter and any officer of SCRA to whom he has delegated any of his functions under section 131(1) of the Local Government etc. (Scotland) Act 1994. The same definition is given in the Children (Scotland) Act 1995. Reporters come from a wide variety of backgrounds, including teaching, law and social work. If a reporter is not legally qualified, provided he or she has one year's experience (Reporters (Conduct of Proceedings before the Sheriff) (Scotland) Regulations 1997), they are entitled to appear and conduct hearings in the sheriff court (*Miller* v. *Council of the Law Society of Scotland*, 1999).

The Reporter and Hearing

The reporter is the 'lynch-pin' of the system (Thomson, 1991), receiving all referrals and making the initial decision regarding the child. If there appears to be sufficient prima facie evidence to establish a condition of referral the reporter has the discretion to decide whether or not a child may be in need of compulsory measures of supervision in light of all the circumstances. Compulsory supervision includes measures taken for the protection, guidance, treatment or control of the child (section 52(3), Children (Scotland) Act 1995).

Anyone can refer a child (defined in section 93(2)(b), 1995 Act) to the reporter, although the law enforcement agencies (primarily the police) have remained the main sources of referral since the inception of the system. In 1999/2000, the police were the source of 79.3 per cent of referrals to the reporter (SCRA, 2001: 6, Table 2). Annual statistics since 1996 have been calculated on the period 1 April to 31 March. Social work, education and health are further sources of referral to the reporter. In the year 1999/2000, 33 837 children were referred to the reporter (SCRA, 2001: 4). Rates of referral are higher for boys than girls with rates per 1000 of the population under 16 of 39.5 for boys and 26.5 for girls in 1999/2000 (SCRA, 2001: 6).

The annual statistics also highlight the changing pattern of referrals to the children's hearings system where there has been an increase in referrals on care and protection grounds (grounds (a) to (g)) of 238 per cent between 1989 and 1999/2000 (the definition of a care and protection referral was extended by SCRA to include ground (a) where a child is seen as beyond parental control). In the same period the number of alleged offence referral grounds increased by 26.5 per cent (SCRA, 2001: 4). The grounds or conditions of referral are set out in the Children (Scotland) Act 1995, s.52(2) and are as follows, that the child:

(a) is beyond the control of any relevant person;
(b) is falling into bad associations or is exposed to moral danger;
(c) is likely –
    (i) to suffer unnecessarily; or
    (ii) be impaired seriously in his health and development,
    due to a lack of parental care;
(d) is a child in respect of whom any of the offences mentioned in Schedule 1 to the Criminal Procedure (Scotland) Act 1995 (offences against children to which special provisions apply) has been committed;
(e) is, or is likely to become, a member of the same household as a child in respect of whom any of the offences referred to in paragraph (d) above has been committed;
(f) is, or is likely to become, a member of the same household as a person who has committed any of the offences referred to in paragraph (d) above;

(g) is, or is likely to become, a member of the same household as a person in respect of whom an offence under sections 1 to 3 of the Criminal Law (Consolidation) (Scotland) Act 1995 (incest and intercourse with a child by step-parent or person in position of trust) has been committed by a member of that household;

(h) has failed to attend school regularly without reasonable excuse;

(i) has committed an offence;

(j) has misused alcohol or any drug, whether or not a controlled drug within the meaning of the Misuse of Drugs Act 1971;

(k) has misused a volatile substance by deliberately inhaling its vapour, other than for medicinal purposes;

(l) is being provided with accommodation by a local authority under section 25, or is the subject of a parental responsibilities order obtained under section 86, of this Act and, in either case, his behaviour is such that special measures are necessary for his adequate supervision in his interest or the interest of others.

The 1995 Act introduced one new ground (j) and extended the incest ground to include boys. There is also some overlap between public and private law in relation to children and families. The 1995 Act allows courts in 'relevant proceedings' to refer a child to the principal reporter if it deems that any of the conditions of referral (except section 52(2)(i) – that is, the child has committed an offence) are satisfied (section 54, 1995 Act). Relevant proceedings include, amongst others: divorce actions; proceedings related to parental responsibilities or rights; adoption proceedings, including freeing for adoption. The reporter will then investigate the case and, if he or she decides that compulsory measures of supervision are necessary, will arrange a children's hearing.

The reporter has extensive discretion in decision-making and may request social work and school reports from the local authority (section 56(2), 1995 Act). Provided there is evidence to establish grounds of referral the reporter may decide:

- a children's hearing does not need to be arranged and the child, any relevant person and the referrer must be advised of this decision (section 56(4)(a), 1995 Act). Essentially no further action is taken; or
- a children's hearing does not need to be arranged but the reporter may refer the child and his/her family to a local authority for advice guidance and assistance (section 56(4)(b), 1995 Act); or
- arrange a children's hearing if it appears compulsory measures of supervision are necessary in relation to the child (sections 56(6), 65(1), 1995 Act).

If the reporter decides there are ground(s) of referral and that compulsory measures of supervision may be necessary she or he will arrange a children's hearing, notifying the child and 'relevant persons' of the date and time of the hearing and the grounds (Rules 5, 6, 7, Children's Hearings (Scotland) Rules 1996). A social background report (or supplemental report) from the local authority social worker and any other relevant professionals will be obtained (section 56(7), 1995 Act).

Following the decision of the European Court of Human Rights in *McMichael* v. *United Kingdom*, 1995 criticizing the UK for refusing to give parents the right to see any written reports provided by professionals, the law was changed in 1996. Each relevant person (and the genetic father of the child, if he is living with the genetic mother) receives a copy of all the reports, and other documents sent to the panel members (rules 5(3), 7(3), 12, Children's Hearings (Scotland) Rules 1996).

Children are not legally entitled to receive a copy of reports, however, prior to the case, *S* v. *Principal Reporter and Lord Advocate* [2001], the Principal Reporter issued interim practice guidance indicating circumstances where reports, subject to certain protective measures, would also be given to some children where they made such a request. Further guidance will be introduced following consultation and the evaluation of a proposed pilot scheme in relation to access to reports.

The children's hearing itself involves three lay members of the children's panel (one of whom chairs the meeting), the relevant person(s), the child in the majority of cases, representatives from social work and the reporter who provides legal advice to the hearing but does not take part in decision-making at this stage. There must be at least one female and one male member of the hearing panel present (section 39(5), 1995 Act).

Relevant persons are defined in section 93(2)(b), 1995 Act and are (a) parents with parental responsibilities and rights; (b) any person who has parental responsibilities and rights vested under or by virtue of the 1995 Act; (c) any person who appears to ordinarily have charge of, or control over, the child (except by reason only of his employment). The latter could include for example unmarried fathers who live with the child, as currently they do not automatically have parental responsibilities and rights in Scots law. Relevant persons have a right and an obligation to attend the children's hearing, although they can be released from the obligation to attend in certain circumstances (s.45(8)(b), 1995 Act).

The child has an absolute right and obligation to attend their hearing (section 45(1), 1995 Act). Although they can in some circumstances be released from the obligation to attend (section 45(2)(a), (b), 1995 Act) they cannot be prevented from doing so. Relevant persons and their representatives can be excluded from part of the hearing in certain circumstances (section 46(1)), though not at the initial stage where the chair sets out the ground(s) of referral. The chair must inform the excluded person of the substance of what has taken place in his or her absence (section 46(2)) so there is no confidentiality offered to the child.

There is provision for relevant persons and the child to each bring a representative who may be a friend or a solicitor (Rule 11, Children's

Hearings (Scotland) Rules 1996) although the latter is rare as legal aid is not available at this stage. In the recent case *S* v. *Principal Reporter and Lord Advocate*, 2001 this restriction on legally-aided representation for children at hearings could not be seen to be in compliance with Article 6(1) of the ECHR, although a formal declaration of incompatibility was not found necessary at a subsequent hearing (*S* v. *Miller (No.2)*, 2001).

The Scottish Executive has indicated that they will consult on a long-term solution, which may include a proposal to introduce hearings rights officers, publicly funded lawyers to represent children at some hearings. In the mean time safeguarders and curators *ad litem* who are legally qualified may be appointed to represent children at some hearings: where a residential supervision requirement may be necessary and the child may meet the criteria for secure accommodation; or where representation is needed to allow the child to participate effectively, Rule 3, The Children's Hearings (Legal Representation) (Scotland) Rules 2002.

The chair has the responsibility for the formal aspects of the proceedings and puts the grounds of referral to the child and his or her family. If the child is old enough, and able to understand what is going on and accepts the grounds of referral as true, and if the relevant persons(s) accept the grounds (fully or in part) the hearing proceeds (section 65(4)(5)(6), 1995 Act).

However, if the child and/or relevant persons do not accept the grounds fully or in part, the hearing can decide to discharge the referral or direct the reporter to refer the matter to the sheriff for proof of the grounds which are not accepted (section 65(7), 1995 Act). If the child is not capable of understanding the explanation of the grounds of referral, often if the child is very young, the hearing can make the same decision as above (section 65(9), 1995 Act). A formal court hearing will be heard in the sheriff's chambers, to establish if the conditions for the grounds are met, and must begin within 28 days of the reporter lodging an application. Legal aid is available at this stage.

The basic rules of evidence are observed at the proof hearing. Although Kilbrandon (1964) strove to place the emphasis on 'needs' rather than 'deeds', the continuing differentiation between offenders and non-offenders has always remained and is reflected in the different standards of legal proof. Children who are offended against require grounds to be established on the civil standard of proof (the balance of probability) whilst, for child offenders, the criminal standard (beyond reasonable doubt, section 68(3), 1995 Act) has been retained. If the child has been offended against, proceedings do not have to await the outcome of any criminal prosecution (see, for example, *P* v. *Kennedy*, 1995).

If the grounds are established, the case is remitted back to the children's hearing for disposal; if the grounds are not upheld the case is discharged. The hearing can continue a case for further investigation, discharge the child's case or place the child under a supervision requirement with conditions attached (section 69, 70, 1995 Act). Such conditions may include, for example, that the child resides at a certain place (for instance, with foster carers). The hearing when making a supervision requirement may consider imposing conditions regarding medical examination or treatment in relation to the child. The regulation of contact must be considered (section 70(2), (5)(a)(b), 1995 Act).

The majority of children under supervision are living at home with a parent or guardian (67 per cent of all supervision requirements in 1999–2000, SCRA, 2001: 4). Although implementation of the supervision requirement is a corporate responsibility of the local authority it is the social work department/division who is generally responsible for the care and supervision of the child.

There is a review system to examine progress and ensure that compulsory measures of supervision continue to be required. Review must be annual unless it is requested earlier by the child and/or relevant person(s) or social work department/division (section 73, 1995 Act). Research by Ball (1995) indicated that panel members wanted the power to request early reviews. This was instituted under the Children (Scotland) Act 1995 (s.70(7)), which gives hearings the power to determine when a supervision requirement may be reviewed during the currency of that requirement.

Panel members can hold a 'business meeting' prior to a hearing to discuss aspects of procedure, for example, in the case of sexual abuse where the alleged perpetrator may be attending the hearing, the child may be released from the obligation to attend. The detailed aspects are set out in Rule 4 of Children's Hearings (Scotland) Rules 1996. The business meeting now has a role in deciding whether legal representation may be necessary for the child (Rule 3, Children's Hearings (Legal Representation) (Scotland) Rules 2002). Children and their families must be advised that the business meeting is to take place and have a right to ask the reporter to convey their views on the issues to be discussed.

Safeguarders

Safeguarders come from a variety of backgrounds and are appointed to look after the child's interests in a particular case, providing an independent report assessing the child's needs. Since the 1995 Act came into force all children's hearings and sheriffs dealing with hearings case have to consider whether a safeguarder should be appointed; previously there had to be a prior conflict of interest before this could arise. The number of appointments of safeguarders has increased, recent figures indicate that a safeguarder was appointed in 9.3 per cent of disposals in 1999/2000 (SCRA, 2001: 18, Table 15). This compares with 4.8 per cent of disposals in 1994 (*Statistical Bulletin*, 1995: 20, Table 12D). Safeguarders are more likely to be appointed for children referred to a hearing on non-offence grounds (86.3 per cent of all safeguarder appointments made in 1999/2000, SCRA, 2001: 18).

Appeals

Appeals lie in relation to dispositive decisions of a hearing such as the imposition of a supervision requirement or against the issue or renewal of a warrant for detention. Hearings can issue warrants to detain a child in a place of safety if there is concern that the child will fail to attend the hearing or where there are concerns for a child's safety. The child and relevant person(s) have the right to appeal to the sheriff but this must be exercised within three weeks of the hearing's decision (section 51, 1995 Act). The sheriff can only allow the appeal if he or she is satisfied the hearing's decision was not justified in all the circumstances of the case, meaning essentially that there was a procedural irregularity or that the hearing failed to take account of an important matter (see *D* v. *Sinclair* [1973]).

If the appeal is allowed, the sheriff can remit the case back to the children's hearing for further consideration, with a note of the reasons for his decision (section 51(5)(c)(i)). The sheriff cannot give directions on how the hearing should dispose of the case; these decisions are seen to lie with the hearing (Norrie, 1997, citing *Kennedy* v. *A* [1986]). The sheriff can decide to discharge the child from any further hearing or proceedings (section 51(5)(c)(ii)). The 1995 Act introduced a new power to allow the sheriff to make a supervision requirement on the terms and conditions available in section 70 of the Act. In effect this latter provision (section 51(5)(c)(iii)) gives the sheriff the power to substitute his or her own decision for that of the hearing.

This option appears to give wide latitude to sheriffs to decide what is in the best interests of the child, and was seen at the time as a potentially significant change in the law. The separation of the court's function to determine the facts of a case and the hearing's function to decide what is in the best interests of the child are central elements of the hearings system. However, to the author's knowledge there has not been significant use of this provision.

A new layer of appeal to the sheriff principal on a point of law or in respect of an irregularity in the conduct of the case was introduced by the 1995 Act. A further appeal to the Court of Session (with the consent of the sheriff principal) is allowed. Alternatively, a direct appeal from the sheriff to the Court of Session on a point of law or in relation to a procedural irregularity is possible (section 51(11), 1995 Act). There is no further appeal to the House of Lords.

Issues in the Hearings System

Since its inception the children's hearings system has given rise to debate about the balance to be struck between justice, the rights of parents and the rights and welfare of children (Adler, 1985). This is perhaps most apparent in child protection cases where the interests of parents may be in conflict with those of the child. This remains an issue although the hearings system is seen to be in conformity with Article 6 of the ECHR in all matters except that relating to legal aid for children (*S* v. *Miller (No.2)*, 2001).

Until recently there has been limited empirical research in relation to the hearings system. Hallett and Murray (1998) in a study of decision making noted that professionals and panel members saw a lack of resources as a weakness of the system; and that the system had difficulties in dealing with persistent offenders. A study of over 1000 children referred to the reporter in 1995 found the children principally came from households where there was social and economic disadvantage (Waterhouse et al., 2000).

Children (Scotland) Act 1995

The Children (Scotland) Act 1995 is split into four parts with five schedules. Part I (private family law) came into force from 1 November 1996 and Part II (public child care law) from 1 April 1997. Some minor provisions were introduced from 1 November 1995. The 1995 Act reflected the general consensus that child and family law in Scotland was in need of reform in the light of widespread changes in society. The Act was widely welcomed albeit that the opportunity to locate the majority of the law relating to children and families within one statute was not taken. The 1995 Act is not a complete codification of the law in this area, a range of other statutes remain relevant.

Part I Children (Scotland) Act 1995

Part I of the Act deals with the relationship between parents and children in the area of private law. The emphasis has moved from the view of the child in Scots law as a 'possession' of the parent(s) towards parents having responsibilities towards their children. Although parental rights are still delineated (section 2, 1995 Act), they are seen to allow the exercise of parental responsibilities. Parents have the responsibility:

(a) to safeguard and promote the child's health, development and welfare;
(b) to provide, in a manner appropriate to the stage of development of the child
    (i) direction,
    (ii) guidance, to the child;
(c) if the child is not living with the parent, to maintain personal relations and direct contact with the child on a regular basis; and
(d) to act as the child's legal representative.
(Section 1(a), (b), (c), (d))

Residence and contact orders (section 11, 1995 Act) emphasize the maintenance of parent–child contact and the continuing involvement of both adults in the child's care and upbringing even when parents are living apart.

The child's mother automatically has parental responsibilities and rights, but the birth father only has them if he was married to the child's mother at the time of conception or subsequently (section 3(1)(a), (b)). The 1995 Act introduced a new arrangement for unmarried fathers to gain parental rights, with the written agreement of the mother. This agreement must be in a prescribed form and registered, there is no court involvement (section 4). The Scottish Executive (2000a) has indicated an intention to change the law to give parental responsibilities and rights to unmarried fathers who jointly register the birth with the mother.

In court decisions relating to parental responsibilities and rights, the welfare of the child remains the paramount consideration (section 11(7)(a)); children have a right to have account taken of their views if they so wish (section 11(7)(b)); and the 'no order' principle is relevant (that is, a court order should not be made unless it is considered that this is a better course of action than making no order at all).

Part II Children (Scotland) Act 1995

Part II of the 1995 Act includes the promotion of children's welfare by local authorities and children's hearings. Chapter 1 outlines provisions for local authorities to support children and their families. Local authorities have a duty to provide a range of services to safeguard and promote the welfare of 'children in need' and to promote the upbringing of such children by their families (section 22(1)). Children in need is broadly defined and includes those children affected by the disability of another member of the family (section 93(4)(a)).

The Act places a range of other duties on local authorities including, for example, publishing information about children's services, increased duties to care leavers and producing children's service plans. The provision of short-term refuge for children is also found in this part of the 1995 Act (section 38).

The 1995 Act replaced the concept of children 'in care' with that of being 'looked after' by the local authority; this change in terminology appears to be an attempt to reduce stigmatization. Section 17(6) of the 1995 Act sets out the categories of children included in the definition of 'looked after', which is as follows:

1　children 'accommodated' by local authorities under section 25 of the 1995 Act;
2　children subject to a supervision requirement;
3　children under warrants, orders or authorizations (for example, child protection orders) and parental responsibilities orders;
4　children from other jurisdictions.

Local authorities have a duty and in some cases a power to provide accommodation for children in their area (sections 25(1), 25(2)). The duty is owed where the child has no one with parental responsibility, or where he or she has been abandoned or lost, or where the parent or carer can no longer provide suitable accommodation or care (section 25(1)(a)(b)(c)). The power to provide accommodation extends to young people who are 18 years but less than 21 years (section 25(3)) if this would safeguard or promote their welfare. The local authority has a range of duties towards 'looked after' children, which are set out in section 17 and include *inter alia*:

1   safeguarding and promoting the child's welfare (this is of paramount concern according to section 17(1)(a));
2   maintaining contact between the child and anyone with parental responsibilities towards him or her (section 17(1)(b));
3   providing advice and assistance to prepare a child for when he or she is no longer 'looked after' by the local authority (section 17(2)).

In making decisions about a child who is 'looked after' or is proposed to be so, due regard must be paid to the child's views, as well as those of the parent(s) and others who have parental responsibilities or whose views are relevant. Attention must also be paid to the child's religious persuasion, racial origin, cultural and linguistic background (section 17(4)). However, protecting the public from 'serious harm' may allow a local authority to override these duties (section 17(5)).

The child's welfare 'throughout his childhood' is the paramount consideration for courts and children's hearings making decisions about children under Part II of the 1995 Act (section 16(1)). Regard must also be given to the child's views if she or he wishes to express them (section 16(2)). A child of 12 years is presumed to be of sufficient age and maturity to form a viewpoint. Furthermore, a court order or supervision requirement should not be made unless it is considered that this is a better course of action than making no order at all (section 16(3)). These provisions and others promote important children's rights set out in the United Nations Convention on the Rights of the Child, especially Articles 3 and 12.

Protecting Children

Chapter 3 of the 1995 Act addresses the protection of children. Three new child protection measures were introduced by the 1995 Act reflecting developments in Scottish child-care law. A child assessment order (section 55) allows for the assessment of the child on application by a local authority to a sheriff where there is 'reasonable cause' to suspect that the child is being treated or neglected in a way that he is 'suffering or likely to suffer significant harm'. This order may be used in cases where the parents are refusing access to the local authority to assess a situation. Research by Francis and McGhee (2000) found little use of this order by local authorities in the first two years of the 1995 Act.

Leading up to the 1995 Act there had been increasing public concern about procedures in Scotland for protecting children from harm in urgent situations. Lord Clyde's Report of the Inquiry into the Removal of Children from

Orkney in 1991 (Scottish Office, 1992), highlighted concerns about the rights of parents and natural justice in relation to state intervention and its impact on children, their families and communities. The scope of discretion allowed in relation to the grounds for removal under the previous legislation (section 37(2), Social Work (Scotland) Act 1968) was seen as excessive and running counter to Article 8 of the European Convention on Human Rights (Scottish Office, 1992: 288). The outcome was the introduction of the child protection order (CPO, sections 57–62, 1995 Act), which sets out clear criteria for and legal challenge against the emergency detention of children.

Application for a CPO may be made to a sheriff by 'any person', which includes local authorities (section 57(1)), or by local authorities under section 57(2), the grounds are slightly different. The sheriff may grant an order if he or she is satisfied that there are reasonable grounds to believe that a child is being treated or neglected to the extent that he is suffering 'significant harm' or that he will do so unless he is removed to a place of safety (or kept where he is). The order must also be necessary to protect the child from harm or further harm (section 57(1)). The sheriff can attach directions to the CPO, including those relating to contact between the child and his or her parents/carers and medical examination (section 58).

A child, however, retains the right to consent or withhold consent to medical examination (section 90, 1995 Act, and the Age of Legal Capacity (Scotland) Act 1991, section 2(4)). The 1991 Act sets out the legal capacities of children but also provides exceptions to the general rule that children under 16 years old lack legal capacity. One such exception is the child's capacity to consent to medical procedures. The medical practitioner (doctor, dentist, and surgeon) who is treating the child has to decide whether the child is of an age and maturity to understand the proposed treatment and possible consequences. If he or she so decides, then the child can consent to treatment on his or her own behalf.

The 1995 Act also inserted a new subsection 2(4A) into the 1991 Act providing that a child under 16 years will be able to instruct a solicitor in relation to civil matters if he or she has a general understanding of what it means to do so (Schedule 4, para. 53, 1995 Act).

The reporter to the children's hearings (the principal reporter) must be told immediately of the implementation of the CPO and he or she can subsequently decide to liberate the child (for example, if conditions have changed). If not a children's hearing must be arranged on the second working day after the implementation of the CPO (section 59(2)).

At the second working day hearing the continuation or cessation of the CPO will be decided and, if it is continued and compulsory measures of supervision are perceived to be necessary, grounds of referral must be put to the child and relevant persons at a further hearing on the eighth working day after implementation. The timescale and provision for recall (that is, discharge) or variation of the CPO is complicated. Application to recall (discharge) the CPO is possible to a sheriff once in the eight-day period, either before or after the second working day hearing which makes the initial examination of the need to continue the order or not.

There has been a continuing reduction in the use of emergency protection measures in Scotland. In 1990 there were 1373 'place of safety orders' (under the 1968 Act) in 1990, compared to 754 in the year April 1996 to March 1997 (SCRA, 1999: 7). This reduction has increased following the implementation of the 1995 Act, where there were 454 CPOs in 1997/98 and 461 in 1998/99 (SCRA, 1999: 7).

Where it is 'not practicable' to make an application to a sheriff for a CPO, emergency authorization can also be made to a Justice of the Peace (similar to a lay magistrate). However, a CPO would have to be applied for within 24 hours (section 61).

Exclusion orders (sections 76–80) are a new development in the range of legal options available to protect children under the 1995 Act. They are largely modelled on the orders available to spouses subject to domestic violence under the Matrimonial Homes (Family Protection) (Scotland) Act 1981. However, under the 1995 Act, it is only the local authority that may apply for the exclusion order. The grounds are set out in section 76(2): the court must be satisfied that the child has suffered, is suffering or is likely to suffer 'significant harm'; it must be necessary for the protection of the child and that the child's welfare is better safeguarded at home than if removed from home; there must be someone capable of caring for the child in the family home. Finally, the sheriff cannot make an exclusion order if it appears to him to be 'unjustifiable or unreasonable' to do so (section 76(9)). The order can last for a maximum of six months (section 79(1)).

It is possible to gain an emergency exclusion order, on a temporary basis, excluding an alleged abuser without notice being given to that person, pending a full hearing. Francis and McGhee (2000) found in a survey of local authorities in Scotland (27 out of 32 responded) a total of 25 exclusion orders were reported as obtained in the first two years of the operation of the 1995 Act. The case of *Russell* v. *W*, 1998 outlines the first reported case of a local authority making an application for an exclusion order. This prevented a man potentially returning to live with his ex-partner and children on release from prison.

Longer Term Provisions

Chapter 4 of the 1995 Act deals with parental responsibilities orders (PROs) under the 1995 Act (sections 86–89). This replaced the widely criticized previous system whereby an administrative resolution of the local authority social work committee could deprive parents of their rights in relation to their child. Local authorities must apply directly to the sheriff for an order to take over the parental responsibilities and rights in relation to a child (PRO). The grounds for dispensation were changed by the 1995 Act to those, which apply to freeing for adoption and adoption. The parental responsibilities order lasts until the child is 18 years unless discharged and the child should also be allowed reasonable contact with parents and other like persons (section 88(2)). In a recent case a child of 10½ years successfully opposed a local authority's application for a parental responsibilities order in relation to him (*City of Edinburgh Council* v. *H*, 2001).

Community Care

The Social Work (Scotland) Act (SWSA) 1968 (as amended by the NHS and Community Care Act 1990) contains the key legislation providing for community care in Scotland. The 1968 Act places a general duty on local authorities to promote social welfare (section 12) and remains the central legislation in relation to the provision of services to adults. The NHS and Community Care Act 1990 amended the 1968 Act by inserting new sections that set out the legal basis for community care in Scotland. Section 55 of the 1990 Act inserted a new section 12A into the Social Work (Scotland) Act 1968 coming into force on 1 April 1993. This requires local authorities to assess the need for community care services of any persons who appear to require such services; and decide, in the light of the assessment, whether they should arrange any services and, if so, which services. The Community Care and Health (Scotland) Act 2002 amends this section to ensure account is taken of any carers' contribution; and their views and those of the adult being assessed in deciding any services to be provided (section 8). Community care services are defined in section 5A and include, for example, domiciliary care.

The Carers (Recognition and Services) Act 1995 earlier amended section 12A of the SWSA 1968 by adding new provisions relating to the assessment of carers who provide substantial amounts of care at home for adults on a regular basis. The Community Care and Health (Scotland) Act 2002 changes the law so that informal carers will have the right to an assessment of their needs on request to the local authority, independent of whether the cared for person is being assessed (section 9).

Scottish local authorities are empowered to charge for community care services and must charge for residential care (section 87, 1968 Act, and section 22, National Assistance Act 1948). However, this is subject to new provisions in the Community Care and Health (Scotland) Act 2002 which will regulate this area further to take account of the Scottish Executive's plans to introduce free personal care for older people. However, much of the detail will be left to regulation by Scottish Ministers and it is the implementation of this aspect that is expected to take place from 1 July 2002. There has been continuing public debate about the provision and charging for residential care. In particular the concept of notional capital whereby assets such as property given away some years before entering residential care may still be taken into account by local authorities (see *Yule* v. *South Lanarkshire Council*, 1998, *Robertson* v. *Fife Council*, 2001).

The 2002 Act places a duty on local authorities to offer direct payments extending the scope to all community care client groups. It also makes provision for the joint resourcing and management of health and social care services; this will include a single shared assessment. The Scottish Executive has issued guidance to begin the implementation of these aspects initially for older people (see Scottish Executive Health Department Circulars CCD7/2001; CCD8/2001).

Other developments include the enactment of the Adults with Incapacity (Scotland) Act 2000 which makes substantial changes to the law relating to the management of the welfare and finances of adults with incapacity. The Act sets out four general principles to guide intervention which include the following: the action must be necessary and of benefit to the adult; it must be the least restrictive alternative; account must be taken of the adult's views and wishes, and those of certain others such as primary carers; and that the adult should be encouraged to exercise and develop his or her skills in managing their welfare and finances as is reasonably practicable (section 1).

Two new types of power of attorney are created, a continuing power of attorney, which deals with property and financial matters and a welfare power of attorney, which deals with personal welfare and health care decisions. The Office of the Public Guardian has been established whose functions include *inter alia* supervising guardians and others authorized to act in relation to the property/financial affairs of the adult concerned; and investigating complaints regarding the exercise of functions in relation to property or financial affairs by attorneys/guardians.

Guardians (local authorities must apply to be guardians in certain cases, section 57(2)) can be appointed under the Act in relation to welfare, financial or property matters, or all three replacing current provisions including mental health guardianship. Intervention orders are a new provision, which allows for a specific action or decision to be taken in relation to personal welfare and financial matters. Medical treatment is dealt with in Part V of the Act.

Changes in mental health law following the report of the Millan Committee reviewing the Mental Health (Scotland) Act 1984 (Scottish Executive, 2001a) will arise with a new mental health bill, expected early in 2002, replacing the 1984 Act. The broad current framework in relation to compulsory detention in the 1984 Act will be retained, with emergency detention of 72 hours, short-term detention of 28 days and long-term detention of up to six months in the first instance but renewable for a further six months and then annually (Scottish Executive, 2001b: 13). There will be a more flexible form of long-term compulsion, which may allow the patient to remain in a community setting or require him or her to be admitted to hospital. However treatment will only be able to be given forcibly in hospital or in another clinical setting (Scottish Executive, 2001b: 20).

Applications for compulsory intervention will be made to a mental health tribunal with a legally qualified chair (Scottish Executive, 2001b: 23);

currently for long-term detention they are authorized by the sheriff (section 18, Mental Health (Scotland) Act 1984). Patients will be able to nominate a named person (a relative or friend) who will have rights to be involved in legal procedures (Scottish Executive, 2001b: 40). Mental Health Officers (MHOs, similar to approved social workers in England) will continue to be qualified social workers and their responsibilities will be extended by the new Act although they will continue to give consent for emergency and short-term detentions, and co-ordinate the formal application for long-term compulsion (Scottish Executive, 2001b: 71).

Criminal Justice Social Work

Section 27 of the Social Work (Scotland) Act 1968 sets out local authorities duties to provide social enquiry reports to the courts; to supervise offenders on probation, community service and supervised attendance orders; and on release on licence from prison or detention. Local authorities also provide the majority of prison social work services. A total of 27 304 social enquiry reports were provided to the courts in 2000–01, an increase of 3 per cent on the previous year; and 6100 probation orders were made reflecting the substantial demands in this area of social work (*Statistical Bulletin*, 2001). The duties set out in section 27 remain underpinned by section 12 of the 1968 Act, which outlines the general duty to 'promote social welfare'. Adults in need of care and attention following release from prison or detention remain included in the definition of a person in need (section 12(6), 1968 Act).

Legislative change including that prior to devolution increased the role of social workers in the supervision of more serious offenders, for example, the Crime and Disorder Act 1998 amended the law in Scotland introducing provision for 'extended sentences' for sexual or violent offenders allowing for longer periods of post-release supervision (section 86 inserting section 210A into the Criminal Procedure (Scotland) Act 1995). A new criminal justice bill was introduced early in 2002 taking forward *inter alia* the development of a new sentence, an Order for Life-long Restriction for high-risk violent and/or sexual offenders (Criminal Justice (Scotland) Bill).

Drug treatment and testing orders (sections 234B–234K, Criminal Procedure (Scotland) Act 1995) were also introduced by the 1998 Act and are available in the sheriff courts in Glasgow, Fife and Aberdeen. These allow for the supervision of offenders with the aim of addressing drug misuse. A pilot project for a 'drug court'; a specialist court to deal with offenders with drug misuse problems has been set up in Glasgow where there will be access to treatment and support facilities provided under the direction of the social work department, working closely with the Greater Glasgow Health Board (SE1185/2001).

Summary

This chapter provides a brief outline of key aspects of Scottish law, which are relevant to social work practitioners. Despite the differing legal context many of the dilemmas and problems facing social services in England and Scotland such as the adequacy of resources and multidisciplinary working are similar. However, the creation of the Scottish Parliament with its devolved responsibilities does raise an issue as to how far policy and services in Scotland may come to differ from other jurisdictions in the UK.

Table of Cases

Table of Statutes and Statutory Instruments

Statutes

Access to Justice Act 1999
Adoption Act 1976
Adoption and Children Act 2002
Adoption (Intercountry Aspects) Act 1999
Adoption (Scotland) Act 1978
Adults with Incapacity (Scotland) Act 2000
Age of Legal Capacity (Scotland) Act 1991
Asylum and Immigration Act 1996
Bail Act 1976
Bail (Amendment) Act 1993
Bail, Judicial Appointments etc. (Scotland) Act 2000
Care Standards Act 2000
Carers and Disabled Children Act 2000
Carers (Recognition and Services) Act 1995
Child Abduction Act 1984
Child Care Act 1980
Child Support Act 1991
Child Support Act 1995
Children Act 1989
Children and Young Persons Act 1933
Children and Young Persons Act 1969
Children (Leaving Care) Act 2000
Children (Scotland) Act 1995
Chronically Sick and Disabled Persons Act 1970
Civil Evidence Act 1995
Civil Evidence (Scotland) Act 1988
Community Care and Health (Scotland) Act 2002
Community Care (Direct Payments) Act 1996
Community Care (Residential Accommodation) Act 1998
Crime and Disorder Act 1998
Crime (Sentences) Act 1997
Criminal Justice Act 1982
Criminal Justice Act 1988

Criminal Justice Act 1991
Criminal Justice Act 1993
Criminal Justice and Courts Services Act 2000
Criminal Justice and Public Order Act 1994
Criminal Justice (Scotland) Act 1995
Criminal Law Act 1977
Criminal Procedure (Scotland) Act 1975
Criminal Procedure (Scotland) Act 1995
Disability Discrimination Act 1995
Disabled Persons (Services, Consultation and Representation) Act 1986
Domestic Proceedings and Magistrates' Courts Act 1978
Domestic Violence and Matrimonial Proceedings Act 1976
Education Act 1996
Employment Relations Act 1996
Environmental Protection Act 1990
Family Law Act 1986
Family Law Act 1996
Family Law Reform Act 1969
Family Law Reform Act 1987
Guardianship Act 1973
Health Services and Public Health Act 1968
Homelessness Act 2002
Housing Act 1996
Housing and Planning Act 1986
Housing (Homeless Persons) Act 1977
Human Fertilization and Embryology Act 1990
Human Rights Act 1998
Immigration and Asylum Act 1999
Knives Act 1997
Law Reform (Miscellaneous Provisions) (Scotland) Act 1990
Legal Aid (Scotland) Act 1986
Local Authority Social Services Act 1970
Local Government Act 1999
Local Government etc. (Scotland) Act 1994
Matrimonial Causes Act 1973
Matrimonial Homes (Family Protection) (Scotland) Act 1981
Mental Health Act 1983
Mental Health (Amendment) Act 1982
Mental Health (Patients in the Community) Act 1995
Mental Health (Scotland) Act 1984
National Assistance Act 1948
National Assistance (Amendment) Act 1951
National Health Service Act 1977
National Health Service and Community Care Act 1990
Noise Act 1996

Noise and Statutory Nuisance Act 1993
Police and Criminal Evidence Act 1984
Powers of the Criminal Courts Act 1973
Powers of the Criminal Courts (Sentencing) Act 2000
Prisoners and Criminal Proceedings (Scotland) Act 1993
Prosecution of Offences Act 1985
Protection from Eviction Act 1977
Protection from Harassment Act 1997
Protection of Children Act 1999
Race Relations Act 1976
Race Relations (Amendment) Act 2000
Regulation of Care (Scotland) Act 2001
Road Traffic Act 1988
School Standards and Framework Act 1998
Scotland Act 1998
Sex Discrimination Act 1995
Sex Offender Act 1997
Sexual Discrimination Act 1975
Sexual Offences Act 1956
Social Security and Benefits Act 1992
Social Work (Scotland) Act 1968
Special Educational Needs and Disability Act 2001
Supreme Court Act 1981
Youth Justice and Criminal Evidence Act 1999

Statutory Instruments

Admission as a Solicitor with Extended Rights (Scotland) Rules 1992
Adoption Agency Regulations 1983 (No. 1964)
Adoption (Amendment) Rules 1991
Adoption of Children from Overseas Regulations 2001 (SI 2001/1251)
Adoption Rules 1984 (No. 265)
Asylum Support (Interim Provisions) Regulations 1999
Children (Admissibility of Hearsay Evidence) Order 1993 (SI 1993/621)
Children (Leaving Care) Regulations 2001 (SI 2001/3070)
Children (Secure Accommodation) Regulations 1991 (SI 1991/1505)
Children (Secure Accommodation) (No. 2) Regulations 1991 (SI 1991/2034)
Children's Hearings (Scotland) Rules 1986
Children's Hearings (Scotland) Rules 1996 (SI 1996/3261)
Children's Hearings (Legal Representation) (Scotland) Rules 2001 (SSI 2001/478)
Code of Practice on the Mental Health Act 1983 (1999)
Community Care (Direct Payment) Regulations 1997 (SI 1997/734)
Courts (Children Act 1989) (Amendment) Rules 2001

Family Proceedings Courts (Children Act 1989) (Amendment) Rules 2001
Family Proceedings Courts (Children Act 1989) Rules 1991
Family Proceedings Rules 1991
Magistrates' Courts (Advance Information) Rules 1985 (SI 1985/601)
Magistrates' Courts (Children and Young Persons) Rules 1992
Maternity and Parental Leave etc. Regulations 1999 (SI 1999/3312)
Mental Health (Hospital Guardianship and Consent to Treatment) Regulations 1983 (SI 1983/893)
Number of Inner House Judges (Variation) Order 2001 (SSI 2001/41)
Parental Responsibility Agreement (Amendment) Regulations 1994 (SI 1994/3157)
Placement of Children (General) Regulations 1991
Placement of Children with Parents Etc. Regulations 1991
Prosecution of Offences (Youth Court Time Limits) Regulations 1999
Refuges (Children's Homes and Foster Placements) Regulations 1991
Reporters (Conduct of Proceedings before the Sheriff) (Scotland) Regulations 1997 (SI 1997/714)
Sex Discrimination (Gender Reassignment) Regulations 1999 (SI 1999/1102)

Glossary of Legal Terms

Affidavit	Written statement made for the purposes of proceedings and signed and sworn or affirmed before an authorized official.
Applicant	An individual or public body making application for a court order.
Certiorari	Former order of the High Court to review and quash the decision of a lower court which was based on an irregular procedure.
Cross-examination	Questions put to a witness by other parties to test out evidence given.
Discovery of documents	Disclosure of documents to other parties before proceedings.
Doli incapax	Incapable of crime (a rebuttable principle now abolished applying to children aged 10–13).
Estoppel	A rule which prevents a person denying the truth of a statement or the existence of facts which that person has led another to believe.
Ex parte	Application made by one party in the absence of other parties (for example, emergency protection order).
Examination 'in chief'	The interrogation of a witness by the legal representative of the party to a dispute for whom he or she is giving evidence.
Functus officio	The position of a person who having had authority to act has discharged it and is no longer authorized to act.
Guardian *ad litem*	Guardian for the duration of the legal proceedings.
Hearsay evidence	Evidence of facts in issue which are not within the direct knowledge of the witness, but have been communicated to him by another.
In loco parentis	Literally 'in place of a parent'. Used to describe a person acting in a parental capacity.
Indictment	Written accusation charging a Crown Court defendant.
Injunction	Court order requiring someone to do or refrain from doing something. Breach constitutes

	contempt of court punishable by a fine or imprisonment.
Inter partes	Proceedings in which all parties are heard.
Inter vivos	During life.
Interim	Literally 'in the mean time', an order made before the full hearing.
Lacuna	A gap in the law.
Leading question	Question suggesting the required answer, or one which can only be answered 'yes' or 'no'.
Litigation friend	The person through whom a minor or mental health patient acts in legal proceedings.
Locus standi	Recognition of a legitimate interest, and therefore right to be heard, in a matter before a court.
Mandamus	Former order from the High Court to a lower court to do what is required (see mandatory order).
Mandatory order	Command from the Administrative Court to a lower court or public body to do what is required.
Mens rea	The guilty intention to commit a crime.
Obiter dictum	Significant remarks by a judge which go beyond the *ratio decidendi* (see below) and are not directly relevant to the point of law at issue.
Prima facie	On first sight (for example, a *prima facie* case is one which on the face of it appears to be compelling).
Prohibitory order	Order of the Administrative Court preventing a lower court from exceeding its jurisdiction or acting contrary to the rules of natural justice (formerly prohibition).
Putative father	The man not married to the child's mother and alleged to be the father.
Quashing order	An order of the Administrative Court to review and quash the decision of a lower court which was based on an irregular procedure (formerly *certiorari*).
Ratio decidendi	The reason for a judicial decision.
Re-examination	Questions put to the witness by the person calling him after cross-examination.
Respondent	The defendant in civil proceedings.
Statutory instrument	Subordinate legislation made in exercise of a power granted by statute.
Sub judice	During the course of a legal trial or under consideration by a court.
Subpoena	Court order that a person attends court to give evidence or to produce documents.
Ultra vires	An act outside the authority conferred by law.

Bibliography

Adler, R. (1985) *Taking Juvenile Justice Seriously*. Edinburgh: Scottish Academic Press.

Adoption Law Reform Group (2000) *Reforming Adoption Law in England and Wales*, London: British Association for Adoption and Fostering.

Aldgate, J. and Statham, J. (2001) *The Children Act Now: Messages from Research*, London: Stationery Office.

Arnott, H. and Creighton, S. (2000) *Legal Action*, June, 13.

Ashworth, A. (2000) *Sentencing and Criminal Justice* (3rd edn) London: Butterworths.

Ashworth, A. (2002) 'Sentencing', *The Oxford Handbook of Criminology*, Maguire, M., Morgan, R. and Reiner, R. (eds), Oxford: Oxford University Press.

Audit Commission (1996) *Misspent Youth: Young People and Crime*, London: Audit Commission.

Auld, Lord Justice (2001) *Review of the Criminal Courts of England and Wales*, London: Home Office.

Bailey-Harris, R., Barron, J. and Pearce, J. (1999) 'From utility to rights? The presumption of contact in practice', *International Journal of Law, Policy and the Family*, 13: 111.

Bainham, A. (1998) *Children – the Modern Law* (2nd edn) Bristol: Family Law.

Ball, C. (1989) 'The current and future context of emergency protection', *Adoption and Fostering*, 13(2): 38–42.

Ball, C. (1995) 'Youth justice and the Youth Court – the end of a separate system?', *Child and Family Law Quarterly*, 7: 196.

Ball, C. (1998) '*R v B*: paying due regard to the welfare of the child in criminal proceedings', *Child and Family Law Quarterly*, 10: 417.

Ball, C. (1991) 'Children Act 1989: origins, aims and current concerns' in *Social Work and Social Welfare Yearbook No. 2*, Carter, P., Jeffs, T. and Smith, M. eds., Milton Keynes: Open University Press.

Ball, C. (2000) 'The Youth Justice and Criminal Evidence Act 1999, Part I: a significant move towards restorative justice, or a recipe for unintended consequences?', *Criminal Law Review*, 211.

Ball, C. and Connolly, J. (1999) 'Requiring school attendance: a little used sentencing power', *Criminal Law Review*, 183.

Ball, C., McCormac, K. and Stone, N. (2001) *Young Offenders: Law, Policy and Practice* (2nd edn), London: Sweet & Maxwell.

Bartlett, P. and Sandland, R. (2000) *Mental Health Law, Policy and Practice*, London: Blackstone Press.

Biehal, N., Clayden, J., Stein, M. and Wade, J. (1995) *Growing Up and Moving On: Young People Leaving Care Schemes*, London: HMSO.

Birch, D. (2000) 'A better deal for vulnerable witnesses', *Criminal Law Review*, 223.

Black, J., Bridge, J. and Bond, T. (2000) *A Practical Approach to Family Law* (6th edn), London: Blackstone Press.

Blom-Cooper, L. (1985) *A Child in Trust: The Report of the Panel of Inquiry into the Circumstances Surrounding the Death of Jasmine Beckford*, London: London Borough of Brent.

Brown, D. (2001) 'Adoption', *The Guardian*, 29 January, 19.

Brown, S. (1991) *Magistrates at Work*, Milton Keynes: Open University Press.

Bucke, T. and Brown, D. (1997) *In Police Custody: Police Powers and Suspects' Rights Under the Revised PACE Codes of Practice*, Home Office Research Study No. 174, London: Home Office.

Bullock, R., Little, M, and Millham, S. (1998) *Secure Treatment Outcomes: The Care Careers of Very Difficult Adolescents,* Aldershot: Ashgate.

Butler, Lord (1975) *Report of the Committee on Mentally Abnormal Offenders*, Cmd 412, London: HMSO.

Butler-Sloss, Elizabeth (1988) *Report of the Inquiry into Child Abuse in Cleveland*, Cmnd 412, London: HMSO.

Callman, T. (2001) 'Special Educational Needs', in Cull, L.A. and Roche, J. (eds), *The Law and Social Work*, Palgrave,. O.U.

Cavadino, M. and Dignan, J. (2001) *The Penal System: An Introduction* (3rd edn), London: Sage.

CCETSW (1993) *Requirements and Guidance for the Training of Social Workers to be Considered for Approval in England and Wales under the Mental Health Act 1983,* London: CCETSW.

CCETSW (2000) *Assuring Quality for Mental Health Social Work*, London: CCETSW.

Child Poverty Action Group (CPAG) (published annually) *Housing and Council Tax Benefits Legislation; National Welfare Benefits Handbook* and *Rights Guide to Non-means-tested Benefits*, London: CPAG.

Children's Society (1998) *Cause for Complaint*, London: Children's Society

Cooper, J. (ed.) (2000) *The Law Rights and Disability*, London: Jessica Kingsley.

Cretney, S. (2001) *Family Law* (4th edn), London: Sweet & Maxwell.

Cretney, S. and Masson, J. (2002) *Principles of Family Law* (6th edn), London: Sweet & Maxwell.

Darbyshire, P. (1997) 'For the new Lord Chancellor: some causes for concern about magistrates', *Criminal Law Review*, 861.

Department for Education and Employment (1999a) *Employment Statistics*, London: The Stationery Office.

Department for Education and Employment (1999b) *Social Inclusion: Pupil Support*, Circular 10/99, London: Department for Education and Employment.

Department for Education and Skills (2002) *Special Educational Needs Code of Practice*, London: The Stationery Office.

Department of the Environment (1995) *Anti-Social Behaviour on Council Estates: A consultation Paper on Probationary Tenancies*, London: DoE.

Department of the Environment (1996) *Code of Guidance on Parts VI and VII of the Housing Act 1996: Allocation of Housing, Accommodation and Homelessness*, London: HMSO.

Department of the Environment, Transport and the Regions (2001) *Supporting People: Policy into Practice*, London: DETR.

Department of Health (DoH) (1989) *The Care of Children: Principles and Practice in Regulations and Guidance*, London: HMSO.

Department of Health (DoH) (1991a) *Children Act 1989 Guidance and Regulations*, 9 vols, London: HMSO

Department of Health (DoH) (1991b) *Working Together under the Children Act 1989*, London: HMSO.

Department of Health (1991c) *Care Management and Assessment; Practitioners' Guide*, London: HMSO.

Department of Health (DoH) (1991d) *National Health Service and Community Care Act 1990: Managers' Guide to the Implementation of the Act*, London: HMSO.

Department of Health (DoH) (1993) *Adoption: The Future*, Cm 2288, London: HMSO.

Department of Health (1995) *Child Protection: Messages from Research*, London: HMSO.

Department of Health (DoH) (1997) *Final Report of the Children Act Advisory Committee*.

Department of Health (1998) *Caring for Children Away from Home: Messages from Research*, Chichester: Wiley.

Department of Health (1999) *Adoption Now: Messages from Research*, Chichester: Wiley.

Department of Health (2000a) *Listening to People*, London: Department of Health.

Department of Health (2000b) *Protecting Children, Supporting Parents*, London: Department of Health.

Department of Health (2000c) *Adoption: A New Approach*, Cm 5017, London: Stationery Office.

Department of Health (2001) *Getting it Right: Good Practice in Leaving Care*, London: Department of Health.

Department of Health and Department for Education and Employment (1996) *Children's Services Planning Guidance*, London: Department of Health.

Department of Health, Home Office and Department for Education and Employment (1999) *Working Together to Safeguard Children: A Guide to Inter-agency Working to Safeguard and Promote the Welfare of Children*, London: Stationery Office.

Department of Health, Department for Education and Employment and Home Office (2000) *Framework for the Assessment of Children in Need and Their Families*, London: Stationery Office.

Department of Health and the Home Office (2000) *Reforming the Mental Health Act*, Cm. 5016, London: Stationery Office.

Department of Health and Social Security (DHSS) (1976) *Report of the Committee of Inquiry into the Care and Supervision Provided in Relation to Maria Colwell*, London: HMSO.

Department of Health and Social Security (1985) *Social Work Decisions in Child Care*, London: HMSO.

Department of Health (DoH) and Welsh Office (1992) *Review of Adoption Law*, London: HMSO.

Department of Health and the Welsh Office (1992) *Review of Adoption Law*, London Department of Health.

Department of Health (DoH) and Welsh Office (1993), *Code of Practice: Mental Health Act 1983*, London: HMSO.

Department of Health and the Welsh Office (1998) *Memorandum on Parts I to VI, VIII and X, Mental Health Act 1983*, London: HMSO.

Department of Health and the Welsh Office (1999) *Code of Practice, Mental Health Act 1983*, London: Stationery Office.

Disability Alliance (annual) *Disability Rights Handbook*, 25 Denmark Street, London WC2H 8NJ.

Eekelaar, J. (1993) 'White coats or flak jackets: doctors, children and the courts, again?', *Law Quarterly Review*, 182.

Eekelaar, J. (2001) 'Rethinking parental responsibility', *Family Law*, 426–30.

Evans, R. (1993) *The Conduct of Police Interviews with Juveniles*, Research Study No. 8, Royal Commission on Criminal Justice, London: HMSO.

Evans, R. and Puech, K. (2001) 'Reprimands and warnings: populist punitiveness or restorative justice?', *Criminal Law Review*, 794.

Farmer, E. and Owen, M. (1995) *Child Protection Practice: Risks and Public Remedies*, London: HMSO.

Feldman, D. (2002), *Civil Liberties and Human Rights in England and Wales*, (2nd edn), Oxford: Oxford University Press.

Fionda, J. (1999) 'New Labour, old hat: youth justice and the Crime and Disorder Act 1998', *Criminal Law Review*, 36.

Fortin, J. (1998) *Children's Rights and the Developing Law*, London: Butterworth.

Fox-Harding, L. (1991) *Perspectives in Child Care Policy*, London: Longmans.

Francis, J. and McGhee, J. (2000) *Child Protection and Social Work Practice: Exploring the Impact of the Children (Scotland) Act 1995*, University of Edinburgh: Department of Social Work.

Frost, N. and Stein, M. (1995) *Working with Young People Leaving Care*, London: HMSO.

Gelsthorpe, L. and Morris, A. (1999) 'Much ado about nothing – a critical comment on key provisions relating to children in the Crime and Disorder Act 1998', *Child and Family Law Quarterly*, 11: 209.

Gerlis, S. (2002) 'CAFCASS – Twisted knickers', 32, *Family Law*, 144.

Gibbons, J., Gallagher, B., Bell, C. and Gordon, D. (1995b) *Development after Physical Abuse in Early Childhood: A Follow-up Study of Children on Child Protection Registers*, London: HMSO.

Gostin, L. (1975) *A Human Condition: the Mental Health Act from 1959 to 1975: Observations, Analysis and Proposals for Reform*, London: MIND, vol. 1.

Graham, J. and Bowling, B. (1995) *Young People and Crime*, Home Office Research Study, No. 145, London: Home Office.

Hallet, C., and Murray, C., with Jamieson, J. and Veitch, B. (1998) *The Evaluation of Children's Hearings in Scotland,* vol. 1, *Deciding in Children's Interests*, Edinburgh: Scottish Office Central Research Unit.

Harris, N. (2002) 'Special educational needs – the Role of the Councils', 14, *Children's Family Law Quarterly*, 137–56.

Hayes, M. and Williams, C. (2000) *Family Law: Principles, Policy and Practice* (2nd edn), London: Butterworths.

Hilgendorf, L. (1981) *Social Workers and Solicitors in Child Care Cases*, London: HMSO.

Himsworth, C.M.G. and Munro, C.R. (1999) *Greens Annotated Acts: The Scotland Act 1998*, Edinburgh: W. Green/Sweet & Maxwell.

Hodgson, J. (1997) 'Vulnerable suspects and the appropriate adult', *Criminal Law Review*, 785.

Hoggett, B. (1996) *Mental Health Law* (4th edn), London: Sweet & Maxwell.

Holdaway, S. et al. (2001) *New Strategies to Address Youth Offending: The National Evaluation of the Pilot Youth Offending Teams*, Occasional Paper 69, London: Home Office.

Holdaway, S., Davidson, N., Dignan, J., Hammersley, R., Hine, J. and Marsh, P. (2001) *National Evaluation of Parenting Orders*, London: Youth Justice Board.

Home Department (2002) *Justice for All*, CM 5563, London: HMSO.

Home Office (1979) Home Office Circular 138/79.

Home Office (1995a) *National Standard for Attendance Centres*, London: Home Office.

Home Office (1995b) *National Standards for the Supervision of Offenders in the Community*, London: Home Office.

Home Office (1997) *No More Excuses: A New Approach to Youth Justice*, Cm 3809, London: Home Office.

Home Office (1998), Interdepartmental *Guidance, Youth Justice. The statutory principle of preventing offending by children and young people*, London: Home Office.

Home Office (1998a) *Inter-Departmental Guidance on Establishing Youth Offending Teams*, London: Home Office.

Home Office (1998b) *Guidance for Practitioners involved in Drug Treatment and Testing Order Pilots*, London: Home Office.

Home Office (1999) *Interim Report on Youth Offending Teams*, London: Home Office.

Home Office (1999a) *Police and Criminal Evidence Act 1984 (s.60 and s.66) Codes of Practice Revised Edition*, London: Stationery Office.

Home Office (2000) *Criminal Statistics for England and Wales 1999*, London: Stationery Office.

Home Office (2000a) *The Final Warning Scheme: Guidance for the Police*, London: Home Office.

Home Office (2000b) *Guidance Document: Action Plan Order*, London: Home Office.

Home Office, with Lord Chancellor's Department and YJB (2000c), *The Detention and Training Order*, London: Home Office.

Home Office (2000d) *Anti-Social Behaviour Orders – Guidance on Drawing up Local ASBO Protocols*, London: Home Office.

Home Office (2002) *Breaking the Circle: Report on the Review of Rehabilitation of Offenders Act 1974*, London: Home Office.

Howard, H. (2001) 'Children Leaving Care Act 2000' *Solicitors Journal* 145(1): 16.

Hucklesby, A. (1997) 'Court culture: an explanation of variations in the use of bail by magistrates' courts', *Howard Journal*, 36: 129.

Jordan, H. and Williams, K. (1996) *Child and Family Law Quarterly*, 8: 337.

Kaganas, F. and Day Sclater, S. (2000) 'Contact and domestic violence – the winds of change?', *Family Law*, 630–36.

Kilbrandon, Lord (1964), *Report of the Committee on Children and Young Persons (Scotland)*, Cmnd 2306, Edinburgh: HMSO.

Law Commission (1987b) *Wards of Court*, Working Paper No. 101, London: HMSO.

Legal Services Commission (2000a) *A Practical Guide to Community Legal Service funding by the Legal Services Commission*.

Legal Services Commission (2000b) *A Practical Guide to Criminal Defence Services*.

Levy, A. and Kahan, B. (1991) *The Pindown Experience and the Protection of Children*, Staffordshire County Council.

Lord Chancellor's Department (2001) *Adoption Proceedings: A New Approach*, London: Lord Chancellor's Department.

Lord Chancellor's Department (2001) *Judicial Statistics*, London: Stationery Office.

Lowe, N. (2000) 'English adoption law: past, present and future', in Sanford, N., Katz, J., Eekelaar, J. and Maclean, M. (eds), *Cross Currents – Family Law and Policy in the US and England*, Oxford: Oxford University Press.

Lowe, N. and Douglas, G. (1998) *Bromley's Family Law* (9th edn), London: Butterworths.

Lowe, N., with Borkowski, M., Copner, R., Kriew, K. and Murch, M. (1993) *Freeing for Adoption Provisions*, London: HMSO.

Mair, G. and Lloyd, C. (1996) 'Policy and progress in the development of bail schemes in England and Wales', in Paterson, F. (ed.), *Understanding Bail in Britain*, Edinburgh: Scottish Office.

Mair, G. and Mortimer, E. (1996) *Curfew Orders with Electronic Monitoring: An Evaluation of the First Twelve Months of Trials in Greater Manchester, Norfolk and Berkshire, 1995–96*, Research Study 163, London: Home Office.

Masson, J. (1994) 'Social engineering in the House of Lords: *Re M*', *Journal of Child Law*, 6: 170.

Masson, J. (2000) 'From Curtis to Waterhouse: state care and child protection in the UK 1945–2000', in Sanford, N., Katz, J., Eekelaar, J. and Maclean, M. (eds), *Cross Currents – Family Law and Policy in the US and England,* Oxford: Oxford University Press.

Masson, J., Oakely, M.W. and McGovern, D. (2001) *Working in the Dark: The Use of Police Protection*, Warwick: Warwick University School of Law.

Mays, R., Smith, V. and Strachan, V. (1999) *Social Work Law in Scotland*, Edinburgh: W. Green/Sweet & Maxwell.

McColgan, A. (2000) *Discrimination Law: Text, Cases and Materials*, Oxford: Hart Publishing.

McDonald, A. (1997) *Challenging Local Authority Decisions*, Birmingham: Venture Press.

McDonald, A. and Taylor, M. (1995) *The Law and Elderly People*, London: Sweet & Maxwell.

Millham, S., Bullock, R., Hosie, K. and Haak, M. (1986) *Lost in Care: The Problems of Maintaining Links Between Children in Care and their Families*, Aldershot: Gower.

Millham, S., Bullock, R., Hosie, K. and Little, M. (1989) *Access Disputes in Child Care*, Aldershot: Gower.

Ministry of Health (1967) Circular F/P9/1B, 14 April.

Monks, D. (2002) 'Children's rights in Education – Making Sense of Contradictions', *Child and Family Law Quarterly*, 45–56.

Morgan, P. and Henderson, P. (1998) *Remand Decisions and Offending on Bail: Evaluation of the Bail Process Project*, Home Office Research Study No. 184, London: Home Office.

Morris, A. and Gelsthorpe, L. (2000) 'Something old, something borrowed, but something new? A comment on the prospects for restorative justice under the Crime and Disorder Act 1998', *Criminal Law Review*, 18.

Mortimer, E., and May, C. (1997) *Electronic Monitoring in Practice: The Second Year of the Trials of Curfew Orders*, Research Study No. 177, London: Home Office.

Mortimer, E., Pereira, E. and Walter, I. (1999) 'Making the tag fit: further analysis from the first two years of the trials of curfew orders', Research Findings No. 105, London: Home Office.

Morton S., and Masson, J. (1989) 'The use of wardship by local authorities', *Modern Law Review*, 52: 762.

Mullis, A. (2000) '*Barrett v Enfield London Borough Council*: a compensation-seeker's charter?', *Child and Family Law Quarterly*, 12: 185.

Mullis, A. (2001) '*Phelps v Hillingdon London Borough Council*: a rod for the hunch-backed teacher?', *Child and Family Law Quarterly*, 13: 331.

Murray, K. (1995) *Live Television Link: An Evaluation of Its Use by Child Witnesses in Scottish Criminal Trials*, Edinburgh: Scottish Office, Central Research Unit.

NACRO (2002) *Youth Crime Section Update*, London: NACRO.

National Assembly for Wales (2000) *Working Together to Safeguard Children: A Guide to Inter-agency Working to Safeguard and Promote the Welfare of Children*, Cardiff: National Assembly for Wales.

Norrie, K.McK. (1997) *Children's Hearings in Scotland*, Edinburgh: W. Green/Sweet & Maxwell.

Oliver, M. (1996) *Understanding Disability: from Theory to Practice*, Basingstoke: Macmillan.

Oliver, M. and Sapley, B. (1999) *Social Work with Disabled People*, Basingstoke: Macmillan.

Parker, H., Casburn, M. and Turnbull, D. (1981) *Receiving Juvenile Justice*, Oxford: Blackwell.

Parker, H., Sumner, M. and Jarvis, J. (1989) *Unmasking the Magistrates*, Milton Keynes: Open University Press.

Partington, M. (2000) *Introduction to the English Legal System*, Oxford: Oxford University Press.

Parton, N., Thorpe, D. and Wattam, C. (1997) *Child Protection: Risk and the Moral Order*, Basingstoke: Macmillan.

Paterson, A.A., Bates, T.St.J.N., Poustie, M. (1999) *The Legal System of Scotland. Cases and Materials* (4th edn), Edinburgh: W. Green/Sweet & Maxwell.

Plowden, P. and Kerrigan, K. (2001) 'Judicial review – a new test?', *New Law Journal*, 7 September: 1291.

Rashid, S.P., Ball, C. and McDonald, A. (1996) *Mental Health Law* (3rd edn), Social Work Law File, Norwich: University of East Anglia.

Royal Commission on Criminal Justice, Report (1993), Cm. 2263, London: HMSO.

Royal Commission on Criminal Procedure, Report (1981), Cm. 8092, London: HMSO.

Sanders, A. (1997) 'From suspect to trial', in *The Oxford Handbook of Criminology* (2nd edn, M. Maguire, R. Morgan and R. Reiner, eds), Oxford: Oxford University Press.

Sanders, A. and Young, R. (2000) *Criminal Justice* (2nd edn), London: Butterworths.

Scottish Children's Reporter Administration (SCRA) (1999) *Scottish Children's Reporter Administration Annual Report 1998–1999*, Stirling: Care and Justice for Children.

Scottish Children's Reporter Administration (SCRA) (2001) *Statistical Bulletin No. 24, Referrals of Children to Reporters and Children's Hearings*, 1999/00, No. SCRA/MJH 2000/24. Stirling: Scottish Children's Reporter Administration.

Scottish Executive (2000a) *Parents and Children*, Consultation. Edinburgh: Scottish Executive.

Scottish Executive (2000b) *Report of Advisory Group on Youth Crime*, Edinburgh: Scottish Executive.

Scottish Executive (2000c) *Scottish Executive Response to the Advisory Group Report on Youth Crime Review*, Edinburgh: Scottish Executive.

Scottish Executive (2001a) *New Directions: Report on the Review of the Mental Health (Scotland) Act 1984*, chaired by the Rt. Hon. Bruce Millan. Edinburgh: Scottish Executive.

Scottish Executive (2001b) *Renewing Mental Health Law*, policy statement, Edinburgh: Stationery Office.

Scottish Executive Health Department Circular CCD7/2001, 'Joint resourcing and joint management of community care services'.

Scottish Executive Health Department Circular CCD8/2001, 'Single shared assessment of community care needs'.

Scottish Law Commission (SLC) (2002) *Report on the Age of Criminal Responsibility*, Report No. 185, Edinburgh: Stationery Office.

Scottish Office (1992) *Report of the Inquiry into the Removal of Children from Orkney in February 1991*, Edinburgh: HMSO.

SE1185/2001 Scottish Executive press release.

Shiels, R. and Bradley, I. and others (2001) *Criminal Procedure (Scotland) Act 1995*, (3rd edn), Annotated Act, Edinburgh: W. Green/Sweet & Maxwell.

Shooter, M. and Kirby, C. (2002) Letter to *The Times*, 3 July 2002, 21.

Slapper, G. and Kelly, D. (2001) *The English Legal System*, London: Cavendish.

Social Work Services Group (SWSG) (1991) *National Objectives and Standards for Social Work Services in the Criminal Justice System*, reissued in 1996, Edinburgh: Scottish Office.

Spencer, J. and Flin, R. (1993) *The Evidence of Children* (2nd edn), London: Blackstone.

Statistical Bulletin (1995) *Referrals of Children to Reporters and Children's Hearings 1994*, Social Work Series, No. SWK/CH/1995/19. Edinburgh: Scottish Office.

Statistical Bulletin (2001) *Criminal Justice Social Work Statistics, 2000–01*, CrJ/2001/6, Edinburgh: Scottish Executive.

Stein, M. (1991) *Leaving Care and the 1989 Children Act*, London: First Key.

Stone, N. (1999) *A Companion Guide to Enforcement* (3rd edn), Ilkely: Owen Wells.

Stone, N. (2001a) *A Companion Guide to Sentencing: Part Two: General Issues and Provisions*, Crayford, Kent: Shaw & Sons.

Stone, N. (2001b) 'The ambit of the standard community rehabilitation order', *Criminal Law Review,* 214.

Straw, J. and Michael, A. (1996) *Tackling Youth Crime: Reforming Youth Justice*, London: Labour Party.

Sturge, C. and Glaser, D. (2000) 'Contact and domestic violence – the experts' court report', 615–29.

Supperstone, M. and Coppel, J. (1999) 'Judicial review after the Human Rights Act', *European Human Rights Law Review*, 3: 301.

Swindells, H., Neaves, A., Kushner, M. and Skilbeck, R. (1999) *Family Law and the Human Rights Act 1998*, Bristol: Family Law.

Thoburn, J. and Lewis, A. (1992) 'Partnership with parents of children in need of protection', in Gibbons, J. (ed), *The Children Act 1989 and Family Support*, London: HMSO.

Thomson, J.M. (1991) *Family Law in Scotland* (2nd edn), Edinburgh: Butterworths/Law Society of Scotland.

Timmis, G. (2001) 'CAFCASS – a service for children or a service for the courts?', *Family Law* 31: 280.

Tolson, R. (2001) '"Star" turn – care orders after *Re W and B; Re W'*, *Family Law*, 31: 598.

Voice of the Child in Care (1998) *How do Young People and Children Get Their Voices Heard?* London: Voice of the Child in Care.

Wadham, J. and Mountfield, H. (1999) *Human Rights Act 1998*, London: Blackstone Press

Warnock, M. (1978) *Report of the Committee of Inquiry into the Education of Handicapped Children and Young People*, London: HMSO.

Waterhouse, L., McGhee, J., Whyte, W., Loucks, N., Kay, H. and Stewart, R. (2000) *The Evaluation of Children's Hearings in Scotland*, vol. 3, *Children in Focus*, Edinburgh: Scottish Executive Central Research Unit.

White, R. (2001) Family Practice column, *New Law Journal*: 1160.

Williams, J. (2000) 'The inappropriate adult', *Journal of Social Welfare and Family Law*, 22: 43.

Wonnacott, C. (1999) 'The counterfeit contract: reform, pretence and muddled principles in the new referral order', *Child and Family Law Quarterly*, 11.

Youth Justice Board (1999) *Speeding Up Youth Justice,* London: Youth Justice Board.

Youth Justice Board (2000) *Juvenile Secure Estate Placement Strategy*, London: Youth Justice Board.

Youth Justice Board (2000) *National Standards for Youth Justice*, London: Youth Justice Board.

Name Index

Subject Index